Socialism and the Limits
of Liberalism

Socialism and the Limits of Liberalism

Edited by

PETER OSBORNE

VERSO
London · New York

First published by Verso 1991
© Verso 1991
Essays © individual contributors
All rights reserved

Verso
UK: 6 Meard Street, London W1V 3HR
USA: 29 West 35th Street, New York, NY 10001–2291

Verso is the imprint of New Left Books

British Library Cataloguing in Publication Data
Socialism and the limits of liberalism.
1. Socialism
I. Osborne, Peter *1958*–
320.531

ISBN 0–86091–326–0
ISBN 0–86091–543–3 pbk

US Library of Congress Cataloging-in-Publication Data
Socialism and the limits of liberalism / edited by Peter Osborne.
p. cm.
Includes index.
ISBN 0–86091–326–0. — ISBN 0–86091–543–3 (pbk.)
1. Socialism. 2. Liberalism. I. Osborne, Peter, 1958-
HX73.S62 1991
320.5'31--dc20

Typeset in Bembo by Selectmove Ltd, London
Printed in Great Britain by Biddles Ltd.

Contents

Introduction

The idea of socialism is more contested today than at any previous point in its history. No longer just criticized from the outside, probed from the standpoint of competing traditions, it is questioned increasingly, and increasingly fundamentally, from within. The collapse of post-capitalist states in Eastern Europe, the impasse of social democratic politics in the West, and an aggressively neo-liberal international management of the crisis in the world economy, have all set the tone for a pessimism on the left which has turned rapidly from a crisis of confidence to a crisis of belief. It is not that current developments do not contain new possibilities for change, but the issue of what is to count, concretely, as a *progressive* change, and how we are to understand its relations to the socialist tradition, remains more open than ever before.

Socialist ideas are not only in deep trouble, for many they seem to have outlived their historical moment of relevance, and 'thus stand condemned to stumble exhausted into the future, as dying traditions always do'.[1] 'The political productivity of the two conceptions of socialism which have dominated the last seventy years — communism and social democracy', it has become common to insist, 'is exhausted'.[2] It really is now time for a 'bonfire of commitments'.[3] The road to renewal will indeed be hard. Yet there can be no denying

1

the crisis in socialist ideas, or the genuine creativity of some of the thinking which it has stimulated. Current debates about citizenship and democracy, constitutionalism and civil society, communitarianism and social movements, constitute a renaissance in specifically 'political' thought which is apparent not just in the academy, but in the wider spheres of political journalism and intra-party politics as well.

The ideological contours of these debates are complex and shifting. But it would be difficult to deny that they have gained their momentum from a re-evaluation of *non*-socialist, primarily liberal and republican, political traditions. If Marxism, although never dominant, set the terms of debate for the left in Britain in the 1970s, it has now been all but erased as a point of reference in political discussion, save for that obligatory acknowledgement of its redundancy which is increasingly a condition for taking part in the debate at all. To write of the future of liberalism in Britain at the end of the nineteenth century was, of necessity, to write also about socialism. Today, a hundred years later, the reverse is true: it has become impossible to write of the prospects for socialism without raising once more the question of its relation to liberalism. Liberalism survived into the twentieth century in Britain only through its assimilation to socialism. Yet the future of socialism seems now to hang in the balance of its reorientation towards the liberal tradition.

It is important, in this respect, to distinguish between the Communist and social democratic components of the 'crisis of socialism', and between the various elements of the liberal tradition itself. Whereas Marxism (later, Marxism-Leninism) provided the Communist movement with an ideological foundation which distinguished it *in principle* from liberalism, social democracy, in its post-war, anti-Marxist sense, was always much more ideologically heterogeneous. An unstable compound of social liberalism, ethical socialism, labourism, and a technocratic, corporate, welfare-state elitism, its unity was forged pragmatically, on the basis of political opportunity and compromise, in the wake of the populist anti-fascist nationalism of the war years. It is the relationship between the elements of this mix, and their differing relations to capitalism, which is now

2

being re-examined, in the context of a political defeat which has been heralded by some as being of epochal significance.[4] Recent discussions have, however, focused almost exclusively on the problems of the explicitly socialist elements of the mix, rather than on those of their liberal counterparts; more on the virtues of liberalism than the possibilities for a creative development of the socialist tradition which would not involve a wholesale rejection of its past. Yet the classical socialist critique of liberalism, associated pre-eminently with Marxism, retains much of its power.

The essays collected together in this volume originated in talks given at a conference in London in November 1988, organized by the *Radical Philosophy* Group, on the theme of 'Politics, Reason and Hope: Philosophy and History in Liberalism, Marxism and Beyond'. They are connected not by any single topic or approach, nor by an adherence to any particular political programme, but by their common commitment to a critical re-examination of *both* the liberal and Marxist traditions, within the broad perspective of a renewal of socialism which would be as sensitive to its distinctive achievements as to its present dilemmas; as conscious of the need to forge a new form of continuity with the past as of the need to transcend it. The first four essays are primarily historical in focus, while the rest consider issues of principle relevant to current political debates. Each of the former is concerned, in one way or another, with the political legacy of the French Revolution.

The French Revolution has served, for two hundred years, as the contested symbol of an ambiguous legacy. For Marxists, it has been an exemplary instance of a willed transformation of society in the interests of an economically ascendent class: the destruction of the political basis of an outmoded social order and the preparation of the ground for a new one. For conservatives, it has been a history lesson of a wholly different order: the result of a gigantic and unnatural hypertrophy of 'reason', it could not but lead to the self-destructive chaos of a Terror which threatened the existence of society in any recognizable form. Liberals have been more ambivalent towards it. For while its progressive historical role in sweeping away the particularisms of the old order is affirmed, its violent means, and essential class character, are disavowed. The simplicity of the pictures underlying each of these stances has long been contested by historians. Yet their power as symptoms and symbols of different orientations towards history remains — as the clash between Thatcher and Mitterrand at the French Bicentennial celebrations showed. However one views the revolution in detail, the contrast between the images of it sketched by its two main original interpreters, Edmund Burke and Thomas Paine, remains the axis of political debate.

Burke's influence on modern conservatism has long overshadowed those more radical elements of his thought which made it natural for Paine to consider him 'a friend to mankind', prior to that outburst of counter-revolutionary fervour, *Reflections on the Revolution in France*, by which he is now almost exclusively known.[5] Paine's reputation for radicalism has similarly inhibited a more nuanced account of his thought. The opening essays in this volume by Tom Furniss and Anthony Arblaster, on Burke and Paine respectively, reassess their political thought in the light of complexities within it which are revealed by more recent concerns and perspectives. *Both* were bourgeois radicals, yet they came to adopt diametrically opposed positions as to the meaning of the French Revolution. This has much to tell us not only about the specific character of their respective radicalisms, but also about the potentially contradictory structure of bourgeois radicalism in general.

Burke, Furniss argues, did not attack the revolution in France for its threat to the established aristocratic order, but for its threat to the particular way in which *capitalism* was being incorporated into England at the time, via certain traditional political and ideological forms. It was not the social content of liberalism (a 'free' or market society) which he opposed, but the dangers posed for just such a social form by a particular propogation of its ends. Burke's thought thus offers us a case study in the limits and contradictions of bourgeois ideology in England at the end of the eighteenth century, and in the threat to it which was posed by a radical, 'philosophical', or abstractly universalistic interpretation of its principles.

But Furniss's essay is more than an elaboration upon Macpherson's recent Marxist reading of Burke, from which it starts out. It is also a highly original investigation of the links between the aesthetic and the political dimensions of Burke's thought. Burke's aesthetics, it argues, was a political intervention in 'capitalism's hegemonic struggle with aristocratic ideology and . . . the contradictory relation between the bourgeoisie and the "lower orders"', waged in the name of the 'sublime' against the aristocratic virtue of 'beauty'. Central to this struggle was the rebuttal by the new financial classes of the charge of luxury, levelled against them by the old aristocratic order. Burke's early *Enquiry into the Origin of Our Ideas of the Sublime and the Beautiful* (1757), Furniss shows, established the sublime as an aesthetic means through which bourgeois thought was able to identify itself as the locus of individual effort and virtue (labour), in opposition to the debilitating effects of luxury; while at the same time both deflecting the charge of luxury back onto the aristocracy and extending it to the lower orders. There was a problem, however, for the bourgeoisie, built into the structure of the concept of the sublime. For once the bourgeois order had established itself, the revolutionary dimension of the sublime as the experience of an object *without limit*, which had been deployed earlier against the aristocracy (economically), became capable of being turned against the bourgeois order itself (politically). It is just such a working out of the inexorable logic of the sublime that Furniss detects Burke as having recognized in the French Revolution. He was thus led to react against the categories of his own earlier thought in order to preserve the order they had sought to establish. In so doing, however, he implicitly confirmed their inherent tendency to overflow their narrow bourgeois form.

Similar, if more familiar, tensions are to be found between the political and economic dimensions of Paine's thought, located as it is at the crossroads of pre-capitalist, liberal and socialist traditions. Yet it would be a mistake, Arblaster argues, to assume that Paine's radicalism is of only historical interest. It may have been more anti-feudal than anti-capitalist, but many of the political and economic changes Paine wanted to see have yet to happen, especially in Britain. The bourgeois form of Paine's radicalism is no reason for the left to patronize him. Nor is it as constraining as might be thought. For however clear the boundaries between liberalism and socialism may be in theory, Arblaster argues, the radicals of the 1790s were constantly crossing back and forth between them in practice, in response to their experiences of 'the evident poverty and deprivation suffered by the great mass of the people'. It is in this tendency for the political *practice* of a consistently radical liberalism to lead, consciously or unconsciously, to a classical socialist critique of the class constraints of capitalist societies that the ultimate lesson of Paine's thought may be seen to reside.

The dynamics of an actual revolutionary process, and the way in which such processes are located within, yet always exceed, the ideological conditions of their existence, is the subject of Robin Blackburn's chapter on 'The French Revolution and New World Slavery'. It is common, he argues, for commentators to exaggerate or ignore the contribution of the French Revolution to the overthrow of French colonial slavery. Rejecting both the view that slave emancipation followed unproblematically from the *Declaration of the Rights of Man*, and that position which would seek its rationale and dynamics elsewhere entirely, Blackburn provides a narrative sketch of the overthrow of French colonial slavery which highlights the contradictory interaction between the revolutionary process in France and the immanent dynamics of the colonial slave revolts themselves. In so doing, he provides a concrete demonstration of both the limits and the possible achievements of the discourse of an abstractly universal human 'right'.

It is the conceptual structure and status (rather than the historical impact) of the discourse of rights which is the topic of Jay Bernstein's essay, 'Right, Revolution and Community'. Taking issue with the orthodoxy that Marx's critique of bourgeois right in 'On the Jewish Question' is to be understood as leading to a rejection of *all* discourses on rights, Bernstein sets out to re-establish within Marxism the link between 'right' and revolution which was forged in practice during the French

Revolution. There is, he argues, a distinctively Marxian account of rights to be recovered from 'On the Jewish Question', within which all rights are to be understood as *political* rights, which can be exercised only in community, and which have as their content various forms of 'participation in community' — various forms, that is, of practically based mutual recognition. Such a 'communitarian' account of rights, it is argued, has its basis in Marx's dialectical critique of the separation of state and civil society, and, by virtue of this historical basis, is able to avoid the standard objections to the abstractness of liberal theories of right.

The three chapters that follow all focus on recent concern to redefine the relationship between socialism and liberalism in favour of a more liberal socialism. Richard Norman and Anne Phillips approach the problem through the issue of the wider political affiliations of feminism, while Michael Rustin considers the possibility of a democratic alternative to the prevailing liberal and socialist models of resource allocation of market and state, respectively. Central to each essay is the question of the meaning and implications of the concept of equality.

The concept of equality, Norman argues, marks a direct continuity between the liberal, socialist and feminist traditions. Socialist and feminist concepts of equality are not qualitatively distinct from, but only more thoroughgoing applications of, the liberal concept. All objections to the concept of equality from a socialist or feminist point of view, it is suggested, should really be seen as objections to too limited a version of it. More specifically, objections to the ideas of 'equal rights' and 'equal opportunities', where appropriate, indicate problems with the concepts of rights and opportunities rather than with that of equality itself. Norman thus places himself squarely within the tradition of a Fabian socialism, in opposition to Bernstein's essay which develops a materialist conception of rights, whilst reaffirming the Marxian critique of equality.

In contrast to Norman's stress on continuity, Phillips takes off from the *disjunction* between recent theoretical work by feminists and the growing tendency to seek a rapprochement

between socialism and liberalism on the ground of some
kind of reformed social liberalism, which would privilege
individual liberty and democracy over equality, as socialist
values. From this perspective, Norman has failed to detect
the extent to which recent feminist writing represents a
qualitative shift away from the purportedly gender-free, but
allegedly patriarchal, presuppositions of liberal theory, and has
misread the ground of the recent convergence between liberal
and socialist ideas. Phillips's main concern is with the parallels
between Marxist and feminist critiques of liberal individualism,
and why it is that, whilst the former are in decline, the latter
flourish. The class critique of abstract individualism is under
attack from within the socialist tradition, but the critique from
the standpoint of sexual difference increasingly holds the stage.
Phillips feels the strength of this critique, but she is worried
about certain of its implications, if it is understood to lead
to the rejection of *all* notions of the abstract self. Rather, she
suggests, what we require is a finer sense of the contexts in
which difference matters, and those in which the impartiality
of an abstract conception of 'the individual' is more conducive
to a politics of emancipation.

Rustin is also concerned with coming to terms with liberal
individualism, politically, while relocating its virtues, theoretically, within a richer and more socially substantive conception of the relationship between 'the individual' and 'society'.
The problem with recent re-evaluations of the political virtues
of liberalism, he argues, is that they threaten to substitute one
field of competition between individuals and interests (civil
society/political life) for another (the market), whilst leaving
the general model of competitive individualism untouched.
In opposition to such moves, Rustin insists on a theoretical
recovery of the 'social' root of socialism, and a return, in
practice, to the communitarian experiential basis of the socialist
movement. There is, he suggests, a third principle, beyond
state- and market-systems: a principle of normative order,
based on 'identification, shared membership, and consensus'.
It has a philosophical basis in 'organicisms or philosophical
idealisms of the left', and a scientific elaboration in the

sociological and anthropological traditions. What it requires is development at the concrete, political level of working out practical institutional alternatives to existing models of resource allocation. Rustin goes on to outline just what this kind of institutional choice would mean, firstly, with reference to funding a system of universally available provision for pre-school children, and secondly, and in more detail, with regard to the development of a system of appraisal for schools. The emphasis in each case is on the interactive dynamics of a participatory approach which would give concrete social content to ideals of democracy and social rights. Habermas's ideal of a deliberative rational community to which all who have an interest have equal access is here given a down-to-earth political appeal.

My own chapter, 'Radicalism Without Limit?', takes issue with a fashionable theoretical formulation of the importance of 'identity' to a new democratic politics. Unlike Rustin's stress on the densely textured fabric of social identities which are produced, reproduced and transformed through the relatively stable interactive networks of family, workplace, community, and institution, Ernesto Laclau and Chantal Mouffe offer a discursive reduction of identity to the temporary fixing of semantic relations amid the *Sturm und Drang* of a permanently unstable flow of meanings, which they take to be characteristic of democratic societies. The philosophical confusions, discursive instabilities and political implausibility of their model of 'the social', I suggest, make it more of a symptom of the depth of the crisis in radical political thought than the theoretical resolution it purports to be. Its focus on 'identity' as a political problem is, however, important, since it is at the heart of the issue of how to build a broadly based socialist movement out of the diverse array of radical movements characteristic of contemporary capitalist societies. But the problem must be reformulated. It is not so much the discursive articulation of autonomous relations of oppression which is required, as the construction of distinctively *socialist* political identities out of the maze of overlapping social identities which make up the oppositional forces to capital.

Gayatri Spivak's 'Remembering the Limits' is an edited transcript of her talk at the *Radical Philosophy* conference. It is directed at once against the suppression of difference involved in the abstract universalism of bourgeois humanism, and certain misunderstandings of the political implications of an 'anti-foundationalist' emphasis on the importance of difference. Difference, Spivak maintains, is a warning against the identitarian impulse inherent in all emancipatory discourses. It is not, and cannot be, the *basis* for an independent emancipatory project of its own. It can, however, serve as the *name* for a non-coercive universal humanism, if the place where all human beings are similar is seen to be lodged in their being different. This argument is then developed through a series of illustrations which draw out the political implications of ethnic, gender and class differences which mark discontinuities of social experience which cannot be reduced to the mediation of a dialectical play. Such a play must, however, be *fabricated* if oppressed groups are to have access to the political resources of the nation-state. The danger lies in the loss of recognition of the element of discontinuity which underlies the necessity for such fabrications. It is in this context that 'difference' acquires its political importance as a reminder of what lies outside the unity of emancipatory projects. Spivak's talk thus complements Blackburn's discussion of the interaction between the political dynamics of the French Revolution and French colonial slave revolts.[6]

It is this emphasis on the importance of understanding the *limits* of emancipatory projects which is taken up in the context of current ecological concerns by Ted Benton and Kate Soper in the last two essays in the volume. Both address the problem of the mutual suspicion between Marxists and the Green movement with a view to developing the theoretical terms of a green historical materialism. In 'The Malthusian Challenge: Ecology, Natural Limits and Human Emancipation', Ted Benton confronts the dilemma posed for Marxism by a movement which on the one hand seems to embody a form of natural-limits conservatism, yet on the other, is an important source of anti-capitalist criticism and action. Starting out from an account of the similarities and differences between Malthus's work and the distinctive neo-Malthusianism of the influential Club of Rome report of the early 1970s, *The Limits to Growth*, Benton goes on to assess the contemporary significance of Marx and Engels's criticisms of Malthus in this light. The main line of this criticism — that Malthus confused natural with socially imposed limits to growth — is affirmed, but idealist and utopian elements of Marx and Engels's writings are identified which undermine their criticism and suggest 'a serious under-theorization or misrecognition of the material limits and preconditions of human interaction with nature'. The problem, Benton argues, has its source in the restrictions imposed on Marx's conceptualization of human interaction with nature by his 'transformative' or craft-based model of the intentional structure of the labour process. Such a model excludes or misrepresents at least two other forms of primary labour process — those of 'selective appropriation' and 'eco-regulation' — which are central to current ecological concerns. Such neglect is not restricted to the explanatory dimension of Marx's thought, but crucially effects his Promethean image of emancipation as a progressive transcendence of natural limits. But the problem is understood to infect only one moment or tendency in Marx's thought. Appropriately modified, Benton argues, Marxian political economy remains the most powerful explanatory theory with regard to the ecological crisis-tendencies of capitalist societies, and the soundest conceptual basis for a critical tran-scendence of neo-Malthusian tendencies in current environ-mental analysis. The task ahead is to build a conception of a natural order which is only *partially* vulnerable to human projects into the core of our idea of human emancipation.

It is this idea of 'Greening Prometheus' which is taken up and developed by Kate Soper in her consideration of those elements within Marxism which resist, and those which enable, a fusion of traditional socialist and ecological demands. There are, she acknowledges, a number of reasons why Marxism might be thought no friend of ecology. But there are also themes in Marx which are not only compatible with, but reinforce, current ecological social critique. Foremost among these are the arguments grouped around the concepts of 'alienation' and 'fetishism' which stress the dialectical interaction of humanity with nature in a process whereby each partakes in the production, reproduction and transformation of the other. Understanding this dialectic, Soper suggests, will be crucial to the mobilization of the political forces necessary to bring about a green revolution. Similar insights are to be found in Marx's account of the dialectic of necessary and surplus labour-time in a socialist economy. The social content of 'necessary' labour, implied by Marx's historical dialectic, opens up the distinction between 'necessary' and 'surplus' labour within a socialist economy to a 'politics of need' within which the possibility of converting 'surplus' labour-time into 'free' time, and thereby of opting for more ecologically sustainable patterns of consumption, takes centre stage. It is true that Marx himself was careful not to project the outcome of this dialectic in any detail, beyond the general idea of the cultivation of a rich, many-sided individuality; and was in any case operating under the assumption of 'abundance'. But the structure of his thought leaves open the option of filling this gap with explicitly ecological demands: 'Where Marx failed to blue-print, we can blue-print green.'

It is fitting that the volume should end with two such emphatic yet critical reassertions of the continuing centrality of Marx's work to political debate on the left. The death of Marxism has been announced too often for such pronouncements to be taken at face value. The times *are* exceptional. But it is precisely because of this that we need to ground our politics in an understanding of the historical development of societies, rather than simply on abstract principles of right. If socialism is to be made anew in the cold climate of the 1990s, as a feasible alternative to capitalism, it will have to do a lot more than mimic the liberal tradition.

Peter Osborne

12

Notes

1. John Keane, *Democracy and Civil Society: On the Predicaments of European Socialism, the Prospects for Democracy, and the Problem of Controlling Social and Political Power*, London: Verso 1988, p. xii.

2. Ernesto Laclau, 'Roads From Socialism', *Marxism Today*, October 1989, p. 41.

3. Ben Pimlott, 'New Politics', in Pimlott, ed., *Fabian Essays in Socialist Thought*, London: Heinemann 1984, p. 6.

4. Stuart Hall, *The Hard Road to Renewal: Thatcherism and the Crisis of the Left*, London: Verso 1988.

5. Thomas Paine, *Rights of Man* (1791–2), London: Penguin 1969, p. 57.

6. Its wider theoretical coordinates are mapped out in an interview with Spivak in *Radical Philosophy* 54, Spring 1990.

Edmund Burke: Bourgeois Revolutionary in a Radical Crisis

Tom Furniss

The history of Burke criticism throughout the two hundred years since the publication of *Reflections on the Revolution in France* in 1790 has been preoccupied with what has become known as 'the Burke problem'.[1] This problem originates with Burke's contemporaries, who found his attack on the French Revolution almost inexplicable given his support for the American colonies and his consistent efforts to limit the powers of the monarchy in Britain.[2] C.B. Macpherson's recent Marxist reading of Burke, elaborating on Marx's observation that Burke 'was an out-and-out vulgar bourgeois',[3] discards the various formulations of such criticism by arguing that 'the central Burke problem which is still of considerable interest in our own time is the question of the coherence of his two seemingly opposite positions: the defender of a hierarchical establishment, and the market liberal.'[4] Macpherson pre-empts one of the explanations of Burke's 'inconsistencies' most often resorted to by pointing out that 'there is no way out by postulating a change in his views over time, for . . . both positions were asserted most explicitly in the same works of the 1790s.' 'Indeed,' he argues, '[Burke's] most explicit statement of his economic assumptions came first in that full-dress defence of the old order, the *Reflections* (1790), and then more fully in the *Thoughts and Details on Scarcity* (1795) and the *Letters on a Regicide Peace* (1796–7).' This is not to argue that Burke did not venerate the traditional order, but that 'his traditional order was already a capitalist order. He saw that it was so, and wished it to be more freely so.' But if this is so, Macpherson asks,

> Why should [Burke] have opposed [the French Revolution] so vehemently, since in the view of most nineteenth-century historians, liberal as well as Marxist, it was essentially a bourgeois revolution, intent on clearing away feudal and absolutist impediments to the emergence of a capitalist order?[5]

For Macpherson, the short answer is that Burke was not a nineteenth-century historian. From his perspective in 1790, the members of the National Assembly 'were not the *haute bourgeoisie* who in England, easily intermarrying with the aristocracy, dominated the House of Commons: they were a *petite bourgeoisie*, who could not be relied on to uphold established property.' Burke either does not see the upheaval in France as a bourgeois revolution, or he sees it as bungling the bourgeois cause by dismantling feudal institutions without having anything to replace them with. Macpherson argues that Burke saw that the transition from aristocracy to bourgeoisie depended on the continuation of class distinctions 'which rested on nothing more than habit and tradition'. Burke is thus driven to disguise the political realities of capitalism by utilizing old social and political forms, and putting 'a new bourgeois content into Natural Law':

> Burke needed the natural and divine law because he had to show not only that the capitalist order was just but also that it was naturally acceptable to the working class. The whole structure of society, Burke insisted, depended on their submissiveness. And he estimated that they would remain submissive if they were protected from the 'rights of man' principles by a counter-barrage of Christian Natural Law principles.[6]

Burke's fear of the Revolution was that it cast off traditional customs and sent capitalism naked into the world. Burke seeks to costume capitalism in traditional garb because otherwise it has no defences against those radical doctrines which would irresponsibly expose its 'defects'. This is why Burke's attacks on the Revolution, with an obvious change of emphasis, often read like Marx's description of the bourgeoisie as that class which 'substituted naked, shameless, direct, brutal exploitation' for exploitation 'veiled by religious and political illusions'.[7]

Although he lacked the perspective of historical hindsight, Burke perceived the Revolution's threat to the particular way bourgeois capitalism was being incorporated into England in an extraordinarily perceptive way. Not only did he realize that Richard Price's rapturous reception of events in France might have serious consequences in an England troubled by the unrest of 'the lower orders', he also pointed out what he saw as the internal contradictions of the National Assembly's political philosophy. He argues, for example, that by telling the peasants that 'almost the whole system of landed property in its origin is feudal . . . [distributed] by a barbarous conqueror to his barbarous instruments', and by allowing them to see that they themselves are the true proprietors of the land they cultivate, the Assembly has given the peasants arguments which may be turned against its own attempts to collect revenue. Similarly, by telling the soldier that he is a citizen with equal rights, the Assembly has 'destroyed the principle of obedience . . . on which the whole of that system depends'. He informs its members that they have therefore 'infused into that army by which you rule, as well as into the whole body of the nation, principles which after a time must disable you in the use you resolve to make of it'. Thus Burke suggests that the founding principles of the Revolution are inimical to its own project: 'You lay down metaphysic propositions which infer universal consequences, and then you attempt to limit logic by despotism.'[8] In other words, Burke claims that by basing itself on 'the rights of man' the Revolution had exceeded the limits of bourgeois liberalism and that it would have to reassert them by means apparently incompatible with its most cherished ideals.

Attempts to 'solve' the Burke problem are misguided in that

they ignore the way in which Burke's position is inextricably bound up with the limits and contradictions of eighteenth-century bourgeois ideology. In order to demonstrate this, I want to concentrate on one of Burke's earlier texts — *A Philosophical Enquiry into the Origin of our Ideas of the Sublime and the Beautiful* (1757; 1759) — whose aesthetic categories, I suggest, contribute to eighteenth-century capitalism's hegemonic struggle with aristocratic ideology and address, in an oblique way, the contradictory relation between the bourgeoisie and 'the lower orders'.[9] This will enable me to suggest that Burke's dilemma in 1790 was that history had confronted him with a revolution that was at once potential within his political philosophy yet fundamentally antipathetic to it. In his texts on the French Revolution, Burke becomes a bourgeois revolutionary in a radical crisis which threatens his ideology from within as well as from without.

The Sublime: A Theory for the Upwardly Mobile

The first edition of Burke's *Enquiry* appeared in 1757. The critical reception it received prompted Burke to publish a second and substantially revised edition in 1759. In the new preface, Burke explains that 'though I have not found sufficient reason, or what appeared to me sufficient, for making any material change in my theory, I have found it necessary in many places to explain, illustrate and enforce it.'[10] That he goes on to repudiate critics for not having attended closely enough to the theory and for not realizing that it was the main point of his treatise, suggests that the theoretical principles developed in the *Enquiry* are particularly important to Burke. By investigating the way in which the *Enquiry* enlists in the rising commercial class's struggle with the traditional order — a struggle which became increasingly urgent in the war years of 1756–63 — I want to demonstrate that Burke defends his theory so passionately because it plays a crucial political role.

Burke's theory is developed through establishing a number of distinctions, some of them common in the eighteenth century, some of them innovative. The first of these, fundamental to all that follows, is the conventional distinction between pain and pleasure. This leads on to the more important and controversial distinction between pleasure and delight — the former being the enjoyment of some 'positive' stimulus of the senses, the latter (Burke claims) the previously undefined feeling 'which accompanies the removal of pain or danger'. These two sensations, which Burke holds to be fundamentally opposed to one another, are in turn associated with another ubiquitous eighteenth-century distinction — that between the passions which accompany or promote self-preservation and those concerning social relations ('the society of the *sexes*' and '*general society*'). Through this series of distinctions, Burke is able to define his aesthetic categories:

> The passions which belong to self-preservation, turn on pain and danger; . . . they are delightful when we have an idea of pain and danger, without being actually in such circumstances. . . . Whatever excites this delight, I call *sublime*.

> beauty . . . is a name I shall apply to all such qualities in things as induce in us a sense of affection and tenderness, or some other passion the most nearly resembling these. The passion of love has its rise in positive pleasure.[11]

These definitions lead Burke to argue that the sublime and the beautiful are utterly distinct from each other: 'They are indeed ideas of a very different nature, one being founded on pain, the other on pleasure; and however they may vary afterwards from the direct nature of their causes, yet these causes keep up an eternal distinction between them.'[12] One of the aims of the present paper is to demonstrate the ways in which this theoretical account of the origin of the sublime in pain or danger, together with the valorization of delight over pleasure, points towards both the political project of the *Enquiry* and its irresolvable problem.

To anticipate somewhat, although Burke argues that the three principal links in 'the great chain of society' are *sympathy, imitation,* and *ambition,* he adds that sympathy and imitation (which are associated with the beautiful) could never in themselves lead to social improvement and would leave men at the level of 'brutes'. Progress comes, rather, through individual ambition and the 'satisfaction [a man feels] arising from the contemplation of his excelling his fellows'. Burke clinches his argument by suggesting that such a feeling is precisely that described by Longinus as the characteristic experience of the sublime — producing 'a sort of swelling and triumph that is extremely grateful to the human mind'.[13]

The sublime, then, is experienced not through sympathy with, but in competition against, and at the *expense* of, other human beings. The implicit claim in this discussion of ambition is that bourgeois processes of individuation are the only means by which social 'progress' (a catchword whose modern figurative sense originates in the early seventeenth century) could occur. In this schema, as we will see, the beautiful becomes associated with the 'luxury' which was thought to threaten the new bourgeois order not only from above and below — through the aristocracy and the labouring poor — but from a fatal tendency within its own ethos.

The sublime's political status seems to have been at stake at least since the formulations it received in early eighteenth-century English discourse in which, Martin Price argues, it features as a mode of revolt against neo-classical principles of order and balance.[14] In Price's reading of Addison's *Spectator* papers of 1712, Beauty ceases to be a term for all aesthetic experience and has to take a diminished place alongside two new categories: 'the Great (which was to become the sublime), [and] the New or Uncommon (which was to become the picturesque)'. The 'Great' produces, in Addison's phrase, 'pleasing astonishment' — this being so because 'the Mind of Man naturally hates everything that looks like a Restraint upon it, and is apt to fancy itself under a sort of Confinement when the Sight is pent up in a narrow Compass. . . . On the contrary, a spacious Horison is an Image of Liberty.'[15] 'Liberty' here is naturalized or made over into private aesthetic experience, but I want to argue that its political accent continues to have force. In the present discussion, it might be suggested that the individual mind's breaking out of narrow confinement only to redefine its bounds as the 'spacious Horison' is indicative of both the liberatory impulse of eighteenth-century bourgeois thought and its reinscription of limits. This double impulse is, of course, inscribed within the etymological structure of the sublime itself: although the sublime gestures towards the infinite, its prefix — from the Latin *sub*, meaning 'under, close to, up to, towards' — suggests that it always respects the *limen*, the threshold or limit.

According to Samuel Monk, the sublime underwent a transformation between 1735 and 1756 from rhetorical style to an aestheticized encounter with nature in its irregular or vast aspects.[16] Such a transition involves a shift from the authority of tradition to an emphasis on the authenticity of individual experience — a shift initiated by Hume's influential discussion of the sublime, in *A Treatise of Human Nature* (1739), in psychological rather than 'literary' terms. These interrelated transitions are said to find their most influential formulation (prior to Burke) in Baillie's *An Essay on the Sublime* (1747), whose analysis is 'centred in the exploration of the subject rather than the description of the object'. And yet, implicit in its impressive bursting of neo-classicism's confining aesthetics in the name of individual liberty is the problem of co-opting the sublime for a social or ethical programme. Monk shows that Baillie regards as sublime not only 'heroism, power, desire for fame, universal benevolence, and patriotism,' but also 'the wholly immoral "ravaging conqueror" . . . so long as the object aimed at is vast and great'.

As this new aesthetic develops, traditional notions of beauty become devalued in comparison. Monk demonstrates how the sublime was instinctively felt to be something beyond the sphere of neo-classical beauty. And yet Price shows that the beautiful itself undergoes important transformations through this period. In Uvedale Price, for example, beauty becomes less a matter of proportion and order and is characterized more in predominantly erotic terms. In Burke's *Enquiry*, the beautiful is defined not in terms of an object's abstract properties but through the *sensation* or *effect* the object produces on the observing subject. Although Burke is at great pains to distinguish this effect ('love') from desire, his conception of the beautiful is primarily defined in terms of *women's* beauty. Dismissing Renaissance theories of ideal human proportion, for example, he suggests that the 'advantage' women have over men in terms of beauty 'will hardly be attributed to the superior exactness of proportion in the fair sex'. Burke marshals similar arguments against received notions that beauty is caused by fitness, perfection, qualities of the mind, or virtue.[17]

But although Burke comes to champion beauty in *Reflections*, it is not at all clear that he does so in the *Enquiry*, where it is distrusted and repressed. Burke's characterization of the beautiful in terms of traditional constructions of the 'feminine' ought to alert us to ways in which the *Enquiry* participates in a crucial hegemonic struggle over the concept of 'luxury' — a term which, as John Sekora has shown, was central to the struggle for power between aristocracy and bourgeoisie in early eighteenth-century England.[18] By placing his aesthetics in such a context, Burke's sublime can be seen as pre-eminently a *bourgeois* aesthetic, at once developing a philosophical theory to valorize individuality, labour and ambition, and defending the new financial classes against traditional charges that the spread of material prosperity (luxury) beyond an aristocratic elite would inevitably lead to political degradation. In this way, we will see that Burke's mid-eighteenth-century aesthetics attempts to marginalize both the aristocracy and 'the lower orders' in one and the same strategy.

Luxury: The Dissolution of Proper Distinctions

Sekora suggests that the concept of luxury is 'one of the oldest, most important, and most pervasive negative principles for organizing society Western history has known', and that the changes in meaning it undergoes in the eighteenth century 'represent nothing less than the movement from the classical world to the modern'. Although late-eighteenth-century bourgeois economists such as Adam Smith helped construct the modern notion of luxury as a positive good by de-emphasizing 'morality in favour of economics, arguing in the main that luxury could increase and redistribute wealth and was therefore a laudable trait in a society', much of the political struggle between England's traditional ruling classes and the upwardly-mobile financial classes in the first half of the century was conducted by each attacking the other for its 'luxury'.[19]

Sekora demonstrates that the social and political meaning of luxury — *anything to which one has no right or title* — derives from the Old Testament, where it is developed as 'a theory of entropy that explains as it describes how men, singly or collectively, lose vitality and fall from grace. For individuals it bears a theory of ethics, for nations a theory of history.' The Hebraic theory is complemented by Graeco-Roman thought, including Socrates' 'memorable attack upon the luxurious quality of democracies' in the *Republic*. For the eighteenth-century ruling classes, the fate of the Roman republic was thought to be, or was represented as, historical evidence of the fate of any society which gave itself up to luxury, and was used to resist all political, economic, and social innovation: 'The upholders of traditional privilege sought first to remind England of the Law known from antiquity that set limits upon what most men *may* do by defining the limits of what they *can* do, and which condemned categorically all forms of luxury.'[20] If the sublime functions to extend, but also to redefine, limits, luxury is that which threatens to transgress all limits.

The metaphors through which this tradition describes the way the luxury of the few comes to endanger the state itself have significant parallels with those through which Burke came to represent the 'dreadful epidemic distemper' of revolutionary thought and economic practice: 'All of these theories,' Sekora writes, make luxury a generic vice . . . using some metaphor like contagion to describe the movement of its corruption from the one to the many. When it strikes a man, it has the fatal power to dissolve his character and to destroy his estate. . . . When it has struck a sufficient number of individuals, luxury will sap a nation's economic and military strength and subsequently bring down the nation itself.[21]

Thus luxury is to be feared because it cannot be limited to the individual or to a particular class; spreading by contagion, it violates the boundaries between bodies and social groupings. We might therefore postulate that fear of luxury is the beginning of the sublime.

The struggle for political power in eighteenth-century England exploited such structures of thought while significantly updating them:

The distinctive use of the concept during the 1730s . . . is as a *specialized* theory of contemporary English history. Reviewing events of the past half-century, various writers of Tory inclination reported finding in luxury the source of a nefarious process that had robbed them and their patrons of their accustomed rank, power, and privilege. In sermon and treatise, broadside and history, they elaborated a series of indictments against the men who had profited from the events of 1688, especially those who were without birth, breeding, formal education, or history of family involvement in government. . . . In the new Whigs and the moneyed interest, they sought to expose a group guilty of the rankest usurpation and insubordination.[22]

For such writers, 'the Revolution of 1688 was a Pandora's box setting loose a spirit of luxury the national order could not contain'. At the same time, however, the assumptions behind such interpretations of the causes of Britain's political and economic problems could be turned against the traditional order. For Mandeville:

It is the sensual Courtier that sets no limit to his Luxury; the Fickle Strumpet that invents new fashions every Week . . . the profuse

Rake and lavish Heir . . .: It is these that are the Prey and proper Food of a full grown Leviathan. . . . [while] He that gives most Trouble to thousands of his Neighbours, and invents the most operose Manufactures is, right or wrong, the Greatest Friend to the Society.[23]

It is this stress on the social benefits that derive from the troublesome and operose nature of 'manufacture' in contrast to the dissolution that stems from the activities of the 'sensual Courtier' that provides the grounds upon which Burke distinguishes the sublime from the beautiful. Writers such as Addison, Steele and Defoe developed Mandeville's arguments into 'an indictment of the upper orders' and a defence of the middle classes' claims upon government. At the same time, however, while such writers can attack the upper classes for their luxury, they share their uneasiness about the 'luxury' of the 'lower orders' — an uneasiness which may have been provoked by a common anxiety about property, since luxury was thought to have 'inspired in the poor a desire for things they may not and cannot have'.[24]

Burke's *Enquiry* can be seen as developing a philosophical ground for the positions adopted by these writers by reworking the sublime in a way that repudiates contemporary charges of luxury against the rising financial class through presenting the endeavours of economic individualism as the very apotheosis of sublimity. As a corollary, all that is 'other' to the new middle class — the aristocracy and what *Reflections* notoriously labels 'a swinish multitude' — is identified as the real source of the political ills brought on by luxury. According to Sekora, the final phase of the struggle for this crucial sign takes place immediately before and during the Seven Years' War (1756–63). It is worthwhile attending more closely to the way the political and economic anxieties of these years were understood by contemporaries because they allow us to realize the buried political import of Burke's *Enquiry* (the first and revised editions of which were published during this period).

To the eighteenth-century upper and middle classes, the poor 'seemed always on the brink of collective insurrection' — a tendency attributed to their unprecedented luxury. In the *London Magazine* (September 1754), 'Civis' writes that,

> Amongst the many reigning vices of the present age none have risen to a greater height than that fashionable one of luxury, and few require a more immediate suppression, as it not only enervates the people, and debauches their morals, but also destroys their substance.

'He denounces in particular,' Sekora comments, 'the rise of the fashion [for luxury] among the lower orders and calls for speedy enforcement of sumptuary laws against urban labourers.' This could seem, or be made to seem, particularly critical after the outbreak of war. In such an atmosphere, the food riots in the summer of 1757 'provided landowners with what seemed to them cogent instances of the depravity of the times'. But if, after the Treaty of Paris, the moral condemnation of luxury as a concept is gradually displaced as England begins to sense the possibilities of expansion through its commercial and industrial revolution and to conceive of itself on a grand scale, the notion of luxury is retained as a means of restricting that expansion and prosperity to the middle and upper classes:

> The coordinate issue — the relationship of luxury, idleness, and insubordination — is explored in James Ridley's . . . *Remarks on the Present State of the National Debt* (1764) . . . its author regards only idleness amongst the poor as *dangerous* luxury; all other forms are mere refinement or innocuous luxury.[25]

Having virtually won its ideological struggle, then, the bourgeoisie in the second half of the eighteenth century set about expanding its own economic, political, and imperial horizons while simultaneously redefining the limits beyond which the 'idle poor' may not go. This is precisely the reason why *Reflections* can assume a collusion of interests between the bourgeoisie and the traditional ruling class when faced with a political movement and philosophy apparently based on the dissolution of the limits both classes set on 'the lower orders'.

The *Enquiry*: Labour Against Luxury

For Burke the experience of the sublime is one of simultaneous terror and delight — 'delightful horror' being 'the most genuine effect, and truest test of the sublime'.[26] The problem of how terror and delight might be experienced at one and the same time was a theme pursued by Burke's contemporary critics, who argued that fear and exultation were mutually exclusive feelings.[27] But this is a question which Burke himself explores, and in doing so articulates his theory most fully. Burke claims that the basis of his argument 'that pain and fear consist in an unnatural tension of the nerves' is drawn from his observations of the effects of pain and terror on human beings and dogs, but we will see that this emphasis on nervous tension allows the sublime to function as a corrective to the overly relaxed state that the eighteenth century identified as the characteristic effect of luxury. Burke's attempt to explain 'how pain can be a source of delight' demonstrates the way in which the sublime is construed as a remedy to this dangerous condition. Apparently abandoning the traditional view of the sublime as an effect of rhetoric, Burke's aesthetics is grounded in a version of eighteenth-century physiology:

> the nature of rest is to suffer all the parts of our bodies to fall into a relaxation that not only disables the members from performing their functions, but takes away the vigorous tone of fibre which is requisite for carrying on the natural and necessary secretions. At the same time . . . in this languid and inactive state, the nerves are more liable to the most horrid convulsions, than when they are sufficiently braced and strengthened. Melancholy, dejection, despair, and often self-murder, is the consequence of the gloomy view we take of things in this relaxed state of the body. The best remedy for all these evils is exercise or *labour*; and labour is a surmounting of *difficulties*, an exertion of the contracting power of the muscles; and as such resembles pain, which consists in tension or contraction, in every thing but degree.[28]

Since Burke characterizes beauty as that which affects the body 'with an inward sense of melting and languor', and which 'acts by relaxing the solids of the whole system. . . . [resulting in] a relaxation somewhat below the natural tone', we can postulate, with Frances Ferguson, that 'the sublime acts as the antidote to the dissolution produced by the beautiful', and that 'all its strainings follow the dictates of the work ethic'.[29] In the *Enquiry*, as in traditional discussions of luxury, beauty is associated with political as well as physical entropy: 'It may be observed,' Burke writes, 'that Homer has given the Trojans, whose fate he has designed to excite our compassion, infinitely more of the amiable social virtues than he has distributed among his Greeks.' Burke goes on to imply that the fall of Troy can be accounted for by the susceptibility of 'Priam and the old men of his council' to what he refers to as Helen's 'fatal beauty'. The fact that, as Ferguson puts it, 'both death and defeat — loss of collective liberty — accompany the amiable virtues', demonstrates the importance of the sublime as a means of staving off the devastating effects of 'luxury'.[30]

Having arrived at the analogy (however dubious or politically problematic) between 'the exercise of the finer parts of the system' and 'common labour', Burke can at last answer his critics and explain how pain or terror can cause or be associated with delight:

> In all these cases, if the pain and terror are so modified as not to be actually noxious; if the pain is not carried to violence, and the terror is not conversant about the present destruction of the person, as these emotions clear the parts, whether fine, or gross, of a dangerous and troublesome incumbrance, they are capable of producing delight; not pleasure, but a sort of delightful horror, a sort of tranquillity tinged with terror; which as it belongs to self-preservation is one of the strongest of all the passions. Its object is the sublime.[31]

Thomas Weiskel suggests that to understand the sublime as a 'homeopathic therapy, a kind of physiological catharsis . . . will hardly do' and transposes Burke's formulations into psychoanalytic terms whereby 'terror is the labour of the mind; the sublime, a purgative therapy of the "finer parts" of the imagination.'[32] Yet the physiological model allows us to see how Burke's aesthetic theory anticipates the figures through which *Reflections* would attempt to constitute the notion of England as a body politic whose preservation depends on keeping at bay revolutionary contagion, and on expurgating it wherever it may have already infected the system. The sublime is said to be the experience of clearing away or purging 'a dangerous and troublesome incumbrance' from 'the parts, whether fine, or gross'; it is an active response to an internal and/or external danger where passivity would be fatal. Today, we might call it a rush of adrenalin which energizes an extraordinary defensive response. It is at once an energy which empowers exertion, and an exertion which releases energy.

It should be noticed that the distinction between terror and the sublime has to be maintained if the sublime is not to be subsumed by terror: 'When danger or pain press too nearly, they are incapable of giving any delight, and are simply terrible; but at certain distances, and with certain modifications, they may be, and they are delightful, as we every day experience.'[33] The 'distance', 'modification', or 'removal' is therefore important in differentiating the sublime experience from unmitigated terror. The notion of 'removal' can imply that the danger is 'removed' (at one remove) and that delight may arise simultaneously with fear because the danger is not quite adjacent. 'Removal' can also imply that the delight *succeeds* the terror *after* the removal of the threat — the sublime experience being akin to the great relief felt at the cessation of pain or the escape from danger. Finally, 'removal' can mean that the act of removal is itself the source of the delight which 'accompanies' it — the sublime therefore being the experience of the threatened self seeming to overcome or *master* danger through *effort*. The sublime may be read, then, variously as a moment or synchronic structure, a succession of alternating states, or as a concerted action or movement.

The peculiar danger of the threat seems to be that it cannot be unambiguously located — that it transgresses the threshold between inner and outer, subject and object, and might therefore be already at work within the human/political body. This is supported by the suggestion that what most threatens 'the person' is not an external danger but 'a dangerous and trouble-some incumbrance' already internal to the system, while the most efficacious remedy for such a danger is something that is itself potentially 'noxious' if not suitably 'modified'. In addition, the disturbing thing for the strong is that their strength is constituted through a moment of 'feminized' weakness or passivity overcome only through an extraordinary effort. It might be, then, that the 'weakness' which is most to be feared is not 'out there' — in the aristocracy, in the undisciplined poor, in women — but insidiously within the bourgeois self or state. The sublimity of the victorious subject is perhaps more a necessary fiction than a genuine transcendence.

Though he grounds his argument in physiology, Burke can revealingly invoke the rhetorical tradition he apparently displaces:

> whatever either on good or upon bad grounds tends to raise a man in his own opinion, produces a sort of swelling and triumph that is extremely grateful to the human mind; and this swelling is never more perceived, nor operates with more force, than when without danger we are conversant with terrible objects, the mind always claiming to itself some part of the dignity and importance of the things which it contemplates. Hence proceeds what Longinus has observed of that glorying and sense of inward greatness, that always fills the reader of such passages in poets and orators as are sublime.[34]

The threat becomes, or is analogous to, the rhetorical 'terror' instilled in us by 'poets and orators' and enables a fantasy of the creative, originating self: 'by some innate power', Longinus writes in a modern translation of the passage Burke alludes to, 'the true sublime uplifts our souls; we are filled with a proud exultation and a sense of vaunting joy, just as though we had ourselves produced what we had heard.'[35] In this way, the sublime seems to be implicated within the eighteenth-century bourgeoisie's attempt to replace reverence for tradition with an emphasis on originality: 'the sublime of nature *or* of text,' Weiskel comments, 'offers an occasion for the mind to establish its superiority or originality.'[36]

Yet the above passages also reaffirm the suspicion raised throughout the *Enquiry* that this sense of 'danger' necessary to the sublime experience is something of a sham.[37] This suspicion is reinforced by Burke's discussion of 'How the Sublime is produced', where he says that 'whatever is fitted to produce such a tension [of the nerves], must be productive of a passion similar to terror, and consequently must be a source of the sublime, though it should have no idea of danger connected with it.'[38] Since a 'passion *similar* to terror' may equally be a source of the sublime as terror itself, it seems that figurative processes are fundamental to the aetiology of the sublime. The 'removal' which is a necessary condition for the sublime might therefore be a removal effected through metaphor — the removal that is, etymologically, the very *modus operandi* of metaphor. In Burke's *Enquiry*, despite his protests to the contrary, the response to 'natural' terror seems always already rhetorical.[39] That the sense of originality which arises out of the sublime is a fictional one seems most clearly registered by its appropriation of a prior text (or natural feature) as a vehicle. At the same time, this sense appears to be a *necessary* fiction, one which the self needs to believe in.

This problem is perhaps endemic to the modern condition which, Weiskel suggests, is to be incurably ambivalent about authority — to be caught up in the unavoidable opposition 'between imitation, the traditional route to authentic identity, and originality, impossible but necessary'. Significantly enough, Burke apparently pivots between the two 'ancient adversaries' of authority and originality in the 'wrong' chronological order. For if the *Enquiry* both champions the aesthetics of originality and is itself a strong bid for originality, in *Reflections* thirty-three years later Burke notoriously reverts to arguments from authority, from precedent, and from the documents of the dead.[40]

If the sublime is a deception which the self passes upon itself, an auto-affective ruse powerful enough to suspend disbelief, we need to ask why Burke, like so many theorists of the eighteenth

31

century, was so committed to it. A summary of the argument
thus far leads towards a response to that question. That which
modifies terror, rendering it neither proximate nor literal, is a
rhetorical displacement effected through a labour of metaphor
or metaphorical labour. Terror, metaphorized into the sublime,
may *seem* to threaten the self, but actually arms it against a
literal threat.[41] That which is thought to literally threaten self
or state is luxury — which the bourgeoisie, at this point, so
strenuously seeks to distinguish itself from and repudiate. Thus
labour is presented as the antidote to the individual and collective
degeneracy of the upper and lower classes. In addition, the
sublime is occasioned by, and occasions, the illusion of original
creativity. Such a reaffirmation of the self's power, however,
seems more a gesture which *constitutes* a new understanding
of the self, rather than simply preserving a pre-given self.[42]
A new model of the self is 'born' through the labour of the
sublime. We might therefore posit that the sublime operates as
an indispensable trope through which the 'self-made man' (in
philosophical and/or economic terms) is constituted. Although
the sublime seems a mere dumb show, its denouement — the
emergence of the individual ('Self begot, self raised / By our
own quickening power' [*Paradise Lost*, V, 860–61]) — bears
an important ideological load.

The problem which faced the rising middle class in the
eighteenth century was to make individual ambition appear
both socially beneficial and natural. That the sublime plays
a part in this project may be seen by examining Weiskel's
account of its philosophical burden in the eighteenth century,
in which he suggests that 'we hear in the background of the
Romantic sublime the grand confidence of a heady imperialism
. . . a kind of spiritual capitalism, enjoining a pursuit of the
infinitude of the private self.' Robinson Crusoe and Milton's
Mammon, 'preferring / Hard liberty before the easy yoke / Of
servile pomp. . . . [working] ease out of pain / Through labour
and endurance' (*Paradise Lost*, II, 255–62), are seen as exemplary
forerunners of economic individualism who demonstrate that
'the founding gesture of the ego was becoming the requisite for
success'. As a complication to this, the natural sublime may be

read, Weiskel argues, as 'a response to the darker implications of Locke's psychology' which, by emptying out the soul, had 'undermined the doctrine of the will' and put anxiety and uneasiness in its place 'as the principle of individuation'.[43]

Putting Weiskel's two observations together, I would suggest that the sublime functions as an aesthetic means through which bourgeois thought establishes itself as the locus of individual effort and virtue in face of the charges of 'luxury' brought against it by traditional writers — a project made all the more urgent by Locke's inadvertently debilitating model of the self. Behind the 'heady imperialism', then, lies a profound anxiety — a reading supported by late eighteenth-century accounts of the 'springs of action'.[44]

Taste: Legislating the Sublime

By grounding the sublime in human physiology, Burke makes it open to all in a way which potentially cuts across social strata, leaving avenues for the rise of those 'men of ability without property' that he himself epitomized.[45] Moreover, by associating the sublime with the experience of pain and labour, Burke can be seen as constructing the aesthetic correlative of the work ethnic.[46] A society organized around the sublime would be a meritocracy (in which individuals might achieve eminence through self-effort), rather than an aristocracy. Yet the disconcerting aspect of Burke's sublime — which becomes even more troubling with the advent of the French Revolution — is that the very way it is constituted makes it a cultural and political vehicle at least equally available to the 'mob' as to the upwardly mobile. This is especially paradoxical for an aesthetic category which is constituted as a mode of distinction — of the elevation of the individual in relation to nature, to past texts, or to other human beings. Burke needs to be able to show how the sublime is at once available to all (through a notion of 'common nature') and yet the means of replacing 'artificial' aristocratic distinctions with 'natural' hierarchical relations between human beings and social classes. A second difficulty which the sublime poses for bourgeois thought is that it can only be problematically harnessed for social stability, since it seems always to bear the marks of its origins in the disruption of the habitual and the regular. It is a principle at once of commonality and individual ascendancy, of stability and insurrection.

Although the sublime appears to encourage the individual to transgress the constraints of custom, the 'truth' of that transgression is guaranteed by an empirical sensationism which claims that 'the true standard of the arts is in every man's power'.[47] In Burke, then, the sublime is caught within a theoretical and ideological impasse: its initial attitude of revolt against custom or habit in the name of individual freedom is made problematic in that such a revolt needs to be authenticated — through an appeal to 'every man' and 'every day' — by that which it claims to repudiate.[48] In this way, the sublime encapsulates a political and cultural paradox which cannot be resolved in any simple way. Given this, that *Reflections* should come to champion the politics of custom and habit is as striking as their denunciation in the *Enquiry*. This cannot be explained away by characterizing Burke as aesthetically radical and politically conservative, nor by claiming that he reversed his position between 1757 and 1790. On the contrary, this shift demands that we recognize both a logical and an ideological contradiction within the very structure of Burke's bourgeois aesthetics and politics.

Burke's revisions of the *Enquiry* for the edition of 1759 seem attentive to these strains and contradictions. In the new 'Introduction on Taste', he insists, perhaps even more than in the body of the text, on the commonality of human faculties as the basis of aesthetic experience and taste. Yet he also emphasizes that there are *differences* in aesthetic response which arise from the uneven distribution of knowledge. The difference which this introduces — which Burke wants to claim is a difference without a distinction — is said to be 'accidental, as it depends upon experience and observation, and not on the strength or weakness of any natural faculty'.[49] Yet this 'accidental' distinction between people becomes all-important. Without it Burke relinquishes the possibility of discriminating the response of the learned from that of 'the vulgar'. Without something which functions like the 'decorum' of the social order he seeks to displace, Burke risks instituting a situation, equally unacceptable to bourgeois as to aristocratic thought, which makes human instincts the standard of aesthetic experience and the social distinctions it underpins.[50] The egalitarian impetus of the sublime has to be limited, then, by the notion of taste, otherwise there is no way of preventing the exaltation of those classes of people completely untrammelled by custom and 'rationality'.

What this reveals, however, is that a democratic revolution, which threatens from within the social order he seeks to institute, is already implicit in Burke's bourgeois revolution as a kind of irrepressible internal momentum. Burke's response to the French Revolution is so fraught because the Revolution can be seen as the political and social extrapolation of possibilities already latent in his early bourgeois aesthetics. As Ferguson suggests, Burke saw the Revolution as an instance 'of the sublime functioning in an unanticipated direction. . . . The ungovernability of the mob turns out to represent rather too much sublimity for Burke's taste when that ungovernability ceases to contribute to the orderly functioning of a productive society.'[51] Burke's reaction is as curious as it is necessary: confronted with an event which foregrounds those aspects of his theory which he attempts to contain in 1757–59, he tries to apply the ballast of custom grounded in aristocratic property and reinvents his aesthetics to meet the crisis he most feared — precisely because it seems an inevitable corollary to his own revolt against the aristocracy.

Burke needs, then, in the *Enquiry*, to be able to make distinctions without abandoning the 'natural' ground of his theory, to which he is heavily committed, since he wants to maintain the principle that aesthetic experience, and hence individual development, is especially open to those uncorrupted by aristocratic culture. He is thus led to argue that although there are no differences in kind between people there are differences in '*degree*' which arise 'from two causes principally; either from a greater degree of natural sensibility, or from a closer and longer attention to the object'. That 'natural sensibility' might vary seems to compromise Burke's claims that aesthetic experience is equally open to all. But his second 'cause' of differences between human beings is even more revealing. He goes on to say that, even if natural sensibility did not vary, in 'nice cases', where distinctions need to be finely discriminated, 'supposing the acuteness of the sense equal, the greater attention and habit in such things will have the advantage'. Thus this 'habit', together with knowledge and 'the reasoning faculty', make up an element of taste which can be used to account for differences in aesthetic response.[52] But although this still allows taste to be acquirable, as Ferguson puts it, 'in exactly the same way that muscles can — by exercise',[53] the facilities for such 'exercise' — made available in a 'liberal' education — are not common to all in the same way that the nervous system is. At the same time, and this is the measure of the irreducible problem Burke wrestles with, such exercise is precisely that which threatens to render the observer insensitive to sensory stimuli and incapable of imaginative activity; for if the judgement 'is improved by . . . the habit of reasoning', Burke repeatedly insists that judgement, habit, and reason are *antithetical* to the experience of the sublime and the beautiful:

> the judgement is for the greater part employed in throwing stumbling blocks in the way of the imagination, in dissipating the scenes of its enchantment, and in tying us down to the disagreeable yoke of our reason: for almost the only pleasure that men have in judging better than others, consists in a sort of conscious pride and superiority, which arises from thinking rightly.

The contradictory demands of Burke's treatise have brought him to an impasse in which the man of judgement is left experiencing an impoverished parody of the sublime sense of vaunting joy. Yet Burke is driven to make one more twist in the argument which, since it seems to flatly contradict the 'egalitarian' principles upon which the treatise is supposedly founded, exposes the difficulties his project involves him in. In a flourish reminiscent of Renaissance thought, he asserts that so far as the imagination and the passions are concerned, I believe it true, that the reason is little consulted; but where disposition, where decorum, where congruity are concerned, in short wherever the best Taste differs from the worst, I am convinced that the understanding operates and nothing else.[54]

Burke's notion of 'Taste' functions as a necessary but trouble-some supplement. Brought in as a standard with which to regulate a new set of social and cultural distinctions, it yet needs to appear different from the 'artificial' or 'arbitrary' measures employed in aristocratic societies. While it actually functions to reproduce a culturally determined meritocracy, taste is represented as a 'natural' acquirement open to all willing to work for it. The difference between this kind of work and productive labour must therefore be made to appear one of degree rather than kind. But although the sublime seems to be grounded in labour, it is a metaphorical labour, not the labour of the masses. This aesthetics, like the politics it forms the counterpart to, is thus based on a division of labour into manual and mental crucial to the development of eighteenth-century manufacturing industry. And yet, as the melancholy aspect of Burke's prose seems to indicate, 'taste', brought in to supplement the sublime to make sure that it functions in the way Burke wishes, renders the sublime unavailable to the 'best judges'. This is to expose the perplexity of a class attempting to constitute an aesthetic for itself which is distinguished at one and the same time from the polished artifice of the court and the 'rude' vigour of the child, the savage, or the lower orders. Wishing to retain 'natural sensibility', bourgeois thought nevertheless perceives its limitations: irrevocably committed to its own so-called 'natural' arts and critical skills, its nostalgia inevitably sees them as impairing precisely what it yearns for (but also fears) in the 'natural' state. 'Taste' works to supplement the acute sensibility experienced by the 'rude' in the 'state of nature'. It supplies the judgement and discrimination which they lack (and which makes them dangerous) yet it supplants those 'natural' qualities which make them enviable.[55]

The sublime arises as a symptom of a profound disquiet

within the bourgeois project. For although I have argued that it functions as the aesthetic ground of bourgeois enterprise, the sublime can also be seen as a measure of the way bourgeois thought represents to itself the cost involved in that enterprise. If, as Weiskel contends, 'the sublime appears as a remedy for the languid melancholy, the vague boredom that increased so astonishingly during the eighteenth century',[56] it can be read as the resort of the 'civilized' classes whose lives no longer present sufficient mental and physical exertion or variety to prevent their degeneration into 'luxury'. The labour and pain which formed the daily experience of the majority provides the material ease which at once allows and makes it necessary that the new ruling classes transform labour and pain into aesthetic experience. It is therefore possible to argue that Burke's sublime acts as an antidote against, but also a symptom of, a disease *already internal* to eighteenth-century bourgeois society.

Significantly enough, then, the bourgeois enterprise is not inherently sublime. Although its great energy in replacing the aristocracy might be initially awe-inspiring, once established, the bourgeois order becomes subject to the same physiological and political entropy as the regime it displaces. Its very success renders the bourgeois social structure vulnerable to the revolutionary potential of the classes it exploits — a vulnerability acknowledged in its agonizing over whether its position would be strengthened or weakened by the education of the workforce.

The Revolution: An Industry Without Limit

Between the Seven Years' War and the Revolution controversy of the early 1790s, the theory and function of the sublime, and of luxury, underwent significant transitions. Yet I would like to conclude by sketching the way that the dynamic interplay between these concepts continues to inform political debate at the end of the century. The Revolution controversy was triggered less by the Revolution itself than by Burke's reaction to Richard Price's *Discourse on the Love of Our Country* (1789), which criticizes Britain's political system for not having perfected the revolutionary principles inaugurated in 1688. Price presents this as a 'defect' which

> renders Britain an object of concern and anxiety. It wants . . . the grand security of public liberty. Increasing luxury has multiplied abuses in it. A monstrous weight of debt is crippling it. Vice and venality are bringing down upon it God's displeasure.[57]

Employing the same terms and assumptions as the *Enquiry*, yet turning the tables on Burke, Price urges the people to 'do [their] utmost to save [their country] from the dangers that threaten it.' Given the example of the French Revolution, he stresses 'the favourableness of the present times to all exertions in the cause of public liberty'. In this way, and by celebrating his having 'lived to see THIRTY MILLIONS of people, indignant and resolute, spurning at slavery, and demanding liberty with an irresistible voice,' Price interpellates 'the people' as a new historical subject called upon, through collective 'exertions', to complete the revolution begun in 1688. Thus it is possible to suggest that radical representations of the Revolution hijack the 'radical sublime' already potential in Burke's political aesthetics, defining Britain's aristocratic-bourgeois system as dangerously luxurious and identifying revolutionary radicalism as its sublime remedy.[58]

Burke's response in *Reflections* is understandably aggressive and contradictory. His celebration of custom and chivalrous manners, embodied in Marie Antoinette's aristocratic beauty, is well known, as is his attempt to ridicule the Revolution's claims to sublimity:

> All circumstances taken together, the French revolution is the most astonishing that has hitherto happened in the world. The most wonderful things are brought about in many instances by means the most absurd and ridiculous; in the most ridiculous modes; and apparently, by the most contemptible instruments. . . . In viewing this monstrous tragi-comic scene, the most opposite

passions necessarily succeed, and sometimes mix with each other in the mind; alternate contempt and indignation; alternate laughter and tears; alternate scorn and horror.[59]

But the fact that the mob *has* become mobile, and that it *has* effected 'the most wonderful things', makes the Revolution a source of 'horror' and 'astonishment' and therefore disturbingly akin to the genuine sublime — astonishment in the *Enquiry* being 'the effect of the sublime in its highest degree'.[60] Thus the above passage is prefaced by Burke's admission that 'it looks to me as if I were in a great crisis, not of the affairs of France alone, but of all Europe, perhaps of more than Europe.' Burke finds himself in such a crisis precisely because history has confronted him with an impossible dilemma and forces him to attend to two perhaps incompatible projects — that of upholding a capitalist order in England by making it appear a traditional order, and that of defending a traditional order in France which, in Burke's political philosophy, is precisely *antipathetic* to economic progress.

Throughout the 1790s Burke remained committed to a laissez-faire economic theory akin to Adam Smith's, with the proviso that the new capitalist practice be accommodated to and ballasted by the landed interest. Indeed, the example of the French Revolution leads him to insist still more emphatically on the primacy of economic 'laws' over interventionist policies in the name of 'humanity'.[61] Yet because the Revolution confronts him with a movement and a rhetoric that, according to his own aesthetic ideology, will prove disastrous to his cause, he is driven to yoke together and defend a class (the aristocracy), an ideology (custom), and an aesthetic category (the beautiful), each one of which is anathema to his thought. But even if Burke is forced to recognize the Revolution's sublimity, and to champion 'the pleasing illusions' of aristocratic forms as the most effective defence against it, he cannot afford to entirely concede the sublime's rhetorical power to revolutionary radicalism, nor overlook the *Enquiry*'s identification of the beautiful and/or luxury as the most insidious threat to political states.

Burke's attempt to resolve this dilemma is to differentiate

between 'good' and 'bad' financial enterprise, sublimity, and
beauty. Although, in the *Enquiry*, the 'shouting of multitudes'
demonstrates that the mob's sublimity is gained at the expense
of individual will — and perhaps leads to an irreverence towards
political edifices akin to that which drove the storming of the
Bastille[62] — the sublime can yet be employed in its 'subordinate
degrees' in order to promote 'awe, reverence, and respect'.[63]
Thus, in *Reflections*, the British constitution is endowed with
sublime qualities that arm it against radical enquiry: 'Always
acting as if in the presence of canonized forefathers, the spirit
of freedom, leading in itself to misrule and excess, is tempered
with an aweful gravity.'[64] By dispelling such 'aweful' illusions,
Burke implies, revolutionary radicalism would abandon a
crucial means of tempering freedom's inevitable momentum
towards 'misrule and excess'.

In a similar manner, Burke strives to distinguish between
those tendencies in the bourgeois ethos which lead towards the
destruction of the state and those which are necessary for its
progress. We have seen that early eighteenth-century critiques
of the upwardly mobile financial classes attacked them for the
luxury which was, in Sekora's words,

> fast begetting new, false, and artificial wealth, a new and noxious
> economic order, and a new and sinister breed of men whose sole
> office was to multiply by some nefarious means the new man-made
> values. Taxes, credit, public funds, stockjobbing, a standing army
> — all of these misbegot, from nothing, the innovators, the moneyed
> men who set out to break the nation to their own ways.[65]

Yet if Burke represents, epitomizes and speaks for that new
order in the second half of the eighteenth century, it is revealing
that his attack on the French Revolution repeatedly condemns,
using the very rhetoric that was originally turned against the
English bourgeoisie, the unbridled luxury and speculation of
the *petite bourgeoisie* whom he identifies as the Revolution's chief
beneficiary:

> if this monster of a constitution can continue, France will be
> wholly governed by the agitators in corporations, by societies

in the town formed of directors of assignats, and trustees for the sale of church lands, attornies, agents, money-jobbers, speculators, and adventurers, composing an ignoble oligarchy founded on the destruction of the crown, the church, the nobility, and the people. Here end all the deceitful dreams and visions of the rights of men.[66]

Bourgeois enterprise is potentially divided against itself, and the Revolution is so critical for Burke precisely because it dramatizes the fundamental antipathy between the radical aspect of the bourgeoisie and traditional institutions. Burke is driven to identify the Revolution as a false sublime (or an example of the sublime gone astray) and to reserve genuine sublimity for the more conservative bourgeois system in Britain; and yet we have seen that *Reflections* often presents the French enterprise as if it were the sublime in its highest degree. An alternative strategy is to figure France as the exemplar of unbridled luxury. But although this serves to distinguish Britain from France, it also foregrounds the destructive potential of any bourgeois system.

Burke's central concern, of course, is not with France but with defending England's *haute bourgeoisie* against the Revolution's 'infectious' principles. One of Burke's problems, however, is that the difference between his own position and that of the French revolutionaries and their English supporters is less clear cut than he would wish. (I have already pointed out that he is himself one of those men of ability without property whom he identifies as the prime movers of the Revolution.) The crucial difference is that Burke stresses that capitalist enterprise ought to be accommodated to the existing order rather than being allowed to destroy it:

Nothing is a due and adequate representation of a state, that does not represent its ability, as well as its property. But as ability is a vigorous and active principle, and as property is sluggish, inert, and timid, it can never be safe from the invasions of ability, unless it be, out of all proportion, predominant in the representation.[67]

Thus the fear of 'invasion' arises less from developments across the English Channel than from the 'invasive' momentum of bourgeois ability itself — which is a 'vigorous and active' principle that is both the greatest threat and most invigorating spur to the state. The fate of the French aristocracy is presented to Burke's readers as an exemplary warning:

> Habitual dissoluteness of manners continued beyond the pardonable period of life, was more common amongst them than it is with us. . . . They countenanced too much of that licentious philosophy which has helped bring on their ruin. There was another error amongst them more fatal. Those of the commons, who approached to or exceeded many of the nobility in point of wealth, were not fully admitted to the rank and estimation which wealth, in reason and good policy, ought to bestow in every country; though I think not equally with other nobility.[68]

If, in the *Enquiry*, the body ought to be ever on the alert against the debilitating effects of luxury, in *Reflections* the bourgeois body politic, if it is to survive the revolutionary crisis which faces it, ought to brace itself against the fatal relaxation that seems almost an inevitable consequence of its own success. The French Revolution makes this seem all the more urgent because it apparently exhibits the 'invasive' power of an unprecedented alliance between radical thought and capitalist enterprise. Just as in the *Enquiry* the self needs to invent a threat in order to tone itself up against the real danger posed by its own supineness, it is possible to see Burke's *Reflections* as opportunistically dramatizing events in France in order to provoke a reaction that will strengthen the 'sinews' of the bourgeois state.[69]

That Burke is caught by history within an inextricable double bind is perhaps most clearly revealed by the way his texts on French affairs produce rapidly alternating and contradictory representations of the revolutionaries, whose danger to the English constitution is figured both as their vigorous and unceasing activity, *and* as the negative example they set of shunning all exertion (and thus being all the more dangerous):

In England we *cannot* work so hard as Frenchmen. Frequent relaxation is necessary to us. You are naturally more intense in your application. . . . At present, this your disposition to labour is rather encreased than lessened. . . . This continued, unremitted effort of the members of your Assembly, I take to be one among the causes of the mischief they have done. They who always labour can have no true judgement.[70]

Their purpose every where seems to have been to evade and slip aside from *difficulty*. . . . Difficulty is a severe instructor, set over us by the supreme ordinance of a parental guardian and legislator. . . . He that wrestles with us strengthens our nerves, and sharpens our skill . . . it is the degenerate fondness for tricking short-cuts, and little fallacious facilities, that has in so many parts of the world created governments with arbitrary powers. They have created the late arbitrary monarchy of France. They have created the arbitrary republic of Paris. . . . The difficulties which they rather had eluded than escaped, meet them again in their course; . . . they are involved, through a labyrinth of confused detail, in an industry without limit, and without direction; and, in conclusion, the whole of their work becomes feeble, vitious, and insecure.[71]

The Revolution endangers 'civilization' because it figures at one and the same time as an instance of the sublime's potential for mobilizing the 'lower orders' and as an example of the possibility that their luxury might be as dangerous to sound capitalist enterprise in Britain as France's ancien régime was traditionally thought to have been.

Burke's shift between 1757–9 and 1790 may be read in terms of the different impetus his aesthetic categories seem to have in radically different historical moments. If the *Enquiry* is produced to help propel an ongoing bourgeois revolution, the *Reflections* is written to defend what has, in the intervening thirty years or so, become a new status quo against revolutionary threats 'from below'. The terror which spurs Burke's later text is the possibility that, just as the aristocracy has been forced to relinquish its sublime role by the bourgeoisie, the 'people' might — through sublime collective effort — overturn traditional/bourgeois institutions by seizing the opportunity presented by the bourgeoisie's very success. From refusing to relinquish his theory in 1759, Burke calls, in 1790, for a resistance to all theory as inevitably leading towards 'misrule and excess'. In doing so, he can be seen as giving a powerful new impetus to a British — or, more accurately, English — resistance to French theory which continues to the present day, whether it be in the form of 'deconstructionism' or the 'socialist' policy of the European community.

Notes

1. For various formulations of 'the Burke problem', see Conor Cruise O'Brien's introduction to his edition of Edmund Burke, *Reflections on the Revolution in France*, Harmondsworth: Penguin 1968, pp. 9–76 (all references to *Reflections* are to this edition); Isaac Kramnick, *The Rage of Edmund Burke: Portrait of an Ambivalent Conservative*, New York: Basic Books 1977; Ronald Paulson, *Representations of Revolution (1789–1820)*, New Haven and London: Yale University Press 1983, pp. 57–73; and Burleigh Taylor Wilkins, *The Problem of Burke's Political Philosophy*, Oxford: Clarendon Press 1967.

2. See, for example, Thomas Paine, *Rights of Man* (1791–92), edited and introduced by Henry Collins, Harmondsworth: Penguin 1969, p. 57; and William Hazlitt, 'Character of Mr Burke' (1817), in P.P. Howe, ed., *The Complete Works of William Hazlitt*, Vol. 7, London: Dent 1930–34, pp. 226–9.

3. Karl Marx, *Capital*, Vol. 1, quoted in O'Brien, p. 9 n.

4. C.B. Macpherson, *Burke*, Oxford: Oxford University Press 1980, p. 7.

5. Macpherson, pp. 4–5, 61, 63.

6. Macpherson, pp. 64, 69–70, 62.

7. Karl Marx, *The Communist Manifesto* (1848), in D. McLellan, ed., *Karl Marx: Selected Writings*, Oxford: Oxford University Press 1977, p. 223.

8. Burke, *Reflections*, pp. 342, 344, 345, 346–7

9. The interplay between Burke's aesthetics and politics has been investigated by a number of commentators — see, for example, Gerald W. Chapman, *Edmund Burke: The Practical Imagination*, Cambridge, Massachusetts 1967, and Neal Wood, 'The Aesthetic Dimension of Burke's Political Thought', *Journal of British Studies* 4, i, 1964, pp. 41–64. The most promising work in this field, however, is that implicit in Frances Ferguson's essays: 'The Sublime of Edmund Burke, or the Bathos of Experience', in *Glyph*, Johns Hopkins Textual Studies 8, 1981, pp. 62–78, and 'Legislating the Sublime', in R. Cohen, ed., *Studies in Eighteenth-Century British Art and Aesthetics*, University of California Press 1985, pp. 128–47.

10. Edmund Burke, *Enquiry* ed. J.T. Boulton, London: Routledge & Kegan Paul 1958; references to the informative introduction (pp. xv–cxxvii) are indicated as 'Boulton'.

11. Burke, *Enquiry* pp. 33–41, 51. For a discussion of the uneasy but necessary attempt to reconcile self-interest and social utility in the eighteenth century, see John Barrell, *An Equal, Wide Survey*, London: Hutchinson 1983, pp. 21–50.

12. Barrell, p. 124.

13. Barrell, pp. 44, 50.

14. Martin Price, *To the Palace of Wisdom: Studies in Order and Energy From Dryden to Blake*, New York: Anchor Books, Doubleday 1965, pp. 361–70; also see Boulton, pp. lvii–lx.

15. Price, *Palace of Wisdom*, p. 362. The quotation from Addison comes from the *Spectator* 412, 23 June 1712.

16. Samuel H. Monk, *The Sublime, A Study of Critical Theories in XIII-Century England* (M.L.A., 1935; Ann Arbor, University of Michigan Press, 1960), pp. 63–83.

17. Burke, *Enquiry*, pp. 91, 98, 106–12.

18. John Sekora, *Luxury: The Concept in Western Thought, Eden to Smollett*, Baltimore and London: Johns Hopkins University Press 1977.

19. Sekora, pp. 1–2, 113.

20. Sekora, pp. 25–6, 31, 77.

21. Sekora, p. 49.

22. Sekora, p. 81.

23. Sekora, pp. 68, 115. The quotation from Mandeville is from *Fable of the Bees* 1, 355–6.

24. Sekora, pp. 5, 107, 117.

25. Sekora, pp. 62, 65, 97.

26. Burke, *Enquiry*, p. 73.

27. These critics included Payne Knight and Dugald Stewart; see Boulton, pp. lxxxviii–xc.

28. Burke, *Enquiry*, pp. 132, 135. Ferguson suggests that 'Whereas Kant will later insist on the importance of detaching the aesthetic object from any thought of the labor that went into its production, Burke sees the aesthetic object as valuable not for the labor that produced it but for the labor it will produce' (Ferguson, 'Legislating the Sublime', p. 134).

29. Ferguson, 'Legislating the Sublime', pp. 149–50; Ferguson, 'Sublime of Edmund Burke', p. 76.

30. Burke, *Enquiry*, pp. 158, 171; Ferguson, 'Sublime of Edmund Burke', p. 76. Ferguson points out that most critics tend to neglect the concept of the beautiful; a neglect which is not without implications for a feminist reading of Burke's project. One reading of the sublime might suggest that it is developed as a mode through which women and femininity are both defined and repressed in the discourse which ushers in the bourgeois capitalist epoch. This in turn might enable a new understanding of the way that patriarchal values were taken up by, and became implicated within, the new order's attempt to legitimize its quest for political power. A rereading of the relation between the sublime and the beautiful might therefore contribute to a feminist critique of the capitalist epoch, while revealing how contemporary interest in

the sublime, insofar as it repeats the sublime's founding gesture, represents a continuation of, as much as a commentary upon, capitalism's relation to the feminine.

31. Burke, *Enquiry*, p. 136.

32. Thomas Weiskel, *The Romantic Sublime: Studies in the Structure and Psychology of Transcendence*, Baltimore and London: Johns Hopkins University Press 1976, pp. 88, 97.

33. Burke, *Enquiry*, p. 40.

34. Burke, *Enquiry*, pp. 50–51.

35. Longinus, 'On the Sublime', in *Classical Literary Criticism*, translated by T.G. Dorsch, Harmondsworth: Penguin 1965, p. 107.

36. Weiskel, *Romantic Sublime*, p. 99.

37. Kant too, Weiskel points out, 'emphasizes as a precondition of the sublime that we not be in physical danger. He postulates a defensive reaction of the mind which will give us "'courage" when there is no danger' (*Romantic Sublime*, p. 84; see Immanuel Kant, 'Analytic of the Sublime', *The Critique of Aesthetic Judgement* (1790), Part 1 of *The Critique of Judgement*, translated by James Creed Meredith, Oxford: Clarendon 1928, pp. 90–203.

38. Burke, *Enquiry*, p. 134.

39. Ferguson also argues, though in different ways to my own discussion, for the 'rhetoricity' of Burke's natural sublime ('Sublime of Edmund Burke', pp. 67–9).

40. See Boulton, pp. lv–lx; and Weiskel, pp. 8, 85–6.

41. In Weiskel's reading, the sublime is characterized as, and produced through, the operation and effect of metaphor: in its 'largest perspective, it was a major analogy, a massive transposition of transcendence into a naturalistic key; in short, a stunning metaphor'. The literal and the sublime seem antithetical, for 'we cannot conceive of a literal sublime' (*Romantic Sublime*, p. 4).

42. For a different discussion of the ways in which 'the autonomous subject, a conceptualization of human subjectivity based on the self-determination of the subject and the perception of the uniqueness of the individual, is the product of a set of discourses present to the period 1756–63, the period of the Seven Years War', see Peter De Bolla, *The Discourse of the Sublime: Readings in History, Aesthetics and the Subject*, Oxford: Blackwell 1989.

43. De Bolla, pp. 6, 9–10, 14–15, 18.

44. Of particular interest to a study of Burke's formulations in the *Enquiry* are the extracts in Alasdair Clayre, ed., *Nature and Industrialization*, London: Oxford University Press and Open University Press 1977; especially those from Bentham's *A Table of the Springs of Action* (pp. 200–2) and Smith's *Wealth of Nations* (pp. 190–8).

45. A point made by Paulson, *Representations of Revolution*, pp. 64–5.

46. See Ferguson, 'Legislating the Sublime', p. 134.

47. Burke, *Enquiry*, p. 54.

48. A point made by Ferguson, 'Sublime of Edmund Burke', pp. 71–2.

49. Ferguson, p. 18.

50. For a discussion of the contradictory political role of decorum in the Renaissance, see Derek Attridge, *Peculiar Language: Literature as Difference*

from the Renaissance to James Joyce, Ithaca, New York: Cornell University Press 1988, pp. 17–21.

51. Ferguson, 'Legislating the Sublime', p. 136.

52. *Enquiry*, pp. 21–23.

53. Ferguson, 'Legislating the Sublime', p. 132.

54. *Enquiry*, pp. 23, 25, 26.

55. Such ambivalences can be found in the most influential apologists for the nascent capitalist system; see Adam Smith, *An Inquiry into the Nature and Causes of the Wealth of Nations* (1776), vol. II, eds R.H. Campbell, A.S. Skinner, and W.B. Todd, Oxford: Clarendon 1979, pp. 774–82.

56. Weiskel, *Romantic Sublime*, p. 97.

57. Richard Price, *A Discourse on the Love of Our Country*, London: Cadell 1789, pp. 46–7.

58. In radical thought of the 1790s right exertion is a sublime remedy not only for that majority subjected to misery by the existing order of things, but also for those groups (aristocrats and middle-class women) whose luxurious, debilitating life perpetuates the suffering of the majority. Wollstonecraft's *A Vindication of the Rights of Man*, J. Johnson: London 1790, astutely identifies the interrelation between Burke's aesthetics and politics and attempts to rewrite those aesthetics for a radical politics (see, for example, pp. 1–6). The *Vindication of the Rights of Woman* (1792) generalizes this insight by realizing that both the traditional order in England and the philosophical forerunners of the Revolution in France figure women in terms of Burkean beauty and so urges that 'it is time to effect a revolution in female manners . . . and make them . . . labour by reforming themselves to reform the world' (*Rights of Woman*, ed. Miriam Brody Kramnick, Penguin: Harmondsworth 1975, p. 132).

59. Burke, *Reflections*, pp. 92–3. It is significant that Burke's rhetoric here is reminiscent of that which was employed against Walpole. 'To the Opposition,' Sekora writes, 'the most bitter proof of Walpole's venality was that he had given a voice in public affairs to men "whose talents would scarce have recommended them to the meanest office in the virtuous and prosperous ages of the commonwealth", men "who had not, either from their obscure birth, or their low talents, or their still lower habits, the least occasion ever to dream of such elevation"' (*Luxury*, p. 88, quoting Bolingbroke).

60. Burke, *Enquiry*, p. 57.

61. Burke's most polemical formulation of physiocratic, laissez-faire economics comes in his *Thoughts and Details on Scarcity* of 1795.

62. Boulton suggests that Burke's observation of this effect might derive from his 'experiences during a student attack on the Black Dog prison' in 1747 (Boulton, p. xvii).

63. Burke, *Enquiry*, p. 136.

64. Burke, *Reflections*, p. 121.

65. Sekora, *Luxury*, p. 68.

66. Burke, *Reflections*, p. 313.

67. Burke, *Reflections*, p. 140.

68. Burke, *Reflections*, p. 244.

69. Paine claims that 'I cannot consider Mr Burke's book in scarcely any other light than a dramatic performance' (*Rights of Man*, p. 81).

70. Edmund Burke, 'A Letter from Mr. Burke to a Member of the National Assembly' (1791), *The Works of the Right Honourable Edmund Burke*, London: Rivington, 1815–27, vol. VI, pp. 67–8.

71. Burke, *Reflections*, pp. 278–9.

2

Thomas Paine: At the Limits of Bourgeois Radicalism

Anthony Arblaster

Whether the French Revolution is best, or even accurately, described as a bourgeois revolution is endlessly debated by historians of a more theoretical bent, and no doubt the discussion will continue. I am not in this essay concerned with the class alignments displayed during the Revolution; or even with the lasting material consequences of the Revolution — whether it decisively displaced feudalism and replaced it with a society and a political system dominated by the bourgeoisie — though I am not anxious to disown such an interpretation either. But whatever may be true elsewhere, it seems clear to me that in the field of ideology the 'bourgeois' label is in fact very appropriate: the ideas of the Revolution and its most thoroughgoing supporters represent bourgeois ideology in its most radical form. It is a form still challenging and relevant, but with certain crucial limitations and impediments which precisely expose the essentially bourgeois character of that form. This radical ideology points both backwards and forwards — backwards to pre-capitalist notions of a 'moral economy', forward to socialism — but it also intersects with the central liberal ideology of the market. All three elements are present in Paine, but also in the French and American radicalism of this period. It is illuminating to set Paine in this wider context.

But it would be wrong to see Paine as a purely historical figure, belonging exclusively to the past. Many of the radical political changes he argued for remain unachieved, and have been, I shall suggest, mistakenly neglected by the left. His continuing relevance ensures that he still enjoys a controversial reputation — in Britain at any rate. It is not many years since the *Daily Telegraph* thought it worthwhile to devote a leader to attacking him. Under the heading 'A Radical Rascal', the author (probably T.E. Utley) reminded us that 'Among decent Englishmen in his time, his name was a synonym for treason, blasphemy and (whether justly or not) debauchery.' He was, the paper claimed, 'an agent of destruction', and one of those 'who laid the intellectual foundations of modern Communist dictatorship'.[1] In a competition to discover which political thinkers have been most abused and misrepresented, Thomas Paine, whom Theodore Roosevelt once called a 'dirty little atheist', would undoubtedly be a strong contender.

It is his tone and style, as much as his ideas, which can still enrage and exhilarate. From this distance his 'actual political proposals' can be seen, in Hobsbawm's words, as being 'almost ridiculously moderate',[2] even though many of them have not in fact been carried out. But his attitudes were another matter. It is hard to think of a sharper mismatch of minds than that between Burke and Paine, for Paine had not a scrap of reverence for existing institutions or traditions in him. What Gwyn Williams has well called the 'contempt and jovial ferocity' of his attack on the British monarchy,[3] on the supposed English (or British) constitution, on aristocracy, on the Old Testament and the Christian religion, can still seem slightly shocking, and must have sounded entirely scandalous to the respectable classes of the 1790s. On the other hand, as the phenomenal success of each of his three most famous works testifies, this liberated style of assault on the hallowed institutions of ruling-class Britain was music to the ears of a huge popular audience, which included manufacturers and merchants as well as crafts-folk and artisans. Paine's writing had a lasting and highly significant influence; Hazlitt remarked in 1792: 'Paine was so great, or so popular an author, and so much read and admired, that the Government was obliged to suspend the Constitution and go to war to counteract the effects of his popularity.'[4] This agreeable hyperbole was not far from the truth.

So what was it that caused such turmoil at the time, and can still stir writers (and readers) of the *Daily Telegraph* to apoplectic mutterings?

Paine's Liberalism

The general character of Paine's radicalism is well known. It is, in a nutshell, more anti-feudal than anti-capitalist. His targets are the familiar Enlightenment ones: kings, aristocrats and priests, and, as much as anything else, the hereditary principle, which he has no difficulty in making look ridiculous. Paine is a sworn enemy of the anciens régimes of eighteenth-century Europe, including the British version, and he is convinced that the overthrow of these regimes is the key which will unlock the prison of human history, and set humanity on the path towards permanent peace, prosperity and enlightenment. The root of most political, economic and social evils lies for him in the character of the existing systems of government. War, argues Paine, provides an outstanding example of this.

It is probably now generally agreed that the European and colonial wars of the eighteenth century were essentially commercial wars, wars over trade and over the control of lucrative colonies outside Europe. And we have become far more aware, in the century since Marx, of the economic causes of wars in general. Paine's view of the causes of war is entirely at odds with this. War, in his view, is caused by the personal and dynastic ambitions and rivalries of kings or monarchs. In *Common Sense* he puts it with his usual bluntness:

> In the early ages of the world, according to the scripture chronology, there were no kings; the consequence of which was there were no wars; it is the pride of kings which throws mankind into confusion.[5]

In *Rights of Man* he enlarges a little on this point:

As war is the system of Government on the old construction, the animosity which Nations reciprocally entertain, is nothing more than what the policy of their Governments excites, to keep up the spirit of the system. . . . Man is not the enemy of man, but through the medium of a false system of Government.[6]

Nor does Paine believe that territorial empire is the outcome of commercial rivalry or ambitions. On the contrary, he argues that the interests of trade and the interests of empire are in conflict with each other:

the most unprofitable of all commerce is that connected with foreign dominion. To a few individuals it may be beneficial, merely because it is commerce; but to the nation it is a loss. The expense of maintaining dominion more than absorbs the profits of any trade . . . it is impossible to engross commerce by dominion.

By the same token, navies do not exist to protect commerce: 'The idea of having navies for the protection of commerce is delusive. It is putting the means of destruction for the means of protection.'[7]

War and empire thus have political, not economic, causes. Their roots lie in the dominance of societies by hereditary monarchs and aristocracies. Abolish these, and the way is open towards international peace and harmony. So far from believing that commercial rivalries led to wars, Paine had great faith in the benign influence of trade:

In all my publications, where the matter would admit, I have been an advocate for commerce, because I am a friend to its effects. It is a pacific system, operating to cordialize mankind, by rendering nations, as well as individuals, useful to each other. . . . If commerce were permitted to act to the universal extent it is capable, it would extirpate the system of war, and produce a revolution in the uncivilized state of governments. The invention of commerce . . . is the greatest approach towards universal civilization, that has yet been made by any means not immediately flowing from moral principles.[8]

It is the restrictions placed on commerce by the old regimes which need to be swept away. Free trade is beneficial to all: 'There can be no such thing as a nation flourishing alone in commerce; she can only participate . . .'; 'the prosperity of any commercial nation is regulated by the prosperity of the rest. If they are poor, she cannot be rich . . .'[9]

International peace and free trade go together. A.J.P. Taylor, in his fine study of the dissenting tradition in British foreign policy, *The Trouble Makers*, was quite right to include Paine in the tradition which perhaps reached its peak in the commercial pacifism of the free traders who led the Anti-Corn Law League to its successful conclusion, Richard Cobden and John Bright. Of course they had a direct interest in free trade, but it was also for them a moral issue. They believed, as Paine did, that wars were made by governments, and for them the supreme example of that was the Crimean war, which they both courageously opposed.

No one would now accept either Paine's view of the causes of war, or his sanguine view of the effects of free trade. But it is a consistent element in his political radicalism: overthrow the old governments, and you will remove at a stroke the principle cause of war and release trade to exercise its pacific influence.

Economically, Paine is a follower of Adam Smith, as was his conservative opponent, Burke; and, like so many radicals of his time (though not William Blake), he was an enthusiast for the amazing advances in productivity and technology then being achieved in the British industrial revolution. He was the designer of an iron bridge, which was built to his specifications, though not over water, and served as the model for the famous bridge over the Wear at Sunderland, which features on so much popular commemorative china of the early nineteenth century. Whether he ever read *The Wealth of Nations* is not clear — Paine was characteristically reluctant to admit to having learnt from other people's books — but he would not have needed to. Smith's ideas rapidly achieved wide currency, and Paine could have picked them up at second or third hand.

Paine's strong belief in the self-regulating character of human social life, and his consequent scepticism about governmental intervention, are set out most clearly in chapter 1 of Part II of *Rights of Man*: 'Government is no farther necessary than to supply the few cases to which society and civilization are not conveniently competent'; and even so, 'how often is the natural propensity to society disturbed or destroyed by the operations of government!' In fact, Paine comes close to an anarchist position in this chapter: 'The more perfect civilization is, the less occasion has it for government, because the more does it regulate its own affairs and govern itself.'[10] Suspicion of government, and a reluctance to allow it more than a minimal role in relation to society, is a consistent attitude with Paine. As he wrote earlier, in *Common Sense*, 'Society in every state is a blessing, but government even in its best state is but a necessary evil. . . . Government, like dress, is the badge of lost innocence.'[11] It might be appropriate to say that this represents a moment of transition between Smith's faith in markets and Paine's friend William Godwin's faith in the collective rationality of humankind, for Godwin's early version of anarchism, published the year after *Rights of Man* Part II, is undoubtedly an extension of liberal ideas about human reason, and about the fundamental conflict between society and government, or the state.

Paine shared the classic liberal suspicion of government, and of government intervention. He shared, too, the classic liberal hostility to taxation. It was an important part of his case against the anciens régimes that they imposed a burden of taxation upon society, and particularly upon the productive, enterprising and hard-working sections of society, which was an obstacle to economic and industrial progress; and which was anyway unjustified, since it was used primarily to support a parasitic aristocracy and to finance wasteful, futile and cruel institutions such as the armed forces:

> The amazing and still increasing expenses with which old governments are conducted, the numerous wars they engage in or provoke, the embarrassments they throw in the way of universal civilization and commerce, and the oppression and usurpation they practise at home, have wearied out the patience, and exhausted the property of the world.[12]

Paine divided society into 'two distinct classes of men . . . those who pay taxes, and those who receive and live upon taxes'.[13] However, Paine's attack on parasitism was not inspired by economic egalitarianism. As someone who had achieved fame and influence by his own efforts and against the grain of the society he was born into, he naturally sympathized with the meritocratic principle. Talent, energy and hard work should be rewarded, and since these are displayed unequally, inequalities in wealth and property will inevitably arise:

> That property will ever be unequal is certain. Industry, superiority of talents, dexterity of management, extreme frugality, fortunate opportunities, or the opposite, or the means of those things, will ever produce that effect, without having recourse to the harsh, ill-sounding names of avarice and oppression. . . . All that is required with respect to property is to obtain it honestly, and not employ it criminally; but it is always criminally employed when it is made a criterion for exclusive rights.[14]

Even in his last and most radical large-scale work, *Agrarian Justice*, Paine did not abandon his belief that some economic inequalities are justified, and even beneficial: 'Though I care as little about riches as any man, I am a friend to riches because they are capable of good. I care not how affluent some may be, provided that none be miserable in consequence of it.'[15]

Paine's Radicalism

So far it might appear that Paine's opinions are impeccably liberal, and could even be quoted with approval by Mrs Thatcher or Lord Young, if they knew where to look. But having said that, it is time to redress the balance. The starting point of *Agrarian Justice* was the anxiety which Paine felt at observing a paradoxical development which seemed not to be catered for within the currently optimistic version of liberal economics.

This was that while poverty appeared not to exist in what Paine calls 'the natural state', it is an undeniable feature of 'the civilized state', to the extent that, in Paine's view, some are worse off in a so-called civilized society than they would be, or would have been, in the state of nature:

> Whether that state that is proudly, perhaps erroneously, called civilization, has most promoted or most injured the general happiness of man, is a question that may be strongly contested. On one side, the spectator is dazzled by splendid appearances; on the other, he is shocked by extremes of wretchedness; both of which it has erected. The most affluent and the most miserable of the human race are to be found in countries that are called civilized.[16]

In observing this glaring contrast between affluence and poverty Paine comes close to another radical writer of the day, William Blake, who wrote these lines in 1793:

> Is this a holy thing to see
> In a rich and fruitful land,
> Babes reduc'd to misery,
> Fed with cold and usurous hand?

Subsequently this becomes almost a commonplace of the critiques of industrial capitalism made both by high Tories like Coleridge and Southey, and radicals like Shelley and Cobbett.[17] But it is greatly to Paine's credit, considering his general position as outlined above, that he was one of the first to worry over this contrast. It is also highly significant. For it is on the question of poverty that Paine diverges most radically from the liberal economic tradition.

Adam Smith had taken a relatively compassionate view of poverty: 'No society can surely be flourishing and happy, of which the greater part of the members are poor and miserable.' He also believed that high wages encouraged people to work better.[18] But most of his followers took a decidedly harsher line. Thus Burke, in his *Thoughts and Details on Scarcity*, a work exactly contemporaneous with *Agrarian Justice*, asserts that mass poverty is inevitable: 'The labouring people are only poor because they are numerous. Numbers in their nature imply poverty'; and that poverty is beyond the power of government to remedy: 'To provide for us in our necessities is not in the power of government.' Indeed, he objects to the very term 'poor', because it seems to imply that as a general condition it is both deplorable and alterable. In another work of the same period, the *Letters on a Regicide Peace*, he writes angrily that 'When we affect to pity as poor, those who must labour or the world cannot exist, we are trifling with the condition of mankind.'[19] Only a few years later, in 1798, this unattractive combination of fatalism and harshness was given a supposedly scientific, and therefore apparently irrefutable, basis by the notorious population theory of Malthus.[20]

This was the direction in which both the theory and practice of liberal economics were already moving in the later 1790s; but it was not a path which Paine could ever have followed. His political solidarity with the poor, and his understanding of poverty and its causes would always have prevented that. In fact, despite his claim to be a 'friend to riches', and his repeated assertion of the inevitability (and justice) of a measure of inequality in wealth, he never lost a certain instinctive suspicion of the rich, which comes out in such incidental remarks as 'wealth is often the presumptive evidence of dishonesty; and poverty the negative evidence of innocence.'[21]

Unlike Burke, and unlike the present-day exponents of laissez-faire economics, Paine would not dream of blaming either nature or 'the Divine Providence', or the poor themselves, for their poverty:

The great mass of the poor in all countries are become an hereditary race, and it is next to impossible for them to get out of that state of themselves. It ought also to be observed that this mass increases in all countries that are called civilized. More persons fall annually into it than get out of it.[22]

Here, clearly, Paine is moving towards an understanding of the class, rather than individual, character of poverty and wealth.

And at many points in his writings he shows a truly sociological grasp of the nature and consequences of poverty; as when he asks, rhetorically: 'Why is it that scarcely any are executed but the poor? The fact is a proof, among other things, of a wretchedness in their condition.'[23] Or when he observed, in his earliest pamphlet, arguing for better wages for customs officers, that 'Poverty, in defiance of principle, begets a degree of meanness that will stoop to almost anything.'[24] And it is notable that in the final chapter of *Rights of Man*, with its remarkable welfare proposals, Paine readily identifies, without the benefit of elaborate social surveys, 'large families of children, and old people past their labour' as the two principal groups of the poor.[25] Two hundred years later the observation has not lost its resonance.

Two things should be particularly noted about Paine's extensive and imaginative proposals for the relief of poverty, which included child allowances, education allowances, and old age pensions, to be paid at the ages of fifty and sixty. The first is that Paine is adamant that 'This support . . . is not of the nature of a charity, but of a right.'[26] In the context of the 1790s, this was a very original and challenging contention. It remains so today. The second is that Paine's plan for a reformed tax system includes a progressive property tax, rising to twenty shillings in the pound on estates worth £23,000 or more. Once again, we see that Paine's respect for wealth is much more qualified than may appear at first sight.

People often marvel at the detailed calculations which Paine enters into when trying to cost his welfare proposals. But the expanation of this is very simple: he is desperately anxious to show that they can be paid for on the basis of savings achieved by ending the wasteful expenditures of the old regime. They must be sustainable on the basis of lower taxation. And presumably he hoped that they would not add unduly to the power and machinery of the state either. So cheap government and social security benefits are compatible, according to Paine.

Of course, with the benefit of hindsight, we know that this is an illusion. But what a significant and historically characteristic illusion it was! Paine clings to his general principles of minimal and cheap government because they are central to the bourgeois assault on feudalism and absolutism, and the liberation of capitalist enterprise; but also because at this point in modern history no one, so far as I know, is formulating a theory of interventionism, of positive state action. So Paine cannot be 'blamed', or patronized for this illusion. In fact what is remarkable is that he should have advocated such a radical practice of interventionism, along with progressive taxation, while remaining under the spell of non-interventionist theory. This is part of what I mean when I say that Paine stands at the most radical edge of bourgeois liberalism in theory, and could even be said to go beyond it in his detailed practical proposals.

I would make the same comment on Paine's handling of the issue of property in *Agrarian Justice*. Here Paine reiterates his view that an equality of property, according to the idea of an agrarian law, is impossible, since the amount of effort that property owners put into cultivating and developing their property is bound to differ. But he qualifies this by distinguishing between two kinds of property: first, 'natural property, or that which comes to us from the Creator of the universe — such as the earth, air, water' (so much for privatized water) which is rightfully the common property of all; and 'artificial or acquired property — the invention of men'.[27] It is only the latter, that is 'the value of the improvement, only, and not the earth itself, that is individual property.' Paine admits that in practical terms it is impossible 'to separate the improvement made by cultivation from the earth itself', and that therefore 'the idea of landed property arose from that inseparable connection'.[28] Nevertheless, he refuses to lose sight of the idea that the earth, the natural world, cannot strictly belong to any single individual, but is 'the *common property of the human race*'.[29] The fault is that land has fallen into the hands of the cultivators without any indemnification being made to the great number of non-owners, 'all those whom it dispossessed'; and this is what has to be remedied. So once again, while disowning any desire to challenge the institution of private property, and any aspiration towards the equalization of property ownership, Paine nevertheless sees the ownership of basic natural resources as a trust rather than an absolute right, and proposes compensatory measures which would in their effect be redistributive. The implications of Paine's treatment of what he partly recognized to be the related issues of property and poverty — 'The contrast of affluence and wretchedness continually meeting and offending the eye, is like dead and living bodies chained together.'[30] — are, surely, more radical than he realized, or could acknowledge, given his conscious primary allegiance to the principles of liberal political economy.

The Unfinished Business of Bourgeois Radicalism

It would be quite wrong, in my view, to represent this as an individual intellectual dilemma which Paine, reprehensibly, failed to resolve. For one thing, the conflict between an ever expanding practice of intervention and continuing adherence to the theory of non-intervention is a feature of British political and intellectual life for at least the following seventy or eighty years. The fact that John Stuart Mill, a far more expert and learned theorist than Paine, allowed his statement that '*laisser-faire* . . . should be the general practice: every departure from it, unless required by some great good, is a certain evil', to appear unaltered in every edition of his *Principles of Political Economy* published between 1848 and his death in 1873, is a celebrated example of this.

But what is even more significant is that the problems Paine wrestled with, and the responses he formulated, however ambivalent or contradictory they may now appear, are so central to, and so representative of, the revolution in its most radical phase. In France in the years 1793–4, the years of Jacobin dominance up to the coup of 9 Thermidor and the fall of Robespierre, the issues of the rights of property in relation to the rights and needs of the poor, of how far political democracy was compatible with gross economic inequalities, were at the very heart of political struggle, and were thus principal preoccupations of the government. Recent vast increases in capitalist power and in the huge wealth of a small minority, coupled with attacks on the poor and their minimal entitlements, have returned these issues to the centre of the political stage.

One constant popular demand during the revolutionary years, as in the pre-revolutionary period, was for legal controls over food prices, and especially over the price of bread. This was a demand which the Jacobins, like their predecessors, were disposed to resist; for, despite their reputation for relentless radicalism, in economic matters they were orthodox liberals. 'People are asking for a law about food supplies,' said Saint-Just in 1792. 'Positive legislation on that subject is never wise.'[31] Robespierre similarly favoured free trade as a matter of general principle:

> Common sense tells us, for example, that such commodities as are not essential to subsistence may be left to unlimited commercial speculation . . . and, generally, it may be assumed that the unrestricted freedom of this trade will redound to the general profit of both the State and the individual.[32]

But Robespierre's qualification was significant. He did, in effect, recognize a right to subsistence, and acknowledged that this must take precedence over the rights of property and the principles of free trade. In the same speech just quoted, he declared:

> Food that is necessary for man's existence is as sacred as life itself. Everything that is indispensable for its preservation is the common property of society as a whole. It is only the surplus that is private property and can be safely left to individual commercial enterprise.[33]

It was in a similar vein that he recognized that formal political rights were inadequate 'if necessity, the most imperious of laws, forces the most sane and the most numerous section of the people to renounce them.' He therefore favoured payment for the performance of public duties such as membership of the National Assembly or jury service.[34] (Payment for public service was also an issue which divided radicals from conservatives in the democracy of classical Athens.) Thus Robespierre, like Paine, was sufficiently conscious of the real needs and problems of the poor majority to be able to qualify, if not contradict, strict liberal economic orthodoxy, when occasion demanded it.

Robespierre's attitude towards economic equality was also strikingly similar to Paine's. He described the agrarian law as 'a bogey created by rogues to frighten fools', and held that 'equality of possessions is fundamentally impossible in civil society'. Yet he did not regard inequality with complacency, and believed that 'extreme disparities of wealth lie at the root of many ills and crimes.'[35] And Saint-Just took much the same line: 'We must give some land to all . . . we must have neither rich nor poor . . . opulence is infamy.'[36]

Although the Jacobin leaders found themselves in political conflict with the Enragés, who often led popular agitation against the government, there was not a wide gulf between the two groups in terms of political attitudes. The Enragés were less restrained, more open in their mistrust of wealth and their hostility to those merchants and employers who exploited their market power at the expense of the poor. They were perhaps a little more forthright in asserting the right to subsistence. But when Théophile Leclerc asserted that 'all men have an equal right to food and to all the products of the land which are indispensably necessary to preserve their existence',[37] he was not saying more than what Robespierre had publicly argued nine months earlier. And the vision of a society containing some inevitable but limited inequalities, outlined by Fauchet in a series of lectures on Rousseau in 1790–91, is essentially the same as that of Robespierre and Saint-Just:

In a society founded on a sound basis . . . citizens will not have the same fortunes, because they have not the same muscles, the same intelligence, the same astuteness; but shocking disproportions will be unknown; the eye will not be saddened by the contrast of the marble of palaces, and the mud of cottages, by the insulting vision of the pauper who is dying of hunger and the rich man who is dying of satiety.[38]

This quite distinctive perspective on property and inequality perhaps finds its clearest and most succinct expression in the programme of demands submitted to the Convention by the *Section des Sans Culottes* on 2 September 1793. This petition asserted that 'property rights, held to be sacred and inviolable . . . are confined to the extent of the satisfaction of physical needs.' Nobody, it argued, 'has the right to do anything that will injure another person'; and therefore there should be price controls, for 'What could be more harmful than the arbitrary power to increase the price of basic necessities to a level beyond the means of seven-eighths of the citizens?' It therefore asked for price controls not only over basic foods, but also over the raw materials essential to the work of the artisan, the craftsman and the manual worker. Other demands were that 'there be a fixed maximum on personal wealth', and that 'no citizen shall possess more than one workshop or retail shop'. The document concluded:

> The *Section des Sans Culottes* thinks that these measures will create abundance and tranquillity, and will, little by little, remove the gross inequalities of wealth and multiply the number of proprietors.[39]

This is a quintessentially petty bourgeois utopia of small independent proprietors and families. Private property as such is accepted, but this attitude is combined with a passionate egalitarianism and sense of justice which demands that property should not be accumulated in the hands of a minority to the point where it becomes a means of exploitation, and that there should be strict limits on the extent of economic inequality. The right to subsistence takes precedence over property rights.

Radicals in Britain in the 1790s were not caught up in such a momentous political drama as their comrades in France, and, as was to be expected, their responses were generally more moderate than those of the sans culottes. There are nevertheless striking similarities of outlook. Generally, the British radicals were insistent that it was 'equality of rights' and not 'equality of property' that they were demanding. A broadside from the Manchester Constitutional Society entitled 'An Explanation of the Word Equality', issued in 1792, made this distinction very clearly:

> The Equality insisted on by the Friends of Reform, is an EQUALITY OF RIGHTS. . . . The *inequality* derived from labor and successful enterprize, the result of superior industry and good fortune, is an *equality* [sic] *essential to the very existence of society.* . . . To render property insecure would destroy all motives to exertion, and tear up public happiness by the roots.[40]

On the other hand, radical respect for property and property rights was not usually unqualified, any more than it was in France. In 1795 the secretaries of the London Corresponding Society wrote that

> It is the reproach of this, as well as every other commercial country, that property is too much respected. As an evidence of industry and economy it is respectable, but it can by no means be considered as a general test of moral rectitude . . .[41]

The response of some historians, such as Norman Hampson and R.B. Rose, to this radical ideology seems somewhat perverse. Fairly enough, they emphasize how much this outlook owes to pre-capitalist notions of a 'moral economy', in which market operations are restrained and restricted by moral and humane considerations deriving, at the theoretical level, from Christian and natural law conceptions. But they seem over-anxious to deny any connection between this outlook and later socialist ideas. Thus R.B. Rose writes of the Enragés that 'in so far as they relied on the state to ensure social justice they were closer to the Ancien Régime than to the socialisms of the nineteenth century.'[42] And Hampson comments, apropos of Saint-Just's hatred of wealth, that 'The egalitarian peasant society he had in mind had more in common with medieval than with socialist ideas.'[43]

These comments seem to me to miss the point. At this early point in the history of industrial capitalism, it was inevitable that popular opposition to the rigours and injustices of the market would ground itself in references to an often idealized pre-industrial and pre-capitalist past. We can see exactly the same response in the writings of William Cobbett a quarter of a century later. But this should not be held to imply that they played no part in the evolution of a socialist critique and response. I would suggest, on the contrary, that there is a significant continuity between the pre-capitalist notion of a moral economy and later socialist ideas of economic equality and a planned or controlled economy. From the time of the French Revolution onwards there is a traceable continuity in popular radical traditions and movements. The responses of Paine and Robespierre, of the sans culottes and the British radicals of the 1790s, to the connected issues of wealth, inequality and poverty, and the rights to food and subsistence, suggest to me that significant elements among 'the people', and later the working class(es), were *never* fully converted to the merits of the market, laissez faire and unlimited inequalities of wealth and property; but moved, without too much difficulty, from a belief in the older moral economy to the more thoroughgoing egalitarianism and critique of capitalism which was developed within the socialist tradition.

In the past, the nature of Paine's radicalism, and of what is too loosely called 'Jacobinism' was not well understood. Writers like Eric Foner and Isaac Kramnick have done us a service in drawing attention to Paine's commitment to economic liberalism; and undoubtedly this casts light over his whole politics. But in so doing they have perhaps underestimated the significance of those moments when he contradicts or qualifies his economic liberalism. And much the same might be said, I think, of certain historians of the French Revolution. What such moments of divergence indicate is that those who were seriously committed to the idea of popular democracy, and to the cause of the poor, could not, finally, accept economic liberalism without qualification in detail and in practice, if not in theory. They were unable to reconcile active political democracy with unlimited economic inequality, and popular welfare with the unlimited operation of the market; and in both respects they were surely right. Their instinctive egalitarianism and their sense of social well-being as something more than the sum of individual interests may hark back to the older moral economy, and inevitably evokes the looming presence of Rousseau. Nevertheless, it also points forward to socialism.

Perhaps, finally, it is my own title that I am criticizing, and in two different but connected respects. My final impression is that the boundary between bourgeois or liberal on the one hand and radical or socialist on the other, however clear it may be in theory, is constantly being crossed and re-crossed by the revolutionaries and radicals of the 1790s, who, whatever their general theoretical commitments or perspectives, often responded with generous indignation to the evident poverty and deprivation suffered by the great mass of the people. Many of them saw clearly enough that sets of liberal rights which did not include the basic right to subsistence were inadequate and even meaningless to the hungry and the illiterate. In seeing this they were seeing one of the central weaknesses of liberalism itself, and, consciously or unconsciously, embarking on the classic socialist critique of liberalism. Furthermore, Paine, as we have seen, was never tempted to blame the poor themselves for the general condition of poverty — unlike economic liberals, then and now. He saw mass poverty as a structural phenomenon which required a structural, or governmental, response. This alone sets him at a considerable distance from the orthodoxy of bourgeois liberalism.

Yet even if we do not, finally allow this to alter our categorization of Paine, Robespierre and others as, in the last analysis, bourgeois radicals, it would be a serious mistake to take this label as a licence for patronizing them. To suppose that 'we' have made such strides in the past two centuries as to have rendered bourgeois radicalism, or even bourgeois liberalism, wholly obsolete and irrelevant, would be an absurd delusion — and especially in Britain. For Britain is an outstanding, and in some ways unique example of a supposedly modern liberal democracy which has failed to achieve even that degree of constitutional liberalism and political democracy which was inaugurated in the United States and France two hundred years ago, and which has, with variations, become the norm in the advanced capitalist democracies.

The survival of a conspicuously un-democratized monarchy, of a second legislative chamber composed in the main of hereditary aristocrats, the absence of a written constitution or any legally guaranteed civil liberties — these and many other aspects of the contemporary British state would shock and scandalize Paine as much today they did two centuries ago. For a long time the left contrived to ignore or dismiss these anachronisms and inadequacies as matters of no great importance — the preoccupations of bourgeois liberals, no doubt. It would be an exaggeration to say that the experience of Thatcherism has changed all that. But there are at least significant signs that liberals and the left are waking up to the great danger they have placed themselves in by allowing the unreconstructed, unconstitutional, pre-modern British state to survive so long. For it is this survival that made possible the erosion without redress of so many civil and collective rights during the 1970s, and even more drastically in the 1980s. The campaign for constitutional reform focusing on Charter 88 is the most important and encouraging sign of this awakening.

Our recent experience of growing authoritarianism would not have surprised Paine. He would say that it vindicates all his arguments in favour of a written constitution and the most open and accountable system possible of representative democracy; and he would be right. Britain has still not achieved the kind of political system he was contending for, and we have paid and are still paying dearly for that failure. Paine's radicalism, bourgeois or not, still retains much of its relevance.

Notes

1. *Daily Telegraph*, 23 January 1982.

2. E.J. Hobsbawm, *Labouring Men*, London: Weidenfeld and Nicolson 1964, p. 1.

3. Gwyn A. Williams, *Artisans and Sans-Culottes*, London: Edward Arnold 1968, p. 14.

4. Hazlitt quoted by Michael Foot, *The Guardian*, 15 January 1982.

5. Thomas Paine, *Common Sense* (1776), Harmondsworth: Penguin 1976, p. 72.

6. Thomas Paine, *Rights of Man* (1791/2), Harmondsworth: Penguin 1984, p. 146.

7. Paine, *Rights*, p. 126.

8. Paine, *Rights*, pp. 212–3.

9. Paine, *Rights*, pp. 213, 214.

10. Paine, *Rights*, pp. 163–4.

11. Paine, *Common Sense*, p. 65.

12. Paine, *Rights* p. 161.

13. Ibid.

14. Thomas Paine, *Dissertation on First Principles of Government* (1975), in Michael Foot and Isaac Kramnick, eds, *The Thomas Paine Reader*, London: Penguin 1987.

15. Thomas Paine, *Agrarian Justice* (1797), in Foot and Kramnick, eds, *Reader*, p. 482.

16. *Reader*, pp. 474–5.

17. This is well charted in Raymond Williams, *Culture and Society 1780–1950*, London: Chatto and Windus 1958, chapters 1–3.

18. Adam Smith, *The Wealth of Nations*, Book 1, chapter VIII.

19. Quoted in C.B. Macpherson, *Burke*, Oxford: Oxford University Press 1980, p. 55.

20. Malthusian ideas have recently been revived as part of the re-emergence of economic liberalism as an influential doctrine. They are discussed by Ted Benton in chapter 10 of this volume.

21. *Reader*, p. 461.

22. *Reader*, p. 484.

23. Paine, *Rights*, p. 218.

24. *Reader*, p. 47.

25. *Reader*, p. 240.

26. *Reader*, p. 243.

27. *Reader*, p. 472.

28. *Reader*, p. 476.

29. Ibid.

30. *Reader*, p. 482.

31. Quoted in Norman Hampson, *The French Revolution: A Concise History*, London: Thames and Hudson 1975, p. 52.

32. Quoted in George Rudé, *Robespierre*, London: Collins 1975, p. 133.

33. Ibid.

34. Rudé, *Robespierre*, p. 102.

35. *Robespierre*, p. 151.

36. Quoted in Norman Hampson, *A Social History of the French Revolution*, London, Routledge 1963, p. 228.

37. Quoted in R.B. Rose, *The Enragés: Socialists of the French Revolution?*, Sydney: Sydney University Press 1968.

38. Rose, *The Enragés*, p. 85.

39. Printed in D.G. Wright, *Revolution and Terror in France 1789–1795*, London: Longman 1974, p. 120.

40. Cited in Eric Foner, *Tom Paine and Revolutionary America*, Oxford: Oxford University Press 1976, p. 227.

41. Quoted in Gwyn A. Williams, *Artisans*, p. 71.

42. Rose, *The Enragés*, p. 90.

43. Hampson, *A Social History*, p. 228.

3

The French Revolution and New World Slavery

Robin Blackburn

In the 1989 commemorations, the French Revolution was sometimes commended for abolishing French colonial slavery. Not infrequently slave emancipation was tagged on to a list of consequences thought to flow from the proclamation of the principles of 1789 and of the *Rights of Man and the Citizen*. In a natural association of ideas, it is apparently thought that the slogan of 'liberty, equality and fraternity' spelt the end for slavery.

Such ideas do the Revolution both too much and too little honour. Too much because the Revolution of 1789, or for that matter of 1791, actually did nothing about slavery — neither the National Assembly nor the Constituent Assembly even staged a debate on colonial slavery as such. But too little also because the epic achievement of the eventual French Republican conversion to revolutionary emancipationism is seldom properly acknowledged. Not only is the French emancipationist contribution ignored in most general histories of abolitionism, but even specialist scholarly debate — such as that which raged in the *American Historical Review* between 1985 and the end of 1987 — treats anti-slavery as an exclusively white, Anglo-Saxon and Protestant affair. The main protagonist in that dispute was Thomas Haskell who argued that slavery was challenged thanks to the spread of the market in the Atlantic

73

zone. In three lengthy contributions, each weighed down by hundreds of citations, there was not a single mention of Toussaint L'Ouverture, or Dessalines, or Sonthonax or Victor Hugues or Julien Fedon or any of those associated with French Republican emancipationism or black Jacobinism. A more forgivable lapse is often made of simply saluting the great black revolutionary Toussaint L'Ouverture and seeing in him the very figure of an irresistible revolt against cruel tyranny. Such a romantic approach does not ask how it is that the slave rebellion in Saint Domingue came to triumph as one of the very few successful large-scale slave revolts in history — some would say the only one. The true story of how French colonial slavery came to be overthrown is sufficiently remarkable and important to justify a narrative sketch.

I

In order to do justice to the French revolutionary contribution it is important not to exaggerate or misconstrue it. Slavery was indeed deprecated by leaders of French opinion in the early phase of the Revolution. Mirabeau and Lafayette were supporters of the abolitionist society — the 'Amis de Noirs' — founded in 1788, whose Secretary was Brissot de Warville and whose President was Condorcet; so abolitionism did not lack for prominent supporters in the middle or pre-Jacobin phase of the Revolution. But for reasons to be explored below these men chose to take their stand on advocacy of the civic rights of free men of colour and did not launch direct attacks on colonial slavery or the slave trade. Moreover, in deploring slavery Brissot and Condorcet were not boldly espousing a new and unacceptable doctrine but rather echoing something like a consensus in enlightened circles in the Atlantic world. It is true that slavery only began to be questioned by moralists and philosophers as late as the mid eighteenth century — Montesquieu's *Esprit des Lois* being a pivotal work. But subsequent to this, the case against slavery had been endorsed or developed by many thinkers, including Scottish economists

74

and jurists, contributors to the *Encyclopédie*, religious leaders like Wesley, and by the widely read French colonial expert the Abbé Raynal in his bestselling work the *Histoire des Deux Mondes*.

By the year 1789 several major political figures had already declared a sympathy for anti-slavery thought — not only William Pitt, the Prime Minister of Britain, and Benjamin Franklin, but also the slaveowners Thomas Jefferson and George Washington. In France itself the formation of the Amis des Noirs belongs as much to the last reforming spasm of the ancien régime as it does to the revolutionary impulse of 1789. One quarter of the members of the Amis des Noirs were in fact high officials of state, mainly in the financial departments. Louis XVI himself graciously received an abolitionist deputation; Necker and other senior ministers or advisers were known to be sympathetic. To someone influenced by Condorcet, anti-slavery was symbolic of a new ideal order and a new integrity without odious distinctions and privileges. As the ancien régime tried to jump out of its own skin it was a widely appealing vision.

Just as remarkable as this consensus was the paucity of action flowing from it. However lamentable New World slavery was thought to be, it was nevertheless protected by interests and doctrines capable of neutralizing and blocking it. The slave plantations might embody great inhumanity but they also constituted a crucial source of national wealth, above all in the United States, Britain and France. In these countries, national commerce largely depended upon an intercourse with the slave plantations. The knot of New World slavery had been tied by national interest, an intense respect for the sacredness of private property and racial disregard of those of African descent. The form of capitalism which thrived in the Atlantic zone in this epoch still entailed extensive exchanges with the slave plantations which were the chief or only suppliers of such coveted produce as sugar, tobacco, coffee, and cotton. Those statesmen who deplored slavery might be ashamed of their state's involvement in slavery, and find it difficult openly to justify denying Africans the attributes of men and women, but they refused to countenance unilateral actions that were hostile to national interests or that tended to put property rights in question. Thus the British abolitionist movement chose to attack the slave trade rather than slaveowners' property, in the first instance; and they found themselves blocked by the argument that if Britain abandoned the slave trade then this would simply provide new openings for their commercial rivals.

The protective complex to which I have referred effectively defended French colonial slavery for three or four years after 1789. The French colonies were the richest and most dynamic in the Americas, and thanks to their monopoly of French colonial trade, the merchants of Bordeaux and Nantes were continental Europe's chief suppliers of plantation produce. As it happened, the organization of both Girondins and Jacobins drew upon the commercial networks radiating out from the Atlantic seaboard. In the Assembly itself as many as a tenth of the deputies owned property in the colonies. Thus it is scarcely surprising that it was not thought possible to make any head-on challenge to colonial slavery. Brissot and other supporters of the Amis des Noirs did, however, eventually bring themselves to press for a modest quasi-abolitionist measure when they undertook to campaign for civic rights to be given to qualified — that is, propertied — free men of colour in the colonies. Restricting the vote to men of property had itself been contentious — denying it to wealthy and respectable coloured proprietors would be more difficult still to justify. And beyond questions of justification there was also the important consideration that the free men of colour were inclined to be much more loyal to the metropolis than were the resident planters of the Antilles. While the white planters dreamt of autonomy, or even independence on the North American model, the free people of colour were open to an alliance with the government in Paris. Girondin attempts to construct a new political order in the colonies did not harm commercial interests, while humanistic rhetoric actually reinforced them in the given circumstances. But this still didn't mean a challenge to slavery as such. Indeed, many mulattoes were slaveowners themselves.

The years 1789–91 witnessed a ragged conflict between metropolis and colonies, and within the colonies, between whites and free mulattoes, royalists and Patriots. Weakening the apparatus of slave domination, this set the scene for the celebrated slave uprising of August 1791 in Saint Domingue. Deservedly famous as it is, this tremendous revolt of the slaves of Saint Domingue's northern plain did not immediately lead to a general assault on slavery as is sometimes supposed. This slave rebellion was remarkable for its scale and stamina but it did not set itself wider objectives than those which characterized other slave revolts — the liberty of those immediately involved. The rebel chiefs did not aim at liberty for all slaves, and they chose to call themselves soldiers of the King, eventually reaching an arrangement with the Spanish monarch. The mass of slave rebels — numbering several tens of thousands — were inspired by the quite specific objective of themselves escaping from an extraordinarily oppressive system. To begin with, they were scarcely concerned at a struggle articulated in terms of French juridical categories. They hoped for liberty for themselves, their families, and those they knew.

In areas the rebellion had not reached, or where it had been contained, there were calls for changes in the plantation regime — for example, for the slaves' free days to be increased from one, or one and a half, to two or three days per week. They also asked for larger garden plots where they could work on their free days; more exceptionally, they might ask for the dismissal of a specially hated overseer. Even those slaves who escaped into the hills and forests would be more likely to be inspired by African memories or ideals than by the *Declaration of the Rights of Man*.

By December 1791 the main rebel chiefs were engaging in a negotiation with the French Commissioner according to which only four hundred of their number would have received outright freedom, the others having to rest content with piecemeal amelioration. The black generals thus adopted a stance towards slavery that might be compared with the modern trade union leaders' approach to wage labour: negotiate for better terms and conditions, not for abolition. In the event the leaders of the black rebels reached a deal with the Spanish King rather than the French Republic. Some French royalist officials and proprietors seem to have been willing to help the black soldiers so long as they fought the Republic and lent themselves to no generalized attack on slavery. There are occasional mentions of black rebel bands accompanied by white curés or even white officers. A number of the black rebels believed that only the King was competent to confer a valid emancipation and that the increasingly bold proposals of Sonthonax, the Republican Commissioner, were a species of trickery without legitimate political sanction. One could even compare the slave uprising in Saint Domingue of 1791–3 with the revolt in the Vendée in that it was anti-Republican in character and eschewed alignment with general emancipationist goals. This having been said, in the long run the revolt did greatly weaken slaveholder power and constitute a continuing pressure on the Republican authorities.

Though the latter managed to pacify much of the northern plain in 1792–3, the rebels maintained themselves in the mountains and border districts. Moreover, there were repeated outbreaks of revolt in different parts of the colony. The factional struggles within the free population weakened the apparatus of slave control and even led to rival groups arming their own slaves. The existence of local markets in slave produce furnished an opportunity for slaves from different plantations to meet. According to legend, voodoo ceremonies also sometimes performed this role. For some slave rebels, simply driving out the whites and claiming what they saw as their land was a quite sufficient programme. But the rebel leaders did use the word liberty and some would certainly have seen the peril and offence of a selective and partial liberty that left vengeful slaveowners in place.

The French Republic belatedly adopted emancipation in February 1794, two and a half years after the slave rebellion in Saint Domingue had made black rebels crucial protagonists in the struggle for the New World. C.L.R. James's magnificent book *The Black Jacobins*, first published in 1938, remains one of the very few works to concern itself with this pivotal moment in the history of New World slavery. James's thesis is not that the rebels were 'black Jacobins' from the outset, but rather that Black Jacobinism eventually emerged as the cement for a precariously negotiated alliance between the most farsighted of the black rebels — notably Toussaint L'Ouverture — and the most consistent and anti-racist of the Jacobins, notably Sonthonax. For a time these two men competed with one another in the liberationist appeals they directed at the mass of blacks, though neither was really in a position to proclaim general emancipation — Toussaint because he was a Spanish General and Sonthonax because he was a representative of the Convention. From the end of 1793 Toussaint began to distance himself from the Spanish authorities, so much so that royalist planters allied to Spain complained that he could not be trusted; they accused the black general of harbouring slave runaways. Sonthonax found that he needed black allies in his struggle against moderate and racist Republicans. He offered freedom and arms to all those who would help him in June 1793, followed up within two months by a local decree of general emancipation. These appeals were issued in Kreyole, the language spoken by the great majority of blacks, instead of in the French that had hitherto been the sole medium of official communication. The great majority of slaveholding whites now abandoned any hope of seeing their interests secured by the Republic and looked instead to Britain for their salvation.

The French Republic had declared war on Britain in February 1793, so this was an appeal heeded by the British government. Britain forthwith dispatched a huge expedition to seize the French Antilles and to rescue the French planters from their own slaves. Both in Saint Domingue and in the Lesser Antilles planters and white militia prepared to welcome the British. As might be supposed, the London government lost interest in abolitionism. Edmund Burke, an erstwhile opponent of the slave trade, declared that he would far rather see a properly regulated slave trade and system of slavery than the abrupt suppression of both or either.

In Saint Domingue, the Jacobin Commissioner knew that the menaced Republican bridgehead could best be defended by his policy of liberating and arming the blacks within his jurisdiction, but to give this credibility it had to be endorsed by the National Convention. At the end of 1793 Sonthonax sent a delegation

— three men, one of whom was a black soldier, another a mulatto — from Saint Domingue to the National Convention to demand general emancipation. This proposal was approved by acclamation in Pluviôse An II. By this time the complex of interests and ideas protective of slavery had broken down. Under the pressure of the sans culottes, private property was no longer sacred; indeed, the rich were now held to be suspect in their patriotism. The emancipation decree was taken up with vigour by the Hebertists and other socially radical currents.

This period also witnessed attacks on merchants, seizure of the property of real or supposed traitors and vigorous attempts to control the market. As Britain moved to capture France's slave colonies with the active collusion of the colonial slaveowners, the argument from national interest no longer militated against emancipation. As for ethnic identification, the universalistic elements in Revolutionary ideology had led to widespread rejection of the notion of an 'aristocracy of skin'. Racist Jacobins were discredited by the unpatriotic behaviour of many white colons. The breakthrough made by the Convention coincided with Toussaint's abandonment of the Spanish and his realignment with the French Republic. In Saint Domingue, revolutionary emancipationism and black power became a formidable — indeed unconquerable — force. The British were compelled to give up their ignominious attempt to grab Saint Domingue and to defend slavery within it. The first British forces had landed in December 1793; despite more than 40,000 reinforcements, they were obliged to evacuate in 1798.

Those who rhetorically invoke the anti-slavery action of the French Revolution do not usually make it clear that the alliance of Jacobinism and black power effected the first major breach in the New World slave systems, and that it dealt a blow to colonial slavery from which it would never recover. Allied to the resources of a great power and revolutionary state, slave insurgence and emancipationism was given a vital breathing space and was harnessed to a programme of general emancipation.

II

Saint Domingue in the early 1790s was the richest and most dynamic slave colony in the Americas. It contained about half a million slaves; adding in the slave populations of Guadeloupe and Martinique there were nearly three-quarters of a million French colonial slaves. Prior to this, anti-slavery had had no impact on the plantation-zone where the large slave populations were to be found. In Britain, the celebrated Mansfield decision of 1772 had prevented an American slaveowner from returning his slave to the colonies, but there were only a few thousand slaves in England at this time and Mansfield did not deny that they owed some service to their masters. In 1780 the state of Pennsylvania had passed an Emancipation Act which seems to have been drafted by Thomas Paine. This was a moment of difficulty and of social radicalization, but even so the emancipation measure was a modest one. Under its terms no existing slave had to be freed. Instead, freedom was to be conferred on children to be born to slave mothers and on them only after they reached the age of twenty-five. Against the extreme modesty and circumspection of measures such as these, the boldness and radicalism of the decree of Pluviôse An II stands out unmistakably. The British government was to wait thirty-nine years before — in the aftermath of the Reform Crisis and pressed by a newly radical working class — it was to introduce its own measure of slave emancipation.

The story would, of course, be simpler and more acceptable if the French Revolution had attacked slavery during its innocent and generous phase. But unfortunately the record shows that vested interests prevented the great orators of the Revolution from forcing the Assembly to attend to the matter — although their fight for the civic rights of the free coloured proprietors did have a value of its own, in so far as it weakened racism and won over coloured partisans to the Republic. It should also be mentioned that Danton immediately welcomed the Pluviôse decree while some Jacobins had sought to prevent the Saint Domingue delegation from addressing the Convention.

The pro-emancipation policy of the French Republic must

be credited firstly to the persistence of the black rebellion —
making it a potential ally against the British; and secondly, to
the more radical French Jacobins, who accepted the decree of
Pluviôse An II, and to the Directory, which upheld the results
of the policy in the Caribbean. It is odd that pro-Jacobin
historians have not, on the whole, made more of this hugely
redeeming act of the period of the Terror; not perhaps so odd
that generations of radical historians have failed to register the
audacious revolutionary deeds of the degenerate Thermidorian
Directory in the Caribbean.

Unfortunately there is much that still needs to be found out
about this fascinating episode in the making of the modern
world. Indeed it is to a novelist, Alejo Carpentier, that we
must turn for the most vivid account of the extraordinary
developments in the Eastern Caribbean in the period after
the decree of Pluviôse. In *El Siglo de las Luces* (*Explosion
in the Cathedral*) Carpentier attempted a narrative of the life
and times of Victor Hugues, the Jacobin Commissioner who
brought the decree of Pluviôse to the New World. But while
this novel yields insight into the mentality of the tropical Patriot,
it does not do justice to the grandeur of Hugues's achievement.
Carpentier wrote this fiction as a Communist still reeling under
the impact of Khrushchev's secret speech to the 20th Congress
of the CPSU. He also seems to have placed too much reliance on
a biography of Hugues — the only one there is — written in the
thirties by a French naval historian. The result is a portrait which
points up the sinister and seamy side of this admittedly flawed
revolutionary, while underplaying the impact of Revolution had
on the Caribbean.

In April 1794 Hugues set out from Brest with a tiny flotilla
of two frigates, five transports and a brigantine; carrying with
him to the New World the emancipation decree, a printing
press and a guillotine. He arrived in the Eastern Caribbean to
face a British force about six times as large as his own which
had occupied the French colonies of Guadeloupe, Desiderade,
and Martinique at the specific invitation of local slaveowners.
The subsequent exploits of the Jacobin not only considerably
outshine the fictional escapades of a Hornblower, but have a

New World significance comparable to Thermopylae or the Battle of Britain.

Hugues established a bridgehead on Guadeloupe and landed a part of his force of 1,200 troops. The British occupation forces on this island alone numbered over 4,000 and were well supplied with war matériel; Benedict Arnold, the American renegade and counter-Revolutionary had set up shop in Basse Terre and was deep in negotiations with local planters. In eight months of fighting, Hugues drove out the British, their American camp-follower and his clients. This triumph over the British and the royalists was achieved thanks to the Revolutionary emancipation measure which enabled the Jacobin leader to arm thousands of blacks and to sow confusion in the British-occupied areas. Once the British had been driven out, Guadeloupe was converted into a springboard for the liberation of Desiderade and a number of smaller islands. The emancipation decree was translated and printed in all the major Caribbean languages. Support was given to slave revolts in St Vincent, Dominica, and Grenada. At one point the Revolutionary forces of Julien Fedon (a coloured proprietor who led the revolt in Grenada) held the whole island save its capital. Recent research shows that the so-called 'War of the Brigands' waged by Hugues and the black revolutionaries of the Eastern Caribbean tied up more British troops and warships than the campaign in Saint Domingue. French propaganda of word and deed inspired slave revolts in Venezuela, Cuba, Jamaica and Brazil.

In the years 1794–9 the French Directory sent substantial supplies to the Caribbean: thousands of troops and impressive quantities of firearms and ammunition. The consolidation of a revolutionary black power in Saint Domingue was decisively assisted by this help and by the diversion of counter-Revolutionary forces to the Eastern Caribbean. The 'War of the Brigands' accounted for two-thirds of the ninety thousand or so British casualties in the Caribbean theatre. British losses in this Caribbean 'sideshow' were greater than in the European theatre.

The truly heroic stature of Toussaint L'Ouverture, the main leader of the black revolutionaries of Saint Domingue, was widely acknowledged, both at the time and subsequently. Toussaint's acceptance as an abolitionist symbol in England dates from the time he became first Napoleon's opponent and then his victim. Without in any way challenging the pre-eminence given to Toussaint, we should point out that the overthrow of slavery in Saint Domingue was owed to the courage and tenacity of many thousands of black rebels who carried the torch of liberty both in the earlier period before Toussaint's role was clear and also following his arrest on Napoleon's orders in 1802. Thus, prior to April 1794, Toussaint, as an officer of the Spanish King, found his room for manoeuvre severely constricted. Recent research by the Canadian historian Robert Stein has shown that the Jacobin Commissioner sent to Saint Domingue in July 1792, Leger Felicite Sonthonax, worked his way quite speedily to a pro-emancipation policy and in the process attracted black allies and a black following. When Sonthonax offered arms as well as liberty to those who would support him against moderate Republicans, amongst those who responded were the followers of the independent black partisan Pierrot, a man who later proved one of Napoleon's most irreconcilable foes. Other black soldiers were given important commands by Sonthonax including Belley, a member of the delegation to the National Convention in February 1794, and many who later fought with Toussaint, like Henri Christophe and Pierre Michel. Sonthonax's orientation towards emancipation was a factor drawing Toussaint to Republicanism; likewise his breach with the Spanish was encouraged by a new and independent slave revolt in the early months of 1794.

Eugene Genovese has argued in his book *From Rebellion to Revolution* that the French Revolution effected a transformation in the character of slave revolts in the Americas. Prior to this period slave revolts and slave maronnage did not aim to overthrow slavery as such but rather to deliver the particular groups involved from the exceptional ferocity of the New World slave systems. The maroons or communities of escaped slaves had their hands full defending their own freedom. Some seem to have recognized traditional forms of bondage, while many made agreements with the slaveowners to discourage or return further runaways. After the victory of the slaves in Saint Domingue the revolts of American slaves could, and often did, have a general anti-slavery character, as in Jamaica in 1831 or Martinique in 1848 or Brazil in 1887. Genovese's argument is a bit schematic but fundamentally accurate.

French Republican anti-slavery policy went far beyond anything witnessed in the American Revolution and far beyond anything envisaged by British abolitionists during the first wave of anti-slavery in Britain in the years 1788 to 1792. It permitted the consolidation of a black army committed to emancipationism and capable of defending this even against France itself. When Laveaux, the senior Republican commander, was recalled to France in 1795 he appointed Toussaint as his successor. By this time the French Republican forces numbered at least twenty thousand, the great majority of them former slaves. Toussaint not only commanded the largest army but had also shown that he could weld an army of former slaves into a highly disciplined and effective force. With rather less success, he also sought to urge black labourers to resume work on the export crops. As is well known, Toussaint never renounced allegiance to France, though as Governor of Saint Domingue he had exercised great autonomy.

When Napoleon sought to destroy the black power in Saint Domingue the prestige of the French Republic was such that he found many coloured soldiers willing to collaborate with him. But black resistance nevertheless welled up and eventually engulfed the occupying force. Napoleon lost more soldiers in Saint Domingue than were to fall at Waterloo, just as the British suffered more casualties in Saint Domingue than in their hard-fought final battle against the French emperor. One of Napoleon's generals recounts in his memoirs the dismay and shame he saw on his soldiers' faces one evening during the siege of Crete à Pierrot. From the clifftop stronghold of this indomitable black irregular could be heard the strains of *La Marseillaise* and the *Ça Ira*. Curiously enough, the black resistance did not adopt the name Haiti until the French had already been defeated.

The Republic of Haiti established in 1804 was not the first independent state in the New World, but it could proudly claim to be the first to ban slavery throughout its territory. This was to be a source of inspiration for later partisans of emancipation. In 1816 Petion, then President of the Haitian Republic, made sure that the torch of slave liberation would be carried further when he gave succour and support to Simón Bolívar in return for a promise that the Spanish American Liberator would himself combine the struggle for independence with the struggle against slavery.

I would like to conclude by considering aspects of this first liberation which might explain the modest role accorded to it in the historical literature.

III

Firstly, the decree of Pluviôse might be thought to have been nothing more than crude realpolitik, a sort of desperate last throw by French colonialism in the Caribbean. I have myself acknowledged that the outbreak of war with Britain and the despatch of a large British expedition to the West Indies meant that French national interest found it easier to accept an emancipation policy that would allow them to recruit black soldiers. However, I would not accept that the course of events left the French Republicans with no other choice, nor that they did not have to accept a price for their commitment to emancipationism in 1794–9. On various occasions the British, Spanish and Portuguese governments felt the need for black soldiers because they were in a tight spot. What they then did was to promise freedom only to those who fought for them: the Portuguese did this in Brazil in the seventeenth century in their war against the Dutch; the British did it during the War of American Independence; the Spanish King, and some French royalists, had done this in Saint Domingue itself. The decree of Pluviôse went decisively further than such limited and opportunistic measures. It also entailed risks and costs. By declaring emancipation, the Paris government knew that it risked alienating some of its remaining white partisans in the Caribbean, as indeed it did — Sonthonax's policy led numbers of white Patriots to defect to the royalists or to seek exile.

Another significant cost of Revolutionary emancipationism was worsening relations with an important potential ally of the isolated and embattled French Republic — the United States, with its influential slaveholding class. The French Revolutionary agents in the Caribbean sought to encourage slave insurgency in other parts of the Americas, and while they didn't directly target the Virginians, this emancipationist policy could not possibly be acceptable to the US government, as soon became apparent. Moreover, Victor Hugues unloosed a flotilla of privateers on the trading, including slave trading, vessels of all other nations, which practised a sort of buccaneering Jacobinism. Indeed, it was largely in consequence that the so-called Quasi-War broke out between France and the United States in which hostilities were confined to the New World. The Directory stuck by Hugues and emancipationism despite these costs. From a national interest point of view there were, of course, gains — the large casualties inflicted on the British. Nevertheless, it is generally true that alternative policy options themselves help to construct rival sets of interests and risks. That the path of Republican virtue also had advantages does not discredit it.

Napoleon's moves to restore slavery in 1802, which met little metropolitan resistance, might be thought to detract from the grandeur of the French Revolutionary contribution. As it happens most of those associated with the emancipationist policy did oppose slavery's restoration, though disgracefully these did not include Hugues, who was then Governor of Guiane. By this time Napoleon had constructed a formidable power and was soon demolishing other Revolutionary gains. Aristocracy was to be recreated and French labourers required to carry a carnet to show they were gainfully employed. The reasons for Napoleon's move to restore slavery are not always properly appreciated. Under the terms of the Treaty of Amiens the British returned to France the captured colony of Martinique in which the slave plantations were in a flourishing condition. Napoleon could not refuse the return of Martinique and he had no desire to see slavery overturned there. The diplomatic record shows that both the United States and Britain were happy to see Napoleon attempt to restore black subordination in the Caribbean. Whether he succeeded or not, they were going to benefit. Pointing out Anglo-American complicity does not absolve Napoleon, but it does help explain how he was drawn into such a dangerous venture. In the event, slavery was restored in Guadeloupe though only after a fierce struggle against a group of the local black military men.

Returning to the Revolutionary period, it seems to me that subsequent events do not cancel out the significance of the decree of Pluviôse any more than the Restoration of Charles II cancels out the significance of the Putney Debates. Moreover, slavery itself was not in fact to be restored in Saint Domingue, or Haiti as it became in 1804.

A final possibility to be considered is that the record of Haiti in the post-Revolutionary period should be seen as somehow diminishing the significance of the emancipation that had been defended at such cost. Thus, the British writer Terry Coleman, writing in *The Guardian*, has suggested that the subsequent poverty and instability of Haiti detracts from the achievement of the 'Black Jacobins'. Some even allege that the mass of Haitian blacks were soon no better off than under slavery. However, anyone at all acquainted with the condition of Caribbean slaves in the eighteenth or nineteenth centuries will know that the post-emancipation condition of the citizens of Haiti was quite transformed. While the Caribbean slave populations invariably had a negative growth rate, with deaths outnumbering births by a considerable margin, Haiti's population recovered and grew. Though the Haitian peasants were poor they did not spend six days a week working for someone else. They built themselves simple but attractive dwellings, enjoyed freedom of movement and developed a rich folklore. Haitian women were not at the mercy of overseers or planters; rather they furnished much of the commercial infrastructure of the peasant economy. The development of Haiti was greatly hampered by two circumstances. First, the Atlantic powers would extend neither diplomatic recognition nor normal trade facilities to the black state. Second, the small free state faced the danger of some new attack by the French or Spanish and was obliged to devote large resources to its armed forces. It may finally be said that the Haitian people themselves do not seem to have shared the view that the post-emancipation order was comparable to slavery — they could always be mobilized by any threat of slavery's return as they had been in 1802–4 when they defeated Napoleon's army.

In Saint Domingue the French Revolution had an enabling force, attracting black partisans who triumphantly defended its emancipationist legacy against the metropolis itself. In saluting the impact of the French Revolution in the Caribbean, therefore, we salute its appropriation by former slaves, few of whom even spoke French, but who found in it both opportunity and inspiration for the first major blow to be dealt to the New World slave systems. It may even be that the blacks of Saint Domingue/Haiti gained more from the Revolution, albeit at huge cost, than did most of the poor or oppressed in France itself. Perhaps this draws our attention to a more general truth. There was a universalistic emancipatory element in the French Revolution, but those who issued the *Declaration of the Rights of Man* were by no means always aware of it, or willing to follow through its logic. Here we may see the limitations as well as the achievements of a formal, abstract mode of reasoning characteristic of increasingly marketized social relations. For the emancipatory promise to be fulfilled there was needed the independent action of formerly excluded, oppressed and exploited social layers — radicalized sans culottes and slave rebels who understood that there should be no peace with slavery or slaveholders.

4

Right, Revolution and Community: Marx's 'On the Jewish Question'

Jay Bernstein

There must be a more than benign irony in the fact that in disavowing the French Revolution Marxism refused the exemplar of the first Western revolution to conceive of itself as explicitly a revolution in the modern sense: that is, as a collective and willed constitution of a new social order.[1] But this refusal is hardly surprising since the French Revolution was fought self-consciously on the terrain of rights, and, indeed, was made possible through the transformation of classical natural law doctrine into a theory of rights.[2] Marx, with his critique of ideology applied to the bourgeois state, his sociological displacement of natural rights, his pungent claim that all rights are rights to inequality, dissolved the link between natural law (right) and revolution. Within the Marxist tradition, only Ernst Bloch in his *Natural Law and Human Dignity* has made the attempt to reconstitute the linkage between right and revolution. According to Bloch, liberty, equality and fraternity 'do not have only a historical but also a progressive, normative weight each time a Bastille is taken'. Applications of the tricolour banner are raised above the level of human rights as such only through the interjection into them of Rousseau's notion of the general will. This, Bloch claims, was the high point of natural law. But 'the epoch in which it flourished was an illusion, for out of the citoyen there came the bourgeois; it was a foreshadowing, for the bourgeois was judged by the citoyen.' This failure was inevitable, for 'all peoples only have and achieve the sort of and degree of revolution that they are ready for on the basis of the human rights they have acquired and preserved.' He continues:

> If, in the four ancient basic rights, a new meaning is given to property — that is, instead of freedom to attain it, it is defined as freedom from attaining it — then, and only then, do liberty and security come to life. And what of resistance to oppression? In the freshness of the revolution and its goals, the Fourteenth of July always infuses a new life and a human face, even after and without the Bastille. The light of 1789 persists everywhere: like the Ninth Symphony, which is so close to the citizen, it cannot be taken back.[3]

If Bloch's strong utopian sensibility makes following his example directly unwarranted, it remains the case that it implies that the ban on rights belongs to the most reductive and economistic aspects of Marx's thought.

Using Marx against himself, I want to begin re-establishing the links between right and revolution by suggesting, however briefly, a Marxian account of right implied by the argument of 'On the Jewish Question', an essay usually read as an attack on the discourse of rights. Such readings are at least partial if not altogether false. Before commencing the examination of this argument, it will prove worthwhile to turn to the 'Critique of the Gotha Programme' to inquire whether the presumed ban on rights as forming a legitimate element of Marxist political theory is fully in accord with the letter of Marx's writing. There is room for doubt.

Communist Rights?

Most readers of the 'Critique' take for granted that it intends to demonstrate that rights belong firmly to the capitalist epoch: that they form both a direct legitimation of private property and a second-order legitimation of capital through their role in underwriting the constitutional state. Yet the explicit target of Marx's critique is the Lassallean thesis that the emancipation of labour requires the conversion of the instruments of labour into the common property and the co-operative regulation of the total labour with a fair distribution of the proceeds of labour. The fairness of distribution, a fairness different from that derivable from market transactions alone, corresponds to the socialist belief that 'the proceeds of labour belong undiminished with equal right to all members of society'.[4] While Marx questions how 'undiminished' these proceeds really are, the core of his questioning of right proceeds from another line of interrogation.

What concerns Marx in Lassalle's normative thesis is the idea that the right of members of society is premised on what they produce. Distribution is still governed by a process of exchange wherein 'a given amount of labour in one form is exchanged for an equal amount of labour in another form'.[5] Although, then, under socialism labourers will receive the proceeds of their labour, minus various necessary deductions, the distribution of those proceeds remains a matter of proportionality. It is quantitative in nature and algorithmically procedural in form. Right here is still bourgeois right, 'stigmatized by a bourgeois limitation', namely, that the 'right of the producers is proportional to the labour they supply; the equality consists in the fact that measurement is made with an equal standard.'[6] Now the reason this is questionable is because it makes natural (or social) endowments — strength, skill, ability, and so on — fundamental criteria for establishing distribution procedures. The exchange mechanism between production and distribution is held in force by criteria that lack moral weight. Why should distribution turn on factors that are not within the control of the labourer? In making natural endowments criteria are we not making genetic endowments or differential social conditioning a means to receiving goods which are incommensurable with them? In treating labour as the measure of desert are we not abstracting one characteristic of human beings as privileged for the purposes of determining desert? By invoking labour in this manner we reduce it to a means to ends external to it, and hence treat intrinsic but differentially distributed characteristics of human beings as fundamentally exchangeable items. This line of thought clearly elaborates and develops what is implicit in Marx's dialectical analysis of use-value and exchange-value: exchangist logic is moral reification.

Capitalist distribution operates the principle of 'to each according to what he and the instruments he owns produces'; this assumes the moral relevance of ownership. By removing ownership as a criterion, socialism removes a morally irrelevant reason from consideration. Hence the advance from capitalism to socialism is a non-reducible moral advance, a progressive formation of right. One way of speaking of ethical progress, surely, is to speak of the historical discovery that certain reasons for moral approbation or disapprobation are empty or idle. These 'discoveries' are not autonomous results of reasoning but occur with fundamental alterations in social formations. But this fact does not entail that these 'discoveries', the knowings that attend social change, are mere reflections of change; to believe that would make all cognition epiphenomenal. In coming to perceive that ownership is not a ground for desert, a fact dimly reflected in defences of ownership which emphasize the risk the capitalist takes and his enterprising spirit, a particular moral equation is found to be false.

An analogous process is at work in the transition to communism. 'From each according to his ability, to each according to his needs' breaks with the principle of the exchangeability of labour, which is why Marx must say that under communism labour is not only a means to life, but life's 'prime want'.[7] Only when we can perceive that the exercise of an ability can be an intrinsic end can we break from the idea that we labour in order to receive benefits external to that labour. And this is only possible when social labour replaces individual labour, since only that alteration makes visible the reductive teleology that has always accompanied the logic of making and producing. Only under communism would labour become an Aristotelian praxis: an activity productive of something but done for its own sake. If 'right can never be higher than the economic structure of society and its cultural development conditioned thereby', then the communist motto is a conception of communist right that crosses the 'narrow horizon of bourgeois right'.[8]

The 'Critique' is systematically ambiguous between a view consigning all right to pre-communist modes of production — the 'all right is a right of inequality' thesis — and a view that anticipates a new stage of right wherein the narrow horizon of bourgeois right is crossed when the exchange relation between production and distribution is broken. Accepting the former view, however, is not really to Marx's credit for it makes sense only on the assumption of the fully liberal construal of the conditions under which questions of justice and right become applicable, that is, according to Hume and Rawls, under conditions of scarcity and lack of benevolence. For Marx, lack of benevolence is a product of scarcity; hence, if one reads Marx as stringently utopian in his outlook, then abundance spells the end of the question of justice and the 'from each . . . to each . . .' motto regresses from a principle to a picture, a picture that leaves no room for political life in any form we might recognize. This picture is complicit with the metaphysical anti-political utopianism of philosophy from Plato to contemporary liberalism.[9] The recurrent questioning of the political in Marx represents the mostly highly rationalistic and utopian element in his thought. And while the conception of right is not the centre of what would constitute a Marxist political philosophy — for that we need a more elaborate understanding of democracy and social autonomy — it can form a pivotal ingredient.

The limits of liberalism, I am contending, should not be equated with the dominion of right as such, but with the reign of equal right that makes human activity exchangeable; and crossing the 'narrow horizon of bourgeois right', something Marx believes impossible even in a socialist society, requires the institution of a new principle of right erected on the communist mode of production. If the new principle of right is not itself going to be a utopian construct, then it must be one which is implicit in the current practice of rights, and hence one which a critique of those practices will reveal. Further, it will have to be compatible with relative scarcity and lack of benevolence while not making either of these a condition for its existence. All this will mean concretely finding a way of grounding the 'from each . . . to each . . .' principle that does not depend solely on a philosophical derivation of the kind just portrayed in the 'Critique'.

Rights, on the view I will propose, are coordinated with modes of production but cannot be construed as merely ideological; at least if ideology is deemed to have only a pejorative sense and the reduction of communism from an anticipated or desired historical state of affairs to a transparent utopia is to be avoided. A Marxist conception of rights will have to possess the following features: first, since rights change with changes in the economic structure of society, they cannot be natural or intrinsic or metaphysical attributes of human beings, nor therefore, will they be discoverable *a priori*. There are no natural rights, not even the Hobbesian right to self-preservation, not to speak of more complex *a priori* attributions like the right to acquire and hold property or the right to exercise one's capacity for self-movement. Rights are not deducible from capacities since the having of a capacity, no matter how universal it is, cannot of itself entail the right to exercise it. Rights are founded or grounded on representations of something that is not a right. Rights are not primitive, but derived. In this Marxism is at one with utilitarianism. Secondly, unlike utilitarianism (which makes persons as such exchangeable against the greatest happiness for the greatest number), a Marxist theory must demonstrate that although rights are derivative or secondary formations, they nonetheless do the work of respecting and protecting the dignity of the individual. This requirement would be satisfied if the account offered turns out to be extensionally equivalent to the 'from each . . . to each . . .' principle. Thirdly, the account must be sufficiently historically and sociologically sensitive so as to be able to explain: (i) that under extreme conditions rights are not worth the paper they are written on, and hence that a mere appeal to, say, human rights, is politically idle because theoretically ungrounded; (ii) that under quite ordinary and usual circumstances rights are or can be rights of inequality, and hence a source of domination or an ideological alibi; (iii) that having rights matters, and can be a source of radical historical change. Of course, fictions can have political significance too, so showing that rights matter must be linked with how they can matter in virtue of their putative ground.

The Political State and the Demands of Reason

In his early writings Marx's account of reason and revolution is premised on the idea, later to be rejected, that what appears in Enlightenment ideology as the abstract demands of reason, what 'ought' to be the case, is best grasped in terms of the dialectical movement of reality itself. In his famous letter to Ruge of September 1843, Marx states:

> Reason has always existed, but not always in rational form. Hence the critic can take his cue from every existing form of theoretical and practical consciousness and from the ideal and final goal implicit in the *actual* forms of existing reality he can deduce a true reality. Now as far as real life is concerned, it is precisely the *political* state which contains the postulates of reason in all its *modern* forms, even where it has not been the conscious repository of socialist requirements. But it does not stop there. It consistently assumes that reason has been realized and just as consistently becomes embroiled at every point in a conflict between its ideal vocation and its actually existing premises.

Marx goes on to claim that just as the theoretical struggles of mankind are represented in religion, so the political state enumerates its practical struggles: 'Thus the particular form and nature of the political state contains all social struggles, needs and truths within itself.'[10]

Marx's strategy here is based on the Hegelian thesis that rational categories, in this case the categories of enlightened reason, are social forms in complex relations of dependency, domination and subordination with respect to other social forms. The totality of these forms constitutes a complex and dynamic totality in which the different components represent progressive or regressive tendencies relative to historical antecedents and current articulation. Marx's critical practice, then, attempts to transfer the ideal concepts of political and moral philosophy from the domain of pure thought to the domain of reality. The demands of reason, the abstract demands of bourgeois, Kantian morality, are not speculative thoughts waiting to be put into practice, but potentialities of reality itself awaiting realization: both awaiting release from their stultification and inhibition by the capitalist economy and awaiting release from their articulation within the categorial determinations of bourgeois thought. Thus the contradiction between philosophy — the demands of right — and reality are formulated as immanent contradictions in reality itself. Marx's practice is neither one of abstract ethical criticism nor one of value-neutral empirical description, but a combining of the two that relativizes the moments of 'is' and 'ought' — empirical science and abstract morality respectively — to contradictory tendencies actually inhabiting the real-in-process.[11]

With good reason, but nonetheless precipitately, Marx gave up this model of analysis as a consequence of the defeats of 1848. From then on the 'merely ideological' conception of the state became dominant. Such a view weakens the significance of non-economic phenomena generally, reduces the meaning of such phenomena en bloc to their class origin, and instrumentalizes political and cultural struggles to economic ends. Yet it is unclear how Marx can criticize Lassalle for instrumentalizing human activity and abilities while not acknowledging the potential intrinsic worth of the products of activity. Conversely, the post-1848 critique surely derives from Marx's insight that within capital, political and cultural phenomena were being instrumentalized to ends wholly external to themselves. By adopting the reductive, sceptical stance of ideological critique Marx accedes to the standpoint against which his critique was lodged. His route of escape from capital's instrumental reification of the political was to double it.

While there is an implacable naivety in the outline of the analytic procedure described in the letter to Ruge, above all in its contention that a true reality can be 'deduced' from existing states of affairs, and hence that the reform of consciousness consists 'entirely' in making the world aware of its own consciousness, in explaining its own actions to it, this is not Marx's actual procedure. It allows for the possibility that the articulation of reason is not just a matter of its form, for example, its being regarded as merely rational, a thought construct, but equally how it is articulated within a given social practice. Reason is not merely misplaced — placed in God or in the political realm as opposed to ourselves or the economy; these displacements deform the concepts themselves. They alter their logical powers. The displacement view, which Marx took over from Feuerbach, does not correspond to his actual practice of dialectical criticism in 'On the Jewish Question'. It has the extra dimension of complexity required in order to think the deformations that accompany displacements.

Rights and Recognition

What readers of 'On the Jewish Question' who regard it as providing a general critique of rights miss is that its complex dialectical argument deploys two senses of ground or foundation: a sense in which civil society represents the real ground or foundation of society as a whole, and a sense in which the state is the ground or foundation, not the mere ideological front, for civil society. In order to make sense of this thought it will be necessary to regard the categories of modernity as incompletely saturated or determined by their instantiation in capital; indeed, it will be necessary to hypothesize that the rationality of these categories is blocked by the way they have become empirically instantiated. Not only are the forces of production inhibited by capitalist relations of production, but so are the categorial forms which constitute the comprehensibility of those relations. This is only to say, minimally, that the meaning of (some of) the categories structuring capitalist practices exceed their empirical determination in a manner logically incompatible with that determination. Such an intentional incompatibility is a premise for the kind of immanent critique carried out by Marx.

Following the line of argument suggested by the letter to Ruge, and simplifying a little, we can say that the duality between state and civil society is described by Marx such that each side of the polarity represents one side of the various dualisms constituting modern philosophy. Capital is a weak Kantian synthesis of empiricism and rationalism wherein civil society is characterized by the categories of empiricism and the state becomes the idealized repository of functions traditionally attributed to reason — rationality, self-consciousness, reflexivity, universality, and so on, or in Marx's own terms, species-life. In tabular form the situation would look like this:

State	Civil Society
mind	body
species-life	individual life
citizen	bourgeois
rights of citizen	rights of man
universal	particular
reason	need
public	private
freedom	necessity
community	egoism
equality	inequality
general interest	private interest
essence	existence
abstract	concrete
idealism	materialism
deontology	teleology
heaven	earth

The dialectical analysis of this dualistic structure forms the core of Marx's enterprise in 'On the Jewish Question'. For a striking statement of the dualism consider:

The perfected political state is by its nature the species-life of man in opposition to his material life. All the presuppositions of this egoistic life continue to exist outside the sphere of the state in civil society, but as qualities of civil society. Where the political state has attained its full degree of development man leads a double life, a life in heaven and a life on earth, not only in his mind, in his consciousness, but in reality. He lives in the political community where he regards himself as a communal being, and in civil society, where he is active as a private individual, regards other men as means, debases himself to a means and becomes a plaything of alien powers. . . . Man in his immediate reality, in civil society, is a profane being. . . . In the state, on the other hand, where he is considered a species being, he is the imaginary member of a fictious sovereignty, he is divested of his real individual life and filled with an unreal universality.[12]

What will be at issue for us is how this oppositional structure affects the question of rights that is the target of Marx's analysis.

Marx, commenting on Bauer's call for the sacrifice of faith for the sake of implementing universal human rights, asks after these 'so-called' rights of man. What are they in reality? What is their basis?

The rights of man are partly political rights, rights which are only exercised in community with others. What constitutes their content is participation in community, in the political community or state. They come under the category of political freedom, of civil rights . . .[13]

Having made this point, Marx quickly turns away from these rights of the citizen to consider the more problematic rights of man. For our purposes, however, it is worth dwelling on the rights of the citizen.

The rights of man are 'partly' political rights. What distinguishes these rights? They are rights exercised only in community and their content is participation in community; they are the rights of citizens, civil rights, enjoining and protecting democratic practice. Each of these three moments requires elaboration and its relations with the other moments made clear. In stating that these rights can only be exercised in community Marx is pressing the thesis that a right, by definition, can only be exercised when there is someone whose duty it is to fulfil the claim the right-holder makes; so, the suggestion is that a certain sense of political community is what it means for something to *be* a right in this context, and *therefore* the material content of these rights is participation in community. In this context, then, political community and right are thought of as co-constitutive of one another; and being a member of the community and being a right-holder are equivalents. For this to be the case political community would have to be both the foundation and goal of civil rights. Thus, to state that rights can only be exercised in community means that these rights denote membership in the community; hence what supports these rights is the mutual recognition of each member by every other member *as* a citizen. Civil rights are not original, natural or metaphysical entities. They are the legal-juridical expression of the mutual recognitions that constitute individuals as citizens of a political state. Rights are a formal expression of the 'as' of citizenship whose ground is nothing other than the mutual recognition of each of the members of the community as a citizen.

Marx's strategy here is just to take seriously the thought that rights are claims and that unrecognized rights are idle. Philosophers attempt to deduce rights which, if the deduction is valid, then, in accordance with the demands of reason, we ought to recognize. Marx inverts the philosopher's paradigm making mutual recognition the foundation and rights the consequents. Community is formed through mutual recognitions, recognitions that typically take the form of the conferment on an individual of a social identity expressive of membership. Individuals individualize themselves or become individuated within communities to whom they owe their possibility of having an identity. Modern rights talk from the outset was intended as a way of articulating the kind of standing an individual should have with respect to its relevant others. The thought behind this was that unless the individual's rights could be credited apart from those others, then the ethical and practical fate of the individual would be at their say-so. But this avoids rather than answers the question: if others fail to recognize one's rights, then what is their purpose? Rights, unlike, say, an ability, have their force and meaning through their being recognized; hence recognition is constitutive of them. Rights are explicit recognitions and are grounded in recognition. An individual's standing in a community cannot be established apart from the community. Unless the 'right' to have rights were recognized the possession of rights would be empty. Being recognized, implicitly or explicitly, as we shall see, is what gives the claim to rights whatever force it might have. Rights presuppose community, and nothing will protect the unrecognized individual. By side-stepping the role of recognition and community in the logic of rights, philosophers provide but theoretical solutions to practical problems.

Rights get their meaning and force from the political community. Rights matter within such a community because conferment of them is recognition of entitlement to participate in the community. Since the idea of political community is given with the concept of rights, then participation in community must exhaust their scope. Civil rights define the necessary entitlements required in order to protect an individual's active participation in the political process. If one could not do those things one would not be a citizen, and being a citizen is doing and being able to do those political things.

By grounding rights in community and restricting the scope of rights to what is compatible with them being so grounded, Marx challenges the individualistic assumptions of liberal theory. In liberalism the individualistic premise of its constructions typically comes out with an individualistic consequent: namely, I have the right to exercise my freedom so long as I do not interfere with others' rights to do the same. On this construction others are the limit of my freedom, and rights the recognition of limits. For Marx the liberal limit is in truth the condition: without the community and its legal-juridical formation there would be no rights for me to exercise. This is perspicuous in the bourgeois state where political life is cut off from its material substrate; and while that makes political life abstract, idle, heavenly, the abstraction equally allows the communal being of rights to come fully into view.

One might object to Marx's argument by contending it embodies some form of verificationism: because only recognition shows that people have rights, then the meaning of rights should be restricted to the logic of mutual recognition. This is inadequate. Marx's argument is not about meaning but concerns the ground and telos of rights. Marx takes the telos of the desire to have a right to attain recognition from others of oneself as having a certain standing, and hence certain entitlements. Crediting an other with a right just is to recognize them as having a standing and the entitlements that go with it. Recognition is the truth of right. Now, if an other were not recognized by me and others in the community as one of our significant others, then there would be no reason to assign them rights whatever characteristics they had. And no one or bundle of characteristics had by others will entail their recognition. Characteristics are always either logically too early or too late for the sake of recognition. Unless I already recognized another individual as one of my others their possession of a characteristic (freedom, self-consciousness, rationality, and so on) would be idle in the field of my concerns. Once recognition is given, characteristics orient concern, but they cannot logically dislodge recognition. This is why Hegel displaced the argumentative strategies of methodological solipsism, especially universality requirements, with *struggle* as essential to the understanding of recognition. Recognition is an achievement of life-praxis, and rights follow the path of recognitions.

The collapse of characteristics as criteria for recognition follows directly from the thought that others are conditions for my possession of, are co-constitutive of, those characteristics in virtue of which recognition and right are to be secured in individualist accounts. The claim that others are the condition rather than the limit of my freedom is implicit in article 34 of the *Declaration of Rights* of 24 June 1793. It states: 'The oppression of each individual takes place when the body of society is oppressed.' This directly entails its logical converse: namely, that the oppression of any single individual destroys, corrupts the legal order as a whole.[14] This thesis is surely equivalent with Marx's own in *The Communist Manifesto* that communism is a form of association 'in which the free development of each is the condition for the free development of all'. *Pace* Marx, however, only the legal formulation of this thesis reveals its truth. Only in a community of rights can the corrupting consequences of oppression be made manifest: the oppression of a single individual corrupts the legal order as a whole. This is the logical core of a communitarian conception of rights.

It is no accident that the theses concerning the exercise and content of right converge on the idea of *political* community. Political community is community in its distinctly modern form as self-conscious and active. The being of a modern community does not reside in anything external to it: God, history, race, language or ties of blood. These and related conceptions conceive of community in passive terms, write human sociality naturalistically and occlude the modern discovery of freedom. In modernity, the community itself explicitly takes on the burden of determining its being and identity as 'this' community, reappropriating to itself what had been projected onto an external determination. Community is political, and hence is nothing outside the activities calling it into and sustaining it in being. Of course, if political life is cut off from its empirical substratum, then it might appear as if this identification of community with the political allowed for the absolute self-constitution of community. The fiction of absolute self-constitution led to the quite real Terror. Political community takes on the *burden* of determining its being and identity, but it can do this only within the confines of history, language and tradition. Political community in its modern sense is a self-conscious historical community.

That rights should first be posed as grounded in and expressive of community in terms of civil rights is not utterly contingent: citizenship is the form of social identity appropriate to a quasi-self-constituting community. The 'we' which is the ground of each and every 'I' becomes active in the idea of citizenship propounded in the French Revolution. Civil rights constitute

105

both the freedom for community and the freedom of the community — its capacity for (collective) self-determination. There is a significant difference between claiming that rights are grounded and express mutual recognitions (which could be true whether that fact was recognized or not) and claiming that at a certain juncture rights were actively conceived of as having that ground and character. That all rights are political rights is the acknowledgement that rights are exercised only in community and have participation in community as their content.

The Dialectical Antinomy of State and Civil Society

This elaboration of the meaning of the rights of the citizen is not a defence of them or of the logic they encapsulate. If there is a historical potentiality latent in the idea of civil rights, this can only be shown through the dialectical unfolding of their relation to the rights of man. Marx reveals the historical potentiality of civil rights by demonstrating that the division between state and civil society is, precisely, a dualism: a duality in which each side is dependent on, and in contradiction with, the other side. This relation between state and civil society represents the dialectical antinomy of a double foundation.

In its simplest terms the fundamental antinomy is not, as it first appears, between abstract and concrete, but rather an antinomy between rational form and irrational content.

> But the perfection of the idealism of the state was at the same time the perfection of the materialism of civil society. The shaking-off of the political yoke was at the same time the shaking-off of the bonds which had held in check the egoistic spirit of civil society. Political emancipation was at the same time the emancipation of civil society from politics, from even the *appearance* of a universal content.
>
> Feudal society was dissolved into its foundation [*Grund*], into *man*. But into man as he really was — into *egoistic* man.
>
> This *man*, the member of civil society, is now the foundation, the presupposition of the political state. In the rights of man the state acknowledges him as such.

Civil society *appears* as natural, as it so conspicuously does to libertarian thinkers, because it lacks the determinations of rationality, reflexivity and universality. It gives the appearance of immediacy and givenness. This appearance is in reality mediated; it is a product of the manner in which the overcoming of feudalism was accomplished. The political overthrow of the ancien régime *released* the economy from political determination. Because no longer politically determined, determined by norms extrinsic to it, the presumption was that a natural core of human activity had been latent within the politico-theological shell of the past. In a sense, the work of political emancipation from the past, by being one-sided, only political, became complicit with capital's own drive to remove the restraining feudal relations of production. Political emancipation from feudalism is the production of a dualistic modernity: 'Political emancipation is the reduction of man on the one hand to the member of civil society, the egoistic, independent individual, and, on the other, to the citizen, the moral person.'[15]

The rights of man are partly civil rights. What of the other part, the rights of mankind itself, the rights to property, security, protection under the law, in short the rights governing and securing civil society? These partake and legitimate the false naturalization of civil society. Marx states that these rights do not go beyond 'egoistic man, man as a member of civil society, namely, an individual withdrawn into himself, his private interest and his private desires and *separated* from community'.[16] Because separation from community is the principle of civil society, the only bond which holds its members together 'is natural necessity, need and private interest, the conservation of their property and their egoistic persons'.[17]

If there is a contradiction here, this will derive from the precise character of these rights as opposed to the rights of the citizen and the manner in which the two sets of rights condition one another (as opposed to being merely contiguous with one another). Here is the core of Marx's analysis:

This fact appears even more curious when we observe that citizenship, the *political community*, is reduced by the political emancipators to a mere *means* for the conservation of these so-called rights of man and that the citizen is therefore proclaimed the servant of egoistic man; the sphere in which man behaves as a communal being [*Gemeinwesen*] is degraded to a level below the sphere in which he behaves as a partial being, and finally that it is man as *bourgeois*, i.e. as a member of civil society, and not man as citizen who is taken as the *real* and *authentic* man.[18]

The rights of man are bestowed on civil society by the political community. And insofar as the political community conceives of itself as having the task of protecting civil society it makes itself a means to ends external to it. Of course, this self-instrumentalization is unavoidable if the real work of society takes place in a sphere independent of political community. This is the significance of Marx's analysis of the origin of the division between state and civil society where the act of political emancipation liberated the spiritual elements of feudal life from their adulterated state in the civil world and thereby constituted 'the sphere of the community, the universal concern of the people', forcing people's particular activity to sink to 'the level of a purely individual significance'.[19]

More to the point, the self-instrumentalization of political community is manifest in both the general characterization and content of the rights of man. For Marx the rights of man are 'so-called' because they are not natural, inalienable rights, not the rights of 'natural', egoistic man. There is no such man. The rights of man are bestowed by political community; hence the true ground of these rights is in political community and the mutual recognitions constituting it. Only a political community could bestow right and legitimacy on a civil society governed by particular interests; only in a political community could the rights of civil society possess the status and force of law. Conversely, the political community had to confer legitimacy on civil society because it was the real, material foundation of society. Categorially, we might say that the universality of political community grounding the particularity of civil society is both there and not there. It is presupposed by civil society in the recognition of each as a right holder, but it is not posited; indeed, it is denied as an explicit moment in the mediations making civil society possible. Rights articulate, implicitly or explicitly, a field of recognitions. If mutual recognition underpins the possibility of rights, then civil society is the recognition (= rights) of non-recognition (= natural rights), and hence a contradiction and miscognition of itself. The declaration of the rights of man as natural rights, and their precise content, is an abstraction from their true ground, hence a reduction and a degradation. By its self-instrumentalization the political community contradicts its own grounding principle while simultaneously legitimating the contradiction and miscognition constitutive of civil society as a domain of right.

Nothing in this analysis speaks against rights. On the contrary, rights represent the fact that community in modernity is no longer given. The state and civil society are both versions of community in modernity; both require and take on legal form. Insofar as legal form is construed as the protection of natural right, the structural and historical conditions of civil society are suppressed. This suppression makes possible the disregard of the way in which civil society is grounded in political community, and so legitimates the instrumentalization of the latter. When the moment of community is suppressed, then legal form becomes a means of oppression. The oppression inhabits both state and civil society because the political community's self-instrumentalization deforms the principle of right constitutive of it. Civil rights become interpreted as formal equivalents of the rights of man leading thereby to the suppression of the moment of recognition and communality. Recognition of significant others as the condition for my liberty and identity, the strictly private and intimate relation now called 'love', becomes opposed to law — the duality of love (particularity) and law (universality) opening up the possibility of morality in its Kantian configuration.

The dialectic of state and civil society is the dialectic of liberal political thought, and hence its limit. In each case an individualist, anti-communal consequence will overturn the logic of its ground. In Locke, for example, the divine ground of equal respect is undermined by the content of rights derived from the self-ownership thesis. In Rawls the benevolence and respect for others that is to give force to the ideal social contract, the terms of which are decided behind the veil of ignorance, is sabotaged by the rational-choice structure of the deliberations concerning the principles of justice.[20] Only a full-scale Hobbesian account can be consistent, but such accounts must necessarily fall foul of free-rider problems.[21] In modern states 'good' liberals provide the ideological alibi for free-riders.

Marx's conclusion, which points to the overcoming of the duality between state and civil society, cannot be construed as recommending the overcoming of rights. On the contrary, the idea of individual man resuming the abstract citizen into himself points rather to individual man taking on in the world of civil society the attributes characterizing the present political community.[22] This would mean extending the construal of right as what can be exercised only in community and whose content is participation in community to civil society, which would *a fortiori*, end its status as a domain opposed to the political. To extend the rights of the citizen to the whole of society is to see that rights are rights to participation in social life as a whole. To deprive anyone of their rights, not to recognize them as a member of the community, is to prohibit them from participating in the life of society as a whole.

Disincorporation and Human Rights

Before a more general evaluation of this analysis can take place one very specific objection must be dealt with. In making community exhaustive of rights this account leaves open the precise characterization of the criteria for membership in the community; or rather, by making the community the arbiter of membership it leaves open the possibility that oppression can take the legitimate form of exclusion. If the moment of universality in the account offered devolves upon citizenship, which can but be the expression of a particular political identity, then real universality is lost. Hence, the massive achievement of making the rights of man inalienable is lost. If natural, egoistic man is an abstraction, it is nonetheless an abstraction which has the virtue of potential universality. Is it possible to sustain some semblance of universality while simultaneously acknowledging the unsurpassability of the role of political community? Two distinct responses to this question are possible: a political, practical response and a theoretical response. At the end of the day the two responses will be seen to converge.

While mutual recognition can be an explicit act, for the most part our recognitions of one another are carried through the concrete practices we engage in. Implicitly, practices whose subject positions are either symmetrically structured or allow for reversibility or leave access to hierarchy open involve mutual recognition from the persons participating in them. In fact, there are few practices that do not have one or another of these characteristics, and reversibility between 'I' and 'You' is of course deeply embedded in our most general practice — that of language. In particular contexts struggles for the acknowledgement of some right rely on just these facts. In practice, mutual recognition is offered and attempts at exclusion necessarily involve the deployment of extraneous considerations, considerations not actually operative in routine dealings. Struggles for right are hence struggles to make what is implicit explicit, to make tacit acknowledgement full recognition. Right is political, and nothing can replace the battle for recognition which ends only when the grounds for refusal are revealed as arbitrary or self-serving.

Of course, the practical character of struggles for right in modernity is governed by the extraction of the self or subject from its encrustation in feudal roles. The modern, abstract subject is a creation of Christianity, Roman law and Capital. The abstract character of the modern subject has supported claims to right whose refusal depends upon considerations less universal than itself: class, colour, sex, et al. It was just this abstract universality implanted in the conception of the rights of man that so terrified Burke, for they extended outside the body politic, outside the traditionally embodied political community. Arguably, this was part of the intention of the French Revolutionaries: to break with the logic of the *body* politic which had conceived of the community as ideally embodied or incorporated in the body of the king. The Revolutionaries wanted to tear this body apart. As Claude Lefort has powerfully argued, in this context modern political revolution signifies

> a phenomenon of disincorporation of power and disincorporation of right which accompanies the disappearance of 'the king's body', in which the community was embodied and justice mediated; by the same token, it signifies a phenomenon of disincorporation of society whose identity, though already figured in the nation, has not yet been separated from the person of the monarch.[23]

Lefort makes this comment in the context of a critique of Marx's account in 'On the Jewish Question'. Whatever the status of Lefort's overall criticism, which takes the traditional anti-right, anti-political reading of 'On the Jewish Question' as hermaneutically correct and theoretically false, he is certainly correct in noting how little Marx comprehended the *critical* significance of the rights of man, their work of disincorporation, which is essential to the disincorporation, the 'nowhere' of power, which is constitutive of a full democratic polity.

Following contemporary convention, let us call these rights 'human rights'. They are not natural rights. 'Human' picks out the scope of these rights, and hence does not specify either their content or the characteristics in virtue of which they are to be applied. This indeterminacy is their strength: on the one hand it prohibits the arbitrary exclusion of any person or group from the community (or community of communities); on the other hand it represents a moment of excess in virtue of which the collective identity of the community can always be put in question; it opens up, and keeps open, the space that separates a community from itself. It is the lack of this difference of the community from itself which makes Burkean communities 'conservative'. As we have already seen, this thought does not depart from Marx's analysis since the difference separating a community from itself is explicit in his thought: that in modernity, community primarily signifies a political entity, one for whom the being and identity of the community becomes the active burden of the community itself. That Marx came to disavow this thesis is one of the disasters of his late thought.

Human rights as substantial entities are fictions. Their moment is the criterional ascription of rights to fellow citizens. Citizenship is ideally, if indeterminately, open to all; the substantiality of such rights is the political force behind them. Human rights are, within political community, the moment of excess that sustains the moment of disembodiment, the groundlessness and the dislocation of power constitutive of democratic practice. This gives to the political community a moving boundary. Human rights, we might say, are never fully within or fully outside political community. Their indeterminacy enjoins the reflective and interrogative movement of a democratic polity. It accomplishes this end by providing each member of the community with an identification or standpoint, which is nowhere, separate from both their particular and social identity. Without the critical moment represented by human rights there exists no structural check on regressive self-identifications by communities. But this is only to say that democratic practice is sustained not through formal procedures alone, but through procedures that continually reenact the dislocation of power that was one of the motives of the French Revolution. That dislocation of power, which is the devolution of the being and being thus of the community onto itself, hence thrusting community into the history it is, occurs through the double inscription of rights: human rights are the rights of the citizen.[24]

This line of thought naturally converges with what was said above about the political reality of struggles for rights. These struggles succeed, when they do, because they demonstrate exclusion to rest upon morally irrelevant criteria. But if in modernity community is political in the active sense, then parochial criteria — race, religion, income, status — will always fall below the level presumed by the community to be political in the modern sense — which is not to deny that most states do fall below the level of their essential presupposition. Nor is this latter fact surprising since the division between state and civil society leads states to misconstrue the character and grounding of the rights they confer upon their citizenry, and hence to miscognize their status as political communities.

Citizenship stands between and mediates the abstract particularity of personal identity and the abstract universality of human rights. Individuals only have rights in community. They are ascribed these rights on the basis of indeterminate criteria whose force is the critical one of revealing unreflected particularity. This nod in the direction of human rights does nothing to alter the fundamental contention grounding rights in community and making participation in community their content.

Love and Law

By providing what is in its essentials a communitarian comprehension of rights we defuse, at a stroke, the standard objections to rights theory which charge it with being too abstract, rationalistic, individualistic and egoistic.[25] Further, because this account does not begin with the individual, it does not oppose rights to the good. The overcoming of the duality of state and civil society, and hence the re-articulation of love and law required for it, provides a conception of the good, or better, is meant to reveal that law and ethics do categorially relate to one another and that their present division is a fragmentation. If there are difficulties for this account they will come from another direction.

First, let me make clear what this account does not claim, namely, that society ought to be revolutionized through the imposition of the model of community found in the state onto civil society. As Marx was aware, 'when political life attempts to suppress its presupposition, civil society and its elements' in order to constitute itself 'as the real, harmonious species-life of man' it inevitably enters into 'violent contradiction to the

114

conditions of its existence.'[26] So long as the state is a separate entity from civil society, and that means so long as there exists private ownership over the means of production, radicalization of the model of political community can but eventuate in either a terror or a totalitarian order. Which is also to say that the modern notion of the state does not exhaust the modern conception of political community.

Nonetheless, one might object to what has been said here that it inverts the very point of our having rights, namely, to protect us from illegitimate interference by society. The problem with this objection is simply that it is very difficult to conceive of significant choices or patterns of actions that would not either be deemed to be 'full participation in the life of society as a whole' or ruled out as seeking personal advantage against the good of the other members of the community. Perhaps aesthetic or sexual preferences might be thought to fall into this category. But this thought is hard to make out, for if such choices matter, then they will matter because pursuing them is among the range of activities that are deemed to constitute full participation in society. If, alternatively, what lies behind this objection is the thought that in 'private' certain activities should be permissible irrespective of their ethical character — a preference, say, for pornographic art and sexual desires matching it — then I fail to see how this objection escapes from the charge of repressive toleration, which, of course, is precisely a charge against extensive rights to liberty individualistically construed.

Any set of rights will rule out certain forms of activity as illegitimate; and certainly communitarian rights will rule out at least some acts of exchange based on private ownership over the means of production between consenting adults. The issue here is not whether in so doing society is imposing itself on the individual, but rather whether that form of activity structurally respects the integrity of those participating in it as full members of the community. The separation between state and civil society that makes civil society a refuge from the state, and rights the positive distancing of self from the demands of community, only appears plausible now against the background of totalitarian

115

regimes: indirect structural oppression is preferable to direct political oppression. But to rehearse that thesis now is to do no more than rehearse the way in which, following the English route now rather than the French, the *Rechtstaat* came into being through the elaboration of the implications of the mechanisms of a nascent civil society. Beginning with the Lockean theory of property as it relates to the bourgeois conception of political economy given by Adam Smith, we should recall how

> possession is initially appropriated in the work performed upon the object, how surplus possessions are then exchanged in trade, and how in this exchange it is then *recognized mutually* as property; how then finally the generalization of the relationship of exchange, and therefore contract, produces a legal state, in which the will of each individual is constituted with private autonomy in the will of all individuals.[27]

Contemporary defences of civil society as a refuge from the state never move beyond the origin of the capitalist state. They do nothing to engage with the place of mutual recognition and political community in the constitution of rights.

This point does, however, raise the issue of how rights are determined. What is and what is not going to count as a right? If rights are communally based and secure participation in community, then their determination cannot be a theoretical issue. Nor is this a fault. For what rights are needed for full and effective participation in community will change over time. It may be the case that full participation will one day require, say, access to an information retrieval system. This will be found to be the case when a significant group of persons discover that although taken to be full members of the community they are in fact excluded from effective participation in it through lack of such a system. On the communitarian approach extant rights protect individuals' ability to participate in the life of the community as a whole, and the struggle for new rights is the political struggle for realizing or transforming what such participation actually amounts to. Communitarian rights are not trump cards in disputes with society, but political signs marking the place where love and law have been united, or where their divergence has become a salient fact for the political community as a whole. Because community can never be given, it is a political entity, an achievement of sorts, a product. And the kind of political entity it is makes conflict endemic to it. Rights are the intersection of conflict and community that is democratic politics.[28]

Communitarian rights both do and do not now exist; they exist in misrecognition, and both their existence and non-existence point to the theoretical immanence of this account of rights, an immanence directly related to its purport for practice. Although mutual recognition does not form the overt characterization of rights in modernity, it is implicit in it in an essential way. Abstract exchange relations are mutual recognitions that disavow themselves, that reduce ethical substantiality to the formality of abstract law. Nonetheless, if right is constitutive of bourgeois exchange relations, and if the reality and force of right is nothing but the reality and force of political community, then even rights whose form and content deny community are based on recognition, are the recognition of non-recognition, and hence even they must contain some radical potential. Once their basis is recognized, their content, *ipso facto*, will be altered. Rights politics now cannot be only the struggle to have existing rights recognized, but fundamentally to transform the meaning of rights discourse by revealing the contradictions and miscognitions present in it.

This critical act of transforming rights discourse would equally be the attempt to transform the nature of the social bonds uniting the members of the community. At present society conceives of itself as instantiating two fundamental forms of social cohesion: the interdependency of needy, preference-maximizing subjects leading to a system of needs, and the legal regulation of the system of needs through individuals who conceive of themselves as juridical subjects who bind themselves to one another and to the polity through contract. Within these social forms affect is either irrevocably individual

117

or a strategic element essentially extraneous to the forms themselves. Which is why contemporary theories of right and justice inevitably come up against the question of motivation. Marx's communitarian conception of right is not a theory of right, but the dialectical revelation of the aporia of love and law, the difficulty of communal forms which operate through their disavowal or suppression of their communal character. If rights are recognitions and recognition in modernity is realized as right, then the recognition of rights would be a first act of political love.

Notes

1. References to Marx's texts in the body of the work are to: 'Critique of the Gotha Programme' (CGP), in D. McLellan, ed., *Karl Marx: Selected Writings*, Oxford: Oxford University Press 1977; and 'On the Jewish Question' (JQ), in Karl Marx, *Early Writings*, translated by Gregor Benton, Harmondsworth: Penguin 1975. I have tried to say something about the significance of revolution for our understanding of modernity in my 'The Headless Community: Art, Genius and Revolution', forthcoming.
2. On this see Jürgen Habermas's splendid 'Natural Law and Revolution', in his *Theory and Practice*, translated by John Viertel, Boston: Beacon Press 1973, pp. 82–120. My debts to this essay are pervasive.
3. Ernst Bloch, *Natural Law and Human Dignity*, translated by Dennis J. Schmidt, London: MIT Press 1986, p. 65.
4. CGP, p. 566.
5. CGP, p. 568.
6. Ibid.
7. CGP, p. 569.
8. Ibid. For this analysis of 'Critique of the Gotha Programme' I am indebted to Michael Green's 'Marx, Utility, and Right', *Political Theory* 11/3, August 1983, pp. 433–46.
9. See my 'The Headless Community'. and more generally, the writings of Cornelius Castoriadis, especially his *The Imaginary Institution of Society*, Cambridge: Polity Press 1988.
10. K. Marx, *Early Writings*, p. 208.
11. This way of interpreting the early Marx is a Lukácsian inspiration. See my *The Philosophy of the Novel: Lukács, Marxism and the Dialectics of Form*, Brighton: Harvester Press 1984, chapter 1; and Andrew Feenberg, *Lukács, Marx and the Sources of Critical Theory*, Oxford: Martin Robertson 1981, chapter 2.
12. JQ, p. 220.
13. JQ, p. 227.
14. Habermas, p. 103.

15. JQ, p. 234.

16. JQ, p. 230.

17. Ibid.

18. JQ, p. 231.

19. JQ, p. 233.

20. For this point concerning Rawls I am indebted to Deborah Fitzmaurice.

21. See my 'Difficult Difference: Rousseau's Fictions of Identity', in Peter Hulme and Ludmilla Jordanova, eds, *The Enlightenment and Its Shadows*, London: Routledge 1990.

22. JQ, p. 234.

23. Claude Lefort, *The Political Forms of Modern Society*, Cambridge: Polity Press 1986, p. 255.

24. This argument is essentially Lefort's; I also learned greatly from a paper he gave on human rights and from conversations with him at the University of Essex in November, 1988.

25. On these matters see Jeremy Waldron's reply to critics of rights in J. Waldron, ed., *Nonsense upon Stilts: Bentham, Burke and Marx on the Rights of Man*, London: Methuen 1987, pp. 151–209.

26. JQ, p. 222.

27. Habermas, p. 127. He is here, of course, paraphrasing an argument of Hegel's.

28. On democracy and conflict see Bernard Yack's 'Community and Conflict in Aristotle's Political Philosophy', *The Review of Politics* 47, 1985, pp. 92–112.

5

Socialism, Feminism and Equality

Richard Norman

I want to defend the view that the concept of equality is, or at least ought to be, a central component of both socialist and feminist thought. Not only is there a concept of equality which is integral to socialism and feminism; there is also, I think, a direct continuity between it and the liberal concept of equality. The former is not a qualitatively different concept from the latter, but a more thoroughgoing application of it. This view has of course been contested. Some socialists and feminists have claimed that equality is an essentially liberal concept, that its limits are the limits of liberalism, and that to espouse it will have the practical effect of diluting the radicalism of socialist and feminist politics. Most of this paper will be devoted to looking at some examples of this argument. I shall try to show that socialist and feminist objections should be directed not at the concept of equality as such, but at particular versions or applications of the concept which are too limited and restricted.[1]

Feminism and Equality

I shall first look at some of the ways in which feminists have formulated their suspicions of equality. Some of these seem to me to rest on fairly standard misconceptions and oversimplifications of the idea of equality — for example, the confusion of 'equality' with 'identity' or 'uniformity'. Thus some feminists, looking back at past struggles to achieve equality with men, such as entry into previously male-monopolized professions, have suggested that these struggles effectively condoned the undervaluation of traditional female spheres such as child rearing and the activities of caring and nurturing. They have then felt that this calls for a re-assertion of sexual difference, a championing of female values and activities, in place of the pursuit of equality.[2] This suggestion, however, may at first appear paradoxical, since the doctrine of 'separate spheres' has historically been employed precisely to legitimate sexual oppression.[3] The opponents of feminism have typically insisted that they are no enemies of womankind; they wish simply to recognize the natural differences between the sexes and to assign each to its proper sphere of activity. How is it that some feminists now seem to be agreeing with them?

The way out of this paradox is to recognize that equality does not require the elimination of difference.[4] Sexual equality, in particular, does not require a denial of the inescapable biological facts of sexual difference, and leaves open what further differences might follow from these. We do not know for certain what psychological differences between the sexes there may be, or how far the tendencies towards differentiated skills and temperaments are biologically or environmentally created. The requirement of equality is the requirement that men's and women's choice of roles should be *genuinely* uncoerced, that is, subject neither to overt bars and compulsions nor to structural and psychologically internalized pressures, and that insofar as particular roles or activities tend to be performed by men or women they should carry with them no inequalities of economic reward, status, or power. That is as radical a feminist agenda as could be devised. It is an agenda for equality, and it leaves open the extent of sexual difference.

Feminists should not, then, jettison the idea of equality on the grounds that it requires women to be more like men and endorses male roles as the norm. A similar misconception is involved, I think, in the suggestion that to pursue sexual equality is to ignore the facts of racial and class oppression.

> Most people . . . think of feminism . . . as a movement that aims to make women the social equals of men. This broad definition . . . raises problematic questions. Since men are not equals in white supremacist, capitalist, partriarchal class structure, which men do women want to be equal to? . . . Implicit in this simplistic definition of women's liberation is a dismissal of race and class as factors that, in conjunction with sexism, determine the extent to which an individual will be discriminated against, exploited, or oppressed.[5]

The implication here is that sexual equality means the equality of middle- and upper-class white women with middle- and upper-class white men. This is again to assume that equality requires keeping one group as it is and assimilating other groups to it. But that is not so. If sexual equality does not mean making women more like men, still less does it mean making women more like middle- and upper-class white men. Sexual equality is not the only kind of equality, and it should go without saying that those who oppose sexual inequality will also oppose inequalities of race and class.

These suspicions of the idea of equality, then, are based on the misconception that equality means eliminating differences and accommodating women to a male norm. More fundamental, I think, is the hostility to equality which stems from identifying it with the demand for *equal rights*. Feminists have looked back at earlier struggles for the right to vote, the right to own and dispose of property, the right to education, and the right to enter the professions. They have seen these rights largely achieved, yet sexual oppression continues. Feminism, they have concluded, must go beyond the liberal demand for equal rights.

I agree. The limitations of the demand for equal rights, however, stem not from the word 'equal' but from the word 'rights', and I want to say something briefly about the limitations of that concept. The idea of 'rights' is essentially a legalistic concept. I do not mean, of course, that it is confined to the concept of legal rights. The whole point of talk about 'moral rights', and in particular of 'human

123

rights', is that they are supposed to be the moral basis for criticism of existing social institutions. Nevertheless, though human rights are said to be distinct from legal rights, the former concept exists, so to speak, within the shadow of the latter. Human rights are idealized legal rights; they are the ideal model for the legal rights which human beings *ought* to have. Consequently a struggle for equal rights is typically one which focuses on the demand for legal entitlements and the removal of legal barriers. What are ignored are the more fundamental non-legal barriers to human fulfilment, barriers constituted by a network of ideological assumptions and power relations. Notoriously, women's right to engage in traditionally male forms of work may be recognized, but their choices are still effectively restricted by self-perpetuating ideas of 'men's work' and 'women's work' often internalized by women themselves and affecting the decisions of (usually male) employers, and by assumptions about women's responsibilities to 'family' and 'home' together with the absence of supportive institutions such as child-care facilities. Facts such as these rightly lead feminists to look for more than just 'equal rights'.

Linked with the legalistic character of the concept of rights is the fact that it is an individualistic concept. To talk of people's rights is to talk of entitlements which they can claim from others, of what is owed to individuals by 'society' or 'the state'. The concept focuses attention on those goods which people enjoy as individuals, on individual liberties and individual needs, rather than on the quality of people's relations with one another and on the structural features of the society. That, at any rate, has been the nature of traditional 'rights' talk. Jay Bernstein, in chapter 4, attempts to give a more communitarian account of rights.[6] Perhaps it can be done; the concept of rights may prove malleable enough. However, I am not sure what it means to say that 'the content of rights is participation in community'. The traditional liberal interpretation of this idea would be that 'participation in community' is embodied in civil rights such as freedom of speech and freedom of assembly, the right to vote and to stand for office. Bernstein wants to draw from Marx a conception of rights which would 'extend the rights of the citizen to the whole of society', overcoming the duality of state and civil society (p. 110). What specific rights would this conception generate? One might argue, perhaps, that all members of the community have a right to the satisfaction of their basic needs such as food and shelter, as well as education, health care, work, and leisure, since without these they cannot play a full and effective part in the life of their community. But how do we decide how limited or extended the list of rights is to be? This brings us up against the most fundamental problem with all versions of the concept of rights: there seems to be no clear and agreed way of determining what these rights are. The concept is hopelessly indeterminate. Bernstein acknowledges the problem of determining what counts as a right, but says that this indeterminacy is not a fault, since 'what rights are needed for full and effective participation in community will change over time'(p. 116). The problem, however, is not just that rights so construed will vary over time and from community to community, but that even in any one community at any one time there is no clear way of drawing the line. It may be that Bernstein, and others who have attempted the task, can rescue the concept from this indeterminacy and can give a satisfactory account of it in communitarian terms. In the meantime I remain sceptical of the concept. I agree with those feminists who, while not discounting the importance of achieving equal legal and constitutional rights, think that feminism requires a great deal more than that. But the 'more' is, in my view, still a matter of more *equality*, and 'equality' should not be identified with 'equal rights'.

Similar points apply to another typical liberal version of equality, the idea of equal opportunities. At first sight this looks more promising than the idea of equal rights. In cases of the kind I have mentioned, where people have a formal right to enter a certain kind of education or a certain kind of job but in practice encounter the informal obstacles created by ideological and institutional pressure, we can say that they have *rights* but do not have real *opportunities*. The concept is thus capable of encompassing more of the real social conditions which affect people's lives. Nevertheless, at least in its commonest form, the

125

idea of 'equal opportunities' also has familiar limitations. The provision of opportunities may give everyone a *chance* to rise to positions of power or status or wealth, but, necessarily, if those positions are themselves limited, then not everyone can *succeed* in reaching them. Like 'equal rights', 'equal opportunities' in this sense exist against a background structure of inequalities. The concept could admittedly be employed in a wider sense. 'Equality of opportunity' could mean not just equal opportunities to get to the top, to get coveted jobs or desirable positions, but an equal opportunity for everyone in society to live a full and unfettered life. In other words there would be no 'top', no substantial inequalities of power and wealth. Equality of opportunity in this stronger sense is, I suggest, the proper goal of feminist and other radical political movements, but the concept is normally used in the narrower and more limited sense.

It seems to me, then, that feminist doubts about equality stem from identifying it with the more limited notions of 'equal rights' and 'equal opportunities'. An example of this is Juliet Mitchell's influential essay 'Women and Equality'. She does not dismiss the struggle for equal rights. Those rights which have been achieved by women are important, and there are others which have yet to be achieved. Nevertheless she argues that feminism has to go beyond equal rights, and she puts the point in these terms:

Equal rights are an important tip of an iceberg that goes far deeper. That they are only the tip is both a reflection of the limitation of the concept of equality and an indication of how profound and fundamental is the problem of the oppression of women.[7]

And again:

The notions of equality, freedom or liberty do not drop from the skies; their meaning will be defined by the particular historical circumstances that give rise to them in any given epoch. Rising as the slogan of a bourgeois revolution, equality most emphatically

denies the new class inequalities that such a revolution sets up —
the equality exists only as an abstract standard of measurement
between people reduced to their abstract humanity under the law.
Those seem to me to be some of the limitations of the concept of
equality.[8]

These passages are puzzling. Why talk of 'limitations' to
the concept of equality? How can the concept itself 'deny
inequalities'? It is precisely by employing the concept of
equality that she draws attention to the contrast between
'equal rights' and underlying *inequalities*. I agree that the
notion of equality 'does not drop from the skies', that it
is a very general concept and that it needs to be given a
more specific content in specific social circumstances. This,
however, as she acknowledges, is true of other broad value-
concepts such as 'freedom'. It is not a limitation of the concept
of equality.

What arguments like Mitchell's really show is that, in a
thoroughgoing version of the concept of equality, the crucial
element must be the idea of equality of *power*. The concept of
equality has to be applied not just to the rights of individuals
within a power structure which is taken for granted, but to
the power structure itself. In particular it has to be applied to
relations of power in the mode of production, and to relations
of power in the family; these would be the distinctively
socialist and feminist interpretations of equality. It is in this
way that the concept of equality links with that of class, for
classes are constituted by structural inequalities of economic
power. Likewise it is within this context that we can properly
understand the concept of oppression. The vocabulary of
'equality' and the vocabulary of 'oppression' are sometimes
counterposed; some feminists have suggested that feminism
should be understood as the struggle to end sexist oppression
rather than the struggle for sexual equality.[9] I do not see how
the two ideas can be separated. Oppression consists precisely
in the unequal relations of power between groups (classes,
sexes, races, and so on). We cannot explain why we oppose
all forms of oppression — still less why we do so if we are

127

not ourselves among the oppressed — except by appeals to the value of equality. This is what makes a reality of the idea of 'the left', as a term to embrace all those political movements which are in their various ways working for a society of equals.

I said at the beginning of this paper that there is a direct continuity between the liberal concept of equality and socialist and feminist concepts of equality. So far I seem to have been emphasizing the discontinuities. Of course the ideas of 'equal rights' or 'equal opportunities' are different from the more thoroughgoing ideas of 'equality of power' and 'equality of material wealth', and in that sense there are different versions of equality. When, however, I speak also of a continuity, what I mean is this: insofar as the moral case can be made for equality of rights or equality of opportunity, it is a case for equality as such, and those who accept it ought therefore, if they are consistent, to accept also the case for equality in its stronger form. The case may not necessarily be regarded as conclusive. It might be argued that the more thoroughgoing equality cannot feasibly be achieved, or that it could be achieved only at too great a price. Nevertheless when we speak of equality in this stronger form we are not redefining equality, but applying the same concept to the most fundamental features of social relations.

Socialism and Equality

I turn now to some uses and abuses of 'equality' in socialist writing. We can, I allow, find examples of socialist writers who use the concept in a weak version which has the effect of correspondingly weakening their conception of socialism, but again I want to argue that this is not inherent in the concept. Properly understood, in its strong version, the concept of equality is at the heart of the case for socialism. A classic presentation of that case is Tawney's book *Equality*. He is marvellously scathing about the way in which talk of 'equality of opportunity' is used to hide underlying inequalities:

It is possible that intelligent tadpoles reconcile themselves to the inconveniences of their position, by reflecting that, though most of them will live and die as tadpoles and nothing more, the more fortunate of the species will one day shed their tails, distend their mouths and stomachs, hop nimbly on to dry land, and croak addresses to their former friends on the virtues by means of which tadpoles of character and capacity can rise to be frogs. This conception of society may be described, perhaps, as the Tadpole Philosophy, since the consolation which it offers for social evils consists in the statement that exceptional individuals can succeed in evading them.[10]

Tawney forcibly puts the view that the underlying inequalities are the divisions between classes. It is not always clear how radical a response he thinks this requires. In one of his more equivocal passages, for instance, he says:

it is by softening or obliterating, not individual differences, but class gradations, that the historical movements directed towards diminishing inequality have attempted to attain their objective. . . . A society which values equality will attach a high degree of significance to differences of character and intelligence between different individuals, and a low degree of significance to economic and social differences between different groups.[11]

But 'softening' class gradations is significantly different from 'obliterating' them, and attaching 'a low degree of significance to economic and social differences' is certainly not the same as eliminating them. Nevertheless Tawney's overall position emerges clearly enough to structure the central argument of the book:

The forces which cut deepest the rifts between classes in modern society are obvious and unmistakable. There is inequality of power, in virtue of which certain economic groups exercise authority over others. And there is inequality of circumstance or condition, such as arises when some social groups are deprived of the necessaries of civilization which others enjoy.[12]

129

The inequality of power is located primarily in the sphere of production, the inequality of circumstance or condition is located in the sphere of consumption, and subsequent chapters go on to show how the latter is to be tackled by progressive taxation and the growth of communal provision for health, education and other social services, and the former by the growth of trade unionism, industrial legislation, and the extension of public ownership and control.

Consider now Juliet Mitchell's verdict on Tawney. To some extent she is generous in her estimate of his achievements, but again I think that she wrongly locates the role of the concept of equality in that achievement. She says:

> Tawney's own recommendations transcend the limitations of his belief in equality: he must argue for redistribution of wealth and for more collective provision of social services. His argument follows the liberal tradition but starts to look beyond it and sees that the freedom of privilege must be controlled; that freedom in a class society is ultimately freedom for one class to exploit another.[13]

But Tawney's ability to see these things does not require any transcending of the belief in equality. It is precisely his commitment to equality that leads him to argue for the redistribution of wealth and collective provision of social services, and to recognize the inadequacies of freedom in a class society.

I have noted some softening of Tawney's position at certain points in the book. A better example of diluting the idea of equality is Anthony Crosland's book *The Future of Socialism*. In his opening chapter Crosland seeks to redefine socialism in terms of its underlying values, and he suggests that 'the most characteristic feature of socialist thought' is the 'distinctive socialist ideal' of

> social equality and the 'classless society'. The socialist seeks a distribution of rewards, status, and privileges egalitarian enough to minimise social resentment, to secure justice between individuals, and to equalise opportunities; and he seeks to weaken the existing

130

deep-seated class stratification, with its concomitant feelings of envy and inferiority, and its barriers to uninhibited mingling between the classes.[14]

I am not at all sure what 'uninhibited mingling between the classes' might be, but it is certainly not socialism. However, it has little to do with equality either, and the fact that Crosland proposes it is no more an indictment of the concept of equality than it is of the concept of 'the classless society' which he also invokes.

Both my examples have been taken from the tradition of socialist thought in the British labour movement. They illustrate the range of socialist positions within that tradition as well as the range of uses to which the concept of equality is put. A recent document from the same stable is the Labour Party's statement of *Democratic Socialist Aims and Values*, and I might remark in passing that this seems to me to be one of the better accounts of the relationship between socialism and equality. The theme of the document is that 'the true purpose of democratic socialism . . . is the creation of a genuinely free society', and that this freedom can be real only if people enjoy effective power to choose and to control their lives. Hence it requires a more equal distribution of wealth and a more equal distribution of power; also, 'the right of all men and women to control the decisions which influence their daily lives must be guaranteed by a major extension of democratic control.'[15] At the general level this seems to me to be absolutely right. I suggest that those who are worried about Labour Party 'revisionism' should direct their criticisms not at the statement of aims and values but at the timidity of the policies which are supposed to put it into effect.

I want finally to look at the most influential critic of equality within the socialist tradition. It is still a matter for debate whether Marx was an egalitarian or an anti-egalitarian, but there is no doubt that his well-known remarks in his 'Critique of the Gotha Programme' provide strong support for those who, like Allen Wood, 'regard Marx as an opponent of the ideal of equality'.[16] Some of the general points which Wood attributes to Marx mirror closely the feminist doubts about the idea of equality: that in practice it may serve as a pretext for class oppression, and that the struggle against oppression does not need to appeal to any ideal of equality; that 'equality' admits of various conflicting interpretations, one of which is the idea of equal rights, and that 'a system of equal rights might lead to a very unequal distribution of wealth, power and well-being'.[17] The passage in the 'Critique of the Gotha Programme' is formulated principally as an attack on 'equal rights', but I think it is plausible to read it, as Wood does, as implying a rejection of the idea of equality altogether. I want to focus on this passage, then, which seems to me to make three main points.

Firstly, Marx's most general point is that talk of equality directs attention to the distribution of goods for consumption and thus ignores the primacy of the mode of production.

> Any distribution whatever of the means of consumption is only a consequence of the distribution of the conditions of production themselves. The latter distribution, however, is a feature of the mode of production itself. The capitalist mode of production, for example, rests on the fact that the material conditions of production are in the hands of non-workers in the form of property in capital and land, while the masses are only owners of the personal condition of production, of labour power. If the elements of production are so distributed, then the present-day distribution of the means of consumption results automatically.[18]

The importance of the ownership and control of the means of production is obviously a central insight of socialist thought, and of Marxist socialism in particular. However, it does not require us to reject the idea of equality. Once again the appropriate conclusion to draw would be that the idea of equality needs to be applied at a more fundamental level — applied to the distribution of the means of production as well as to the distribution of the means of consumption. That insight, then, needs to be retained. It is, however, dangerously overstated in Marx's formulation, that the distribution of the means of consumption 'results automatically' from the distribution of the means of production. Granted the latter sets definite limits to the former, but within those limits there is a range of possible degrees of equality or inequality, and the differences between them may be very important, as we can see if we remind ourselves of present struggles. Think of the campaigns and arguments on such issues as the Poll Tax, the level of child benefit, and the defence and improvement of the National Health Service. These are vital struggles about the distribution of benefits and burdens, and the concept of equality is at the heart of the arguments. It is implicit in such assertions as that taxation should be related to people's ability to contribute, or that good health care should not be the monopoly of the rich. The outcome of such struggles will make a real difference to the lives of millions of people, and what that outcome will be is not a foregone conclusion; it does not follow automatically from the capitalist mode of production (nor even from any sub-species such as 'welfare capitalism' or 'monopoly capitalism' or 'state capitalism' or whatever). Hence, even at the level of the distribution of the means of consumption, arguments about equality are important.

Secondly, Marx's more detailed case against equality distinguishes between two phases of communist society. In the first phase, he says, where distribution still essentially takes the form of rewards for labour, 'equal rights' would have to mean 'equal rewards for the same quantity of labour'. This, he maintains, is still basically a bourgeois notion of right. Its limitations are revealed by the fact that these 'equal rights' would produce real inequalities. People's circumstances differ, and therefore equal rewards for people in differing circumstances will leave them unequal in their standard of wellbeing.

Right by its very nature can consist only in the application of an equal standard; but unequal individuals (and they would not be different individuals if they were not unequal) are measurable by an equal standard only in so far as they are brought under an equal point of view, are taken from one definite side only, for instance, in the present case, are regarded only as workers, and

133

nothing more is seen in them, everything else being ignored. Further, one worker is married, another not; one has more children than another, and so on and so forth. Thus, with an equal performance of labour, and hence an equal share in the social consumption fund, one will in fact receive more than another, one will be richer than another, and so on. To avoid all these defects, right instead of being equal would have to be unequal.[19]

This is needlessly pedantic. In a less cantankerous mood Marx could perfectly well have said that it illustrates admirably the dialectical character of the concept of equality: equality at one level means inequality at another. If that is so, then we have to decide at what level the principle of equality is to be applied. If we were concerned to achieve overall equality of condition, then we should have to modify the simple principle of equal reward for labour, in order to take account of such facts as that one worker has children and another does not. There are familiar ways of doing this, for example a system of child benefit, the provision of child-care facilities, the provision of education, and so on. In fact Marx himself, earlier in the passage, has already said that, prior to the distribution of the proceeds of labour, there would have to be deductions, not only for investment in new production, but also 'for the common satisfaction of needs, such as schools, health services, . . . for those unable to work, and so on'. Here he is already, and rightly, modifying the idea of equality to take account of people's differing needs, and thus bringing in the principle which he says belongs in the 'higher phase of communist society': 'From each according to his ability, to each according to his needs.'

Thirdly, what then are we to say of this 'higher' principle? This is what Wood says:

Marx chooses Louis Blanc's slogan 'From each according to his ability, to each according to his needs!' precisely because it is *not* an egalitarian slogan. It does not treat people equally from any point of view, but instead considers people individually, each with a different set of needs and abilities.[20]

I disagree with this account of the principle. It *is* an egalitarian principle. If people's needs differ, the reason why greater resources should go to those with greater needs is in order to aim at an equal level of wellbeing overall. Equality as a principle of distribution would cease to be relevant only in a situation of unlimited abundance. Marx seems to think that the 'higher phase of communist society' *would* be a situation of unlimited abundance, and that 'To each according to his needs' could in practice mean 'Everyone can have everything they want.' That is how Wood interprets him.

> Marx believes there will be 'defects' and 'inequalities' in distribution even under communism, until the day when 'the springs of co-operative wealth flow abundantly' enough to permit everyone's needs to be fully satisfied. After that day, of course, equality as a device for distributing scarce resources will no longer be needed, since resources will not be scarce.[21]

Since Marx also refers to the abolition of the division of labour and says that labour would have 'become not only a means of life but life's prime want', he is apparently also assuming that work would have become so attractive that there would no longer be any need for economic incentives to work, and thus no need to decide how much people should be paid for their work.[22]

This brings me to the most important point which I want to make about Marx's discussion. His rejection of the idea of equality, and his belief that we can transcend it, is tied to one of the weakest elements in his thought, namely his millenarianism. What are we to say of the idea of total abundance? In these days of greater ecological sensitivity we are bound to take a more sober view of the idea of unlimited resources. As for the transformation of human attitudes which Marx presupposes — an unfettered willingness to engage in necessary labour, and the elimination of all extravagant desires for unnecessary consumption — I hope that, without subscribing to any pessimistic view of human nature, we are more sceptical than Marx. The prospect which we face, as far ahead as we can

135

see, is one of at least relative scarcity. Faced with that prospect, the appropriate socialist response is an appeal to the idea of equality.

Here I want to refer back to my earlier remarks about the relation between 'equality' and 'oppression'. I suggested that 'oppression' can be defined only in contrast to equality of power. What alternative definition might there be? The popular response would perhaps be that 'oppression' is to be defined in contrast with 'liberation', but that is too glib, since it evades the question '*Whose* liberation?' A society without oppression cannot be defined as one of total liberation, for the idea of total liberation is as much of a chimera as the idea of total abundance. Traditional liberal political theory is right in this at least, that freedom in society must mean the maximum freedom for each person that is compatible with an equal degree of freedom for everyone else. The alternative ideal of total liberation would mean the elimination of power altogether, the withering away of the state and of all institutionalized authority, so that 'the government of persons is replaced by the administration of things'.[23] That is Engels's millenarian vision, and presumably Marx's also.

What are we to make of it? I do not know whether it is ultimately possible or impossible, but it is literally millenarian, in the bad sense: whether or not such a state of affairs will last a thousand years when it comes, we shall certainly have to wait for at least a thousand years before we know whether there is any chance of it coming. And the trouble with these millenarian expectations is that they prevent Marx from taking seriously questions about the *distribution* of freedom and of power. He mocks the idea of a 'free state' as simply a contradiction in terms, and he thinks that this absolves him from the necessity to consider how some states might be freer than others.[24] Freedom will be achieved with the withering away of the state. Between now and then lies the dictatorship of the proletariat — and we know how many crimes have been committed in the name of that concept.

The fact is that in any society which we need to worry about, there will have to be institutions in which some people, for specific reasons and in specific respects, exercise power over others. Therefore we do have to take seriously questions about the distribution of power. I suggest that a socialist approach to those questions will consist in considering how we can aim at something like equality in the overall distribution of power. It is precisely the merit of the concept of equality that it is a *distributional* concept, and that it requires us to look at the nature of the *social relations* between people. That is why we need it.

Notes

1. I do not presume to tell feminists how to formulate feminism. However, the disagreement about the relevance of equality is there already, as a debate within feminism. An invaluable source of material on this debate is *Feminism and Equality*, ed. Anne Phillips, Oxford: Basil Blackwell 1987. Anne Phillips provides a very helpful Introduction. I should also like to acknowledge the stimulus of the session at the *Radical Philosophy* conference to which she and I presented first drafts of these papers.

2. Phillips, ed., *Feminism and Equality*, pp. 19–22.

3. See Janet Radcliffe Richards, 'Separate Spheres', in Peter Singer, ed., *Applied Ethics*, Oxford: Oxford University Press 1986.

4. On this see Richards, *Applied Ethics*, and Mary Midgley, 'On Not Being Afraid of Natural Sex Differences', in Morwenna Griffiths and Margaret Whitford, eds, *Feminist Perspectives in Philosophy*, London: Macmillan 1988.

5. Bell Hooks, 'Feminism: A Movement to End Sexist Oppression', in Phillips, ed., *Feminism and Equality*, pp. 62–3.

6. See Jay Bernstein, chapter 4 in this volume.

7. Juliet Mitchell, 'Women and Equality', in Phillips, ed., *Feminism and Equality*, p. 26.

8. Mitchell, p. 30.

9. For example, Bell Hooks.

10. R.H. Tawney, *Equality*, fourth edn, London: George Allen and Unwin 1964, p. 105.

11. Tawney, *Equality*, pp. 57–8.

12. Tawney, *Equality*, p. 112.

13. Mitchell, p. 41.

14. Anthony Crosland, *The Future of Socialism*, revised edn, London: Jonathan Cape 1964, p. 77.

15. The Labour Party, *Democratic Socialist Aims and Values*, Labour Party 1988, p. 3.

16. Allen Wood, 'Marx and Equality', in John Mepham and David-Hillel Ruben, eds, *Issues in Marxist Philosophy*, vol. 4, Harvester 1981, p. 196. On this see also Michèle Barrett, 'Marxist-Feminism and the Work of Karl Marx', in Phillips, *Feminism and Equality*.

17. Wood, p. 196.
18. Karl Marx, 'Critique of the Gotha Programme', in Marx and Engels, *Basic Writings on Politics and Philosophy*, ed. Lewis S. Feuer, London: Fontana 1969, p. 161.
19. Karl Marx, 'Critique of the Gotha Programme', p. 160.
20. Wood, p. 211.
21. Ibid.
22. Marx, 'Critique', p. 160.
23. Friedrich Engels, 'Socialism: Utopian and Scientific', in Feuer, p. 147.
24. Marx, 'Critique', pp. 167–9; cf. Engels, 'Socialism', p. 147.

6

'So What's Wrong with the Individual?' Socialist and Feminist Debates on Equality

Anne Phillips

Equality, like democracy, is something we are all supposed to support, yet over which we patently disagree. And like democracy it has lent itself to a spectrum of opinion from reluctant convert to enthusiastic advocate, dividing us up into pessimists and optimists, realists and dreamers, doubters and those who know. Positions on equality suggest a continuum: a range that starts with the legal and electoral equalities that are the conventional minimum of the day, and extends through increasingly egalitarian stances until no hierarchy at all is acceptable. Where people place themselves on this continuum may seem like psychological quirks; but it is also claimed to be a matter of the limits of their thought. Certainly generations of socialists and radicals have appealed to consistency as a means of securing their case. The liberal dips a toe in the water and considers that quite enough; radicals warn that logic demands further immersion.

Minimal equality is sometimes said to be self-defeating, for once the principles of equality are admitted, they carry more substance than was the original intent. To take just two recent examples: Zillah Eisenstein argues in *The Radical Future of Liberal Feminism* that liberal feminism is potentially subversive, and that qualified as it may seem in its defence of 'mere' equal opportunity, it contains within itself the seeds of a more radical feminism;[1] John Baker suggests in *Arguing For Equality* that 'everything that matters about equality of opportunity points to the much more extensive equality of egalitarianism'.[2] In both cases, the moderate goals of equality before the law or equality of opportunity are said to carry with them considerable equality of condition. Equality is a slippery slope, and once on it, it is hard to get off.

Elsewhere in this volume, Richard Norman argues that there is a direct continuity between liberal, socialist and feminist traditions, and that the last two can be regarded as more thoroughgoing applications of the first. He is mainly concerned with restoring the importance of 'equality', but when he defends liberalism as the worthy progenitor of the egalitarian tradition, the argument can be twisted the other way. Liberalism might deserve some credit for identifying the importance of political and legal equality, but this is a backhanded compliment, for having set things off on the right track, it has been overtaken by more energetic traditions. Pushing the arguments about formal equality towards a more substantial conclusion, socialism and Marxism surely come out with a higher grade. Feminism then zooms in to take top prize. Despite decades of socialist self-congratulation, class was not after all the last word in inequality and subordination, for what about all those further inequalities between women and men? Revealing to astonished gaze how much more remains to be done, feminism exposes the limits of previous thought. The scope and concerns of equality are once more (is this the last time?) enlarged.

The development of ideas does not of course follow this enlightened pattern. There may be individuals who have travelled from liberalism through socialism to feminism, and who felt consistency driving them on at every stage on the way, but the traditions will not arrange themselves so neatly. However attractive the notion of a progressive continuum, the history of equality does not translate as a concept that simply widened in scope. Socialists feel they have have shown up the limits of liberalism times without number; liberals live on to tell their tale. Feminists feel they have completed both liberal and socialist projects; they find their arguments first welcomed and then mysteriously mislaid. This is not just the stubborn obstinacy of those who refuse to recognize reason, but testifies to genuine disagreement over what equality should mean. The continuing debate on the role and legacy of liberalism (to which this book as a whole is a contribution) is a partial reflection of this; my comparison between socialist and feminist views on equality therefore begins here.

It is relatively uncontroversial to say that contemporary notions of equality developed out of seventeenth-century liberalism; but this is uncontroversial precisely because 'developed out of' can mean so many different things. Leaving open almost everything that matters, it does not yet tell us whether the basic tenets were incorporated or more radically transformed. The literature on this has tended to identify the individual as the crucial point of departure, and in exploring the current relationship between socialist and feminist views on equality, I shall broadly follow this lead. To put the questions at their simplest: can socialists do anything with the liberal concept of the individual? Can feminists do anything without it? The main point I want to make is that the respective positions of socialism and feminism have been recently reversed. It used to be socialism that most vigorously challenged individualist versions of equality, while feminism tended towards a more ambivalent stance. In the past decade, however, there has been a marked convergence between socialist and liberal views, which has carried with it a new consensus on the individual and equality; over the same period many feminists have been moving the other way. My concern here is to indicate and substantiate some of these shifts, and then consider their wider implications.

Socialism and the Individual

In the development of the liberal tradition, the individual is abstract and deliberately so. The classical liberalism of Thomas Hobbes or John Locke began from the idea that all men are born equal — even when noting in the same breath tremendous variations in ability and strength. The additional layers of social and economic difference that then accumulate around these individuals were said to be theoretically insignificant. Disregarding the contingencies of social existence, early liberals built their theories around the 'essential' individual as he appeared in the state of nature: free, equal, but lonely and in fear for his life. The argument might be supported by a psychology that attributed particular (usually unpleasant) qualities to human nature, but this was not really the point. The key feature is that liberalism distinguished between the abstraction of the individual and the living realities of actual people, between the very basic and formal humanity in terms of which we were said to be equal, and the multiple differences that in practice kept us apart. The distinction between essential and accidental is central to the liberal tradition. It is a commonplace of political commentary to note that liberals say we are or should be equal, but do not think we are or should be the same. To the irritated critic this can seem like a loss of nerve — to go so far and then quickly draw back. But the argument is entirely deliberate. Notwithstanding any social differences of wealth or status, notwithstanding any biological differences of ability or strength, *as citizens* we should be treated the same. Whatever the differences, they do not matter. They should not be allowed to count.

Socialists have long countered that the point is vacuous, and that while major economic and social 'difference' is left to run its course, it is pious formalism to say we should all be treated the same. Unmasking the false abstractions of the liberal individual, socialists therefore pointed to the class realities through which individuals live their lives. The equal right to vote cannot guarantee an equal distribution of power, for access to political influence is profoundly shaped by the distribution of wealth, while power in the workplace remains securely in employers' hands. The right to equal treatment before the law will not translate into legal equality, for the laws incorporate the privileges of property, while those with money can ensure more favourable terms. Specifically biological difference never attracted much attention from socialists, who tended to argue that inequalities of wealth and power accounted for virtually all the supposedly biological differences of ability, height or strength, and therefore discounted this layer. On that more intransigent difference of sex, they maintained the usual silence. The crux of the argument was that social and economic inequality *does* count, and that as long as 'differences' of property and class exist, political equality remains gesture at most.

The argument that political equality rests on prior social and economic equalities has usually combined with a trenchant critique of liberal individualism that queries its vision of the society we need. Quite apart from their blind refusal to consider economic and social constraints, liberals are said to reduce the dreams of equality to the formalities of equal rights. In doing so they express an impoverished version of human existence, in which individuals are always and inevitably opposed.[3] Egoistic, competitive, self-possessed and self-possessing, the individuals of liberal theory are all too obviously in need of protection, and given the dour premises, equal protection through equal rights may well be the best they can do. But for generations of socialists, this defensive equality — leave me alone to do what I want and I'll leave you alone in your turn — stemmed from the mean-spirited competitive world of contemporary capitalism, a world in which other individuals do indeed threaten our interests and the state does indeed act to constrain and repress. To conflate the specificities of capitalism with the essentials of nature was to give up on our hopes for the future. Liberals had translated the grand ideals of equality into the protective obsessions of equal rights and claims; in the process they had abandoned themselves to a profound fatalism in which individuals had to be separate, atomistic, counterposed.

In abbreviated versions, liberalism was then said to be pro-individual while socialism was pro-society — a summary that did little justice to either tradition, but once spoken, proved hard to correct. Marxists referred repeatedly to the *Manifesto* definition of communism as an association 'in which the free development of each is the condition for the free development of all', but this bid to represent the free individuals signally failed to convince. As far as the sceptics were concerned, socialism — most especially in its Marxist versions — was too closely

143

linked to heavy diatribes against the individualism of the liberal tradition: how could any individual be safe in such hands? And twist and turn as they subsequently did over the relationship between individual, individualism and individuality, socialists had difficulty finding the precise formulation that would cut the last one free. Decades of protestation later, they seem to have given up the ghost. Half the radical intelligentsia is now busy decentering the subject: an approach that cuts through old dichotomies by dropping both individual *and* society in the bin. The other half is bent on winning the individual over.

Anyone who has been following recent debates will be able to furnish examples, and I shall only offer some indications of my own. Part of what I am thinking of is the new emphasis on tensions between equality and freedom, and the various retracings of socialism as being primarily about individual liberty, or primarily about democracy.[4] Socialists have usually contested the way their tradition was characterized as anti-individual or anti-libertarian, but till recently the standard argument was that individuality thrives best in the rich soil of social co-operation, or that freedom becomes possible only when we are equal in power. Within the Marxist tradition, the idea that there might be a conflict between social equality and individual freedom was, typically, brushed aside; or more precisely, it was at the point at which people acknowledged such a conflict that they stopped identifying with Marxist ideas. Today the choices are less painful. Socialists feel more able to voice their suspicions of simple harmony without relinquishing the claim to be socialists still. Freed from some of the pressures to orthodoxy, many now express impatience with the verbal tricks and methodological miracles through which the tradition has resisted complaint.

For example, the commitment to an economic and social revolution once implied disparagement of 'mere' political and legal equalities. I learnt my socialism in an era when liberal democracy was a term of abuse, and military dictatorships were only considered different in degree; socialists often played down threats to existing freedoms, noting that under capitalism no-one was free. Such an easy squaring of the circle is much less practised today. The rights and freedoms of the individual are now regarded as an eminently suitable socialist concern. At the same time there has been a loss of certainty over what economic equality involves. Most contemporary (European) socialists have lost their confidence in centralized planning; many have fundamentally revised their views on the market; the majority probably converge on a critique of statism which attaches heightened importance to individual freedoms and rights. The pursuit of economic equality is increasingly associated with a powerful — and not even efficient — state, and as more and more socialists come to make this equation, they fear that they may be giving up on what is unquestionably progressive in the search for what is dubiously so. Liberals have always insisted on the potential conflict between social equality and individual freedom; the difference with many contemporary socialists is increasingly a matter of degree.

In both epistemology and politics, socialist theory now operates within a more explicitly individualist perspective, as witnessed in the development of rational-choice Marxism, and the growing interest in the language of rights. John Rawls's highly influential *A Theory Of Justice* is a classic of the individualist tradition, deriving a qualified defence of equality from the redistributive principles we might all agree on as fair and just if we did not know whether our personal destiny was to be rich or poor.[5] Taking as its starting point an anonymity of individuals with no interconnection, their rationality devoted only to their own concerns, it is a theoretical construct that breaks every rule in the socialist book — and yet has inspired considerable interest among socialist thinkers today. (One example of this is the Italian theorist Norberto Bobbio, whose writings on socialism and democracy frequently refer to Rawls.[6])

On the terrain of political economy, Alec Nove's *The Economics of Feasible Socialism* offers a polemical challenge to what he sees as the utopianism of much socialist thought, arguing that in the belief that there *should* be no conflict between equality, freedom and growth, socialists have simply turned a blind eye to the warning signs from planned economies.[7] Instead of pretending that the experience of Eastern Europe or the Soviet Union is irrelevant (that is, not really socialist after all) Nove argues that we should be trying to draw the lessons from that experience. The main ones for him are the limits of planning, the continued necessity for a market, the perhaps inevitable conflict (in any time span that will prove significant to us) between equality, efficiency and freedom. In his challenging work on the welfare state in Britain, Julian Le Grand has suggested further lessons from experiences closer to home. Public expenditure on social services has, he argues, proved a profoundly ineffective strategy for securing equality, for it disproportionately favours the middle class, who extract considerably more resources from the educational and health systems than those in greater need. His argument initially favoured a more radical egalitarianism that would directly equalize incomes,[8] but has become more generally associated with voucher systems as a means of equalizing individual claims. In both works there is a noticeable shift from the concerns of the producer to those of the consumer, and whatever we may make of this politically, it is important to observe its theoretical effect. It was part of the ABC of Marxism that 'the consumer' was abstracted from class division, and that presenting us to ourselves only in our roles as buyers and sellers, it glossed over inequalities in power. Compared with the producer, the consumer is a highly abstract and individuated notion, but it is the consumer who leaps out of socialist writing today.

My examples are somewhat random, but together they substantiate a major shift in socialist thought. In terms of equality, they translate into a new emphasis on creating the conditions under which we can act and relate as free and equal consumers, and indeed I would characterize much current thinking as a kind of glorified equality of opportunity. This sounds more disparaging than it should, for any substantial equalizing of our opportunities — whether in access to health care, education, jobs, income, housing — would be a dramatic improvement in our lives. But the change in direction re-arranges the relationship between liberal and socialist thinking, and legitimates an abstraction that socialists once claimed to despise. Socialists initially challenged the liberal distinction between essential man and contingent worker, boss, landlord, tenant; and worked hard to re-clothe those naked individuals in their class-differentiated garments. The abstract individual was thought to be both methodological nonsense and political liability, a construct that had encouraged an ahistorical myopia and led into an impoverished egalitarianism that could not fulfil even its limited claims. Times have changed, and the individual with them. In contemporary socialist thinking, the abstract individual is widely accepted as a meaningful theoretical term.

Feminism and the Individual

What, meanwhile, of feminism? The relationship between liberalism and feminism has followed a different route, and the image of the latter as extension of the former has a plausibility that many writers will confirm. The liberal language of individual rights and freedoms had tremendous resonance for women, and for the nineteenth and much of the twentieth century, it was liberalism rather than socialism that seemed to offer them a way through. The link remains at its most apparent in matters of equal rights, for as victims of often overt discrimination, women can still get mileage out of liberal ideals, still have to operate on what socialists traditionally regarded as that limited terrain of formal equality. More fundamentally perhaps, the individualism that lies behind liberal thinking on equality has a powerful appeal. Much of the personal impetus towards a feminist politics is to do with claiming the space to choose who and what you are — not to be defined, contained and dictated by notions of 'woman'. Or to put it the other way round, the idea that it should not matter who or what you are has been an inspiration to generations of women, as has the associated notion that we should be regarded as individuals, as 'persons', as independent of the contingencies of sex. Liberals abstracted the essential man from the accidents of history and biology, and while the emphasis on 'man' was a bit of a blow, the basic structure seemed to fit. All right, so we are different. These differences should not be allowed to count.

This claim to equality *despite* difference is the point of greatest contact between feminism and liberalism, but as anyone acquainted with the history of feminism will know, it reflects only one strand. For the more socialist inclined, the idea that a woman's sex should not matter is as vacuous in its way as the notion that an individual's class should not count: both of them patently do. A politics that tries to transcend (read ignore) difference is one that confirms the inequalities that exist, and it is precisely the pretence that sexual difference is irrelevant that has denied to women the chance of equal jobs or equal political involvement. For women to be treated as equals with men they need substantial changes in the sexual division of labour, in the conditions under which children are cared for and houses kept clean; it is only when such socially constructed differences are removed that equality can become a meaningful term. 'Equal but different' is from this point of view a nonsense, and merely serves to legitimate separate spheres.

There is a third strand that fits neither of these positions. Feminism has moved recurrently between the emphasis on equality and the focus on difference: between a politics that points out the irrelevance of sex and insists we should be treated the same, and an alternative that takes sexual difference as its starting point. The tension runs through every issue and campaign — often enough through each individual as well — and some of the most obvious examples arise in relation to equality at work. Men and women *are* different, and while some of these differences are socially constructed (to use the language of the 1970s, a matter of gender rather than sex) and therefore open to change, others are more intractable. Women menstruate, get pregnant, give birth: how much should *these* differences be acknowledged when it comes to their positions at work? Legislation that restricts the employment of women in what are regarded as dangerous trades, or limits the hours they can work, or prevents them from engaging in (certain kinds of) night work, can be seen as an unjustifiable restriction on women's earning power. Feminists in the nineteenth century wryly noted that this so-called 'protective' legislation for women was in effect a protection for men, and that it helped secure and maintain the male monopoly in all of the higher paid trades. If women are to be treated as equals, then such legislation might appear to be wrong. But should women have to gloss over the fact that they get pregnant and bear children when the result can be treatment that is *worse* than the man's? The point is similar to that made by Marx in his 'Critique of the Gotha Programme'. As long as people have different needs or capacities, then the kind of equality that metes out exactly the same to each of us in turn will effectively mean inequality: the abstract measuring rod of equal rights is insensitive to varying need.

Feminists will not warm to the example Marx gave, which was that the needs of a single man are less than those of a man with a wife and children to support, but the general question is clearly related. Why should being equal mean being the same? Alone among the wealthy countries of the world, the USA has no national provision for maternity leave, and the only limited protection offered to pregnant women came with the 1978 Pregnancy Disability Act, which established pregnancy as being like 'any other temporary disability'(!). This extended to pregnant women the protections and benefits that are enjoyed by other workers who are temporarily disabled: employers can no longer refuse to hire a woman because she is pregnant, no longer sack her because she is pregnant, or compel her to take maternity leave; and where the state or the firm has some system of benefits to cover temporary disabilities, then these now apply to pregnant women as well. A limited kind of maternity entitlement has thus sneaked in by the back door, though it so far covers less than 40 per cent of working women. But note that the whole philosophy is one that denies pregnancy as something specific to women: 'equal treatment' here means treating pregnant women no better and no worse than any other disabled worker. Feminists in the USA have divided in their responses to this, some feeling that women's interests are indeed best served by gender-neutral legislation, and others arguing that women need sex-specific laws and protections.[9]

Embedded in this issue is the abstract de-gendered individual. The feminisms that most closely approximate the liberal tradition will welcome this character onto their side, for if sexual equality is to be equated with equal treatment regardless of sex, it means we should be 'individuals' and not 'women' or 'men'. This version retains its powerful advocates, but the pendulum has substantially shifted from abstract equality towards engendered difference, and androgynous ideals of de-gendered personhood are by no means so fashionable today.[10] Liberals presented a notion of equality in which differences should not count; socialists tackled this on the terrain of class with the argument that differences should not exist; and neither gives much assistance to feminist debate today. Strategies for sexual equality increasingly emphasize sexual difference as the starting point, arguing that this can be neither discounted nor eliminated.

Equality must instead be theorized to accommodate differences of sex. As Zillah Eisenstein puts it in *The Female Body and the Law*, we must 'pluralize the meaning of difference and reinvent the category of equality'.[11] Discussions of sexual equality have so far silently privileged the male body: when men and women are treated the same, it means women being treated as if they were men; when men and women are treated differently, the man remains the norm, against which the woman is peculiar, lacking, different. This phallocratic discourse has, she argues, pushed women into a corner — or rather into a choice of two equally uncomfortable ones. Feminism has been endlessly locked into an equality/difference dichotomy. These are the only choices on offer and yet neither will do.

Eisenstein argues that instead of *the* difference between male and female we need to recognize the many differences between women, between men, as well as between the two. The pregnant woman is of course different from the never-pregnant man, but she is also different from the non-pregnant woman, and different in many ways from other women who are pregnant. Allowing woman to be subsumed under the category of mother is as bad in its way as claiming she is the 'same' as man; both alternatives reflect the impoverished either/or choice that has so long limited our sense of the options. Equality should not rest on how similar we are, on how closely we approximate the norm. What we need is a 'multiple plurality' in which being different *matters* (this is not the liberal perspective which calls on us to treat difference as simply irrelevant) but no longer weakens our claims on equality.

In such arguments we see not only the emphasis on sexual difference, but another preoccupation of contemporary feminism, which is the challenge to those false unities that have littered the path of previous theory. When the elegant abstractions of 'he' and 'man' gave way to the more clumsy 'he and she', 'women and men', the debate was about more than linguistic usage. (Exactly the same issues were raised over the less overtly sexist 'working class'.) Categories that presumed to deal with both women and men, without even noting if it was more one than the other, necessarily wrote in the experience of one sex as if it automatically embraced the other. A more careful differentiation would establish that sometimes 'men' means men. Very occasionally, it really does mean both women and men, in which case it ought to say so. Most frequently of all, it pretends to mean both women and men when in practice it talks only of the male. It is this last phenomenon that is the most dangerous. A major theme in current feminist writing is that the liberal 'men' once meant exactly that (no women here), but has now shifted into the third, and more devious, camp. The individuals of liberal theory are presented as if they refer indiscriminately to women or men, but have written into them a masculine experience and masculine norm. Their abstraction cloaks a masculine body.

'The "individual" is a patriarchal category. The individual is masculine and his sexuality is understood accordingly.'[12] '(T)he individual is a man, in a male body.'[13] The argument is partly historical, and in Carole Pateman's *The Sexual Contract* involves a major re-assessment of seventeenth-century contract theory as grounded in a prior sexual contract that established new terms for male access to women. I will not here discuss this challenging analysis — and indeed if her argument were only historical, then liberals might still find some means of escape. Scattering profuse apologies around them, they could promise to clean up their concepts and wash off those masculine taints. But Pateman's argument goes further than that. Identity is

151

not something that floats freely through the abstractions of consciousness; it is embodied in physical form. Liberalism tries to deny this in the way it presents its individual, abstracting not only from the social and economic 'contingencies' that have so rightly preoccupied socialists, but from the biological 'contingencies' that make up sexual difference. In doing so, liberals have covered up their equation between individual and man.

> The abstract character of the liberal individual in liberal contract theory has been criticized from the left ever since Rousseau's initial attack. But because the critiques invariably pass silently over the separation of male reason from female body in the original creation of the civil individual, one of his most notable features has also been silently incorporated by the critics. The 'individual' is disembodied.[14]

The body has to be excluded in order to carry off the trick. Under the supposedly abstract guise of the individual, liberalism wrote in a version of sexual mastery in which individuals were perceived as possessing themselves, and wanting and needing to possess others. Carole Pateman's argument builds on C.B. Macpherson's notion of the possessive individual, but she attributes this phenomenon to the demands of patriarchy as much as to the development of the market. Our notions of equality, of fair and just contract, of individuals and how they should relate, are unfortunately extensions of this. Women have tried for centuries to turn this language to their own advantage — demanding, for example, to be treated as individuals and not as women — but when they do so they get caught in an appalling bind. One example Carole Pateman gives relates to recent endeavours by US feminists to construct a 'gender-free' version of the marriage contract, in which two individuals freely and mutually contract — but for what? Given the nature of the 'individual' and the meaning of contract, she argues, this can only mean a contract between two people who own their own bodies and agree to mutual sexual use. Sexual relations then take the form of universal prostitution, marking the political defeat of women as women.

Carole Pateman has long been one of liberalism's most

vigorous critics, and has increasingly identified women as the definitive stumbling block for the liberal tradition. Women, she suggests, cannot be incorporated into the liberal regime of individuals and rights and consent, except in the most uncertain and ambiguous of ways.[15] Existing discourses on equality embody sexual difference, and they confirm the primary status of men. And though may feminists have hoped and believed they could dust down and improve the biased old categories, there are really only two ways to go. Either we carry on with the pretence that the individual is abstract and disembodied, in which case we silently accept his masculine shape. Or we abandon the search for a cleaner abstraction, and admit that there are women and men. 'To take embodied identity seriously demands the abandonment of the masculine unitary individual to open up space for two figures; one masculine, one feminine.'[16] Away with the abstract, the de-gendered, the disembodied. Not the individual, but women and men.

So just as socialists make their tentative moves towards the individual, many feminists have been turning the opposite way. The individual has joined the list of suspect categories, but instead of the traditional socialist argument that stressed his egoism and lack of social context, we have a new feminist critique which stresses his masculinity and liking for men. Let me note again (for feminist critique of dead and gone thinkers always proves more acceptable than contemporary attack) that the argument is not just historical. It says not only that the individual of political theory *has* embraced a masculine experience, but that of its very nature it remains bound to only one sex. We cannot escape the body, and wherever we introduce a disembodied, de-gendered, abstraction, we will be insinuating one or other sex as the norm.

Can We Manage Without Abstraction?

I find much of this argument compelling, and it certainly helps resolve practical dilemmas that arise in the pursuit of sexual equality, where we have been beleaguered by notions of a norm. Categories like 'the individual', 'the citizen', 'the consumer' are indeed extraordinarily abstract, and feminists are right to draw attention to the dangers inherent in their use. When equality is theorized through concepts which simply *presume* we are the same, then it can end up favouring those who most fit, and forcing all others into a singular mould. Last year's socialists (or certainly the Marxists among them) knew this full well in relation to class, which is why they preferred producers to consumers, workers to citizens, classes to individuals, and argued for a historically specific understanding of justice, equality, rights. Feminism has now taken over this mantle, and with its new emphasis on bodily difference, extended the nature and scope of the critique.

What puzzles me is how far the argument should go. The critique of the individual clearly engages with what has become a dominant issue today, which is the space (if any) for universal concepts, and the role left for abstract thought. The bid to universality is much contested these days, and in re-gendering supposedly universal concepts — the individual, citizen, equality, duty, rights — feminism has contributed its fair share to undermining grandiose claims. Social and political theorists are now required to query their hidden assumptions, and even those of most universalistic bent have bowed their head to this need. Jürgen Habermas, for example, acknowledges the challenge in a recent definition of the philosopher's role:

> According to my conception, the philosopher ought to explain the moral point of view, and — as far as possible — justify the claim to universality of this explanation, showing why it does not merely reflect the moral intuitions of the average, male, middle-class member of a modern Western society.[17]

The implication of some contemporary feminist writing is that this simply cannot be done. Or more precisely (since the point is not that average middle-class men are incapable of thinking beyond themselves) that sexual difference can be neither ignored nor transcended, but has to be built firmly into the theories. We cannot pull out some abstract humanity in relation to which we are equal. When we try to do this we impose a part as a norm.

This is where I start to get edgy. For the last three hundred years, every oppressed group has found a lifeline in the abstractions of the individual and has appealed to these in making its claims to equality. 'No, it doesn't matter if I am a woman not a man; it doesn't matter if my skin is black or yellow or brown; it doesn't matter if I am a Catholic or a Hindu or a Jew.' The liberal distinction between an essential 'man' and contingent person has served us reasonably well, for while it buried class and sexual difference as irrelevant and boring, it nonetheless gave us standards of impartiality without which equality is hard to conceive. If we go too far in the opposite direction, we end up with something like Richard Rorty's notion of the self as 'a centreless web of historically conditioned beliefs and desires',[18] and once we get there, how do we ever stand back from our prejudices and predilections to perceive that those who are different are nonetheless deserving of our respect? Generations of feminists quite rightly saw the abstract, disembodied individual as a weapon they could use in their bid for equality, for without even entering into those tedious debates about the size of women's brains or the nature of maternal instinct, they could insist that they were human too. It may be that equality does not require this philosophical underpinning, just as it does not require a humanist foundation that attributes substantial content to the human essence. But there is a risk in this, and it is one I would prefer not to run. If we were to give up on our notions of abstract humanity, what if anything would take its place?[19]

The most radical response is to say that the abstract ideals of impartial justice are themselves part of a male ethic, and that there is an alternative morality premised on understanding, empathy and care. This is part of what Carol Gilligan argues in *In A Different Voice*, where she suggests that psychologists and philosophers have extrapolated from male practices to erect a hierarchy of morals that puts logic and justice on top. Using studies of women facing both real and hypothetical moral dilemmas, she identifies an alternative ethic of responsibility which is based on contextualizing each person involved in the dilemma, trying to understand their options and then minimize everyone's chances of pain:

> The morality of rights is predicated on equality and centered on the understanding of fairness, while the ethic of responsibility relies on the concept of equity, the recognition of differences in need. While the ethic of rights is a manifestation of equal respect, balancing the claims of other and self, the ethic of responsibility rests on an understanding that gives rise to compassion and care.[20]

Here again is the contrast between (male) abstraction and (female) specificity that is running like wildfire through much contemporary feminist debate, and if the implication is that the latter is superior to the former then I simply do not agree. Compassion cannot substitute for the impartiality of justice and equality, for compassion is potentially limited to those we can understand — and hence those who are most like ourselves. For feminists in particular, this would be a risky road to pursue, and it was precisely the demand for equality *across* seemingly impassable barriers of incomprehension and difference that gave birth to the feminist tradition.

Yet Gilligan need not assert one ethic *over* another (from my reading of her work, she does not) and in a sympathetic review of her position, Seyla Benhabib argues that in fact we need both.[21] The very notion of impartial justice (the 'male' standpoint of the 'generalized other') implies being able to put oneself in another's shoes, and acknowledge his/her entitlement to those rights we have claimed for ourselves. But this makes no sense unless we also take the standpoint of the 'concrete other', for until we know the individual's concrete and specific history we cannot say whether the situation is like or unlike our own. We must, in other words, be both abstract and concrete; to relate this to sexual equality, we need both the abstract impartiality implied in 'the individual' and the concrete specificity that tells us whether individuals are women or men.

My only quarrel with this is that it looks remarkably like what juries already do. Equal treatment before the law appeals

at one level to the impartial distribution of powers, benefits
and punishments regardless of sex, race or class; and jurors
are called upon to lay aside those prejudices and sympathies
that will attract them to those most like themselves. At the
same time, jurors are often given considerable information on
the history and background of the accused, and it is seen as part
of the process of justice that these unique circumstances should
be additionally taken into account. Juries are therefore asked to
combine the abstract with the concrete, to blend together the
egalitarianism that is supposed to disregard difference with its
apparent opposite that focuses precisely on what marks people
out. In this sense, our best practices already fit with what
Zillah Eisenstein calls for when she says that 'equality must
encompass generalization, abstraction and homogeneity as well
as individuality, specificity and heterogeneity.'[22]

The point I am making is that feminists — like juries — can
criticize the abstractions of 'the individual' without having to
throw all such concepts away. There are many contexts in
which what matters are indeed the differences between us: the
difference between pregnant and not-pregnant; Muslim and
Christian; shy and confidently verbose. We have to nuance our
understanding of equality to deal with this multiple difference,
but the nuances are required precisely because of an underlying
notion of the human condition which disregards differences of
sex, race, religion or class. This notion may have no substantial
content — there is nothing there if you strip away what makes
us different or unique — yet without it, the mass of complicated
variations would not even begin to enter the debate. We need
both the one and the other.

It is one of the paradoxes of contemporary feminist writing
that so much of it identifies false oppositions, dualisms or
dichotomies as the characteristics of orthodox, masculine
thought,[23] and yet so much of it also reads like straightforward
reversals of what previous writers have said. Feminists are of
course as fond as anyone of creating a theoretical stir, but in
sharpening up the differences between ourselves and orthodox
thought, there is perhaps a tendency to exaggerate the size of the
gap. Thus if men have been abstract, women will be concrete;

if men have talked of the individual, women will talk only of real women and men. In some cases, this sharp dichotomy fits well with the writer's intentions, but in others it does not. When Carol Gilligan, for example, is read as establishing the superiority of the female ethic of caring over the male ethic of justice, it is I think a misinterpretation. When Carole Patemen is interpreted as saying we can no longer use the language of individual rights, her challenge to the orthodoxy is being read in too simple a way. Left to (him)self, 'the individual' may well cut a swathe through our dreams of sexual equality, pushing women into a pattern defined by the male. But this is not to say that we are only women or men.

Richard Norman has approached this from the opposite direction, arguing that feminists have presented the orthodoxy in too simple a way. In his paper in this volume, he suggests that feminist critiques of equality have gone over the top, and that in (rightly) challenging particular versions of the concept, they have (wrongly) dismissed it from use. Without agreeing with all his characterization of the debate, I will end on a similar note. It has been the great achievement of socialism (in the past) and feminism (in the present) to strip away the layers of special pleading to reveal first the class and then the gender of supposedly universal beings, and to challenge what are false abstractions. The risk associated with current socialist developments is that in the desire to accommodate the political importance of the individual, socialists may too readily forget what mattered in the critique of abstraction — and too easily attach themselves to a version of equality that will be only partially applied. The risk associated with current feminist writing is that in the (necessary) critique of gender neutrality, some feminists may give up on any notion of universal humanity, and therefore lose what gives equality its power. The danger may lie more in (mis)readings of feminist argument that in the substantial content of what feminists have to say. But I will just put it on record that abstraction can't be all bad!

Notes

1. Zillah Eisenstein, *The Radical Future of Liberal Feminism*, London: Longman 1981.

2. John Baker, *Arguing For Equality*, London: Verso 1987, p. 148.

3. C.B. Macpherson has probably done most to develop this argument in, for example, *The Political Theory of Possessive Individualism*, Oxford: Clarendon Press 1963. A more recent critique of liberal individualism is Benjamin Barber's *Strong Democracy*, Berkeley: University of California Press 1984.

4. John Keane, *Democracy and Civil Society*, London: Verso 1988, is a prominent example of the latter.

5. John Rawls, *A Theory Of Justice*, Oxford: Oxford University Press 1971.

6. See Norberto Bobbio, *Which Socialism?*, Cambridge: Polity Press 1986; and *The Future of Democracy*, Cambridge: Polity Press 1987.

7. Alec Nove, *The Economics of Feasible Socialism*, London: Allen and Unwin 1983.

8. See Julian Le Grand, *The Strategy For Equality*, London: Allen and Unwin 1982.

9. For an excellent discussion of these debates see Zillah Eisenstein, *The Female Body and the Law*, Berkeley: University of California Press 1989.

10. See, for example, the articles in Anne Phillips, ed., *Feminism and Equality*, London: Basil Blackwell 1987; and the discussion in Lynne Segal, *Is The Future Female?*, London: Virago 1987.

11. Eisenstein, *Female Body*, p. 4.

12. Carole Pateman, *The Sexual Contract*, Cambridge: Polity Press 1988, pp. 184—5.

13. Eisenstein, *Female Body*, p. 77.

14. Carole Pateman, 'The Fraternal Social Contract', in John Keane, ed., *Civil Society and the State*, London: Verso 1988, p. 116.

15. For the development of these ideas over the last decade, see the essays in Carole Pateman, *The Disorder of Women*, Cambridge: Polity Press 1989.

16. Pateman, *The Sexual Contract*, p. 224. The argument, as I understand it, is not that the unitary figure is by definition male (in a matriarchy, for example, it might be woman who becomes the privileged figure) but that it can't be both woman and man. Hence in any conditions that we are likely to experience, it is automatically going to be male.

17. Cited in Richard Rorty, 'Thugs and Theorists: A Reply to Bernstein', *Political Theory*, vol. 15, no. 4, 1987, p. 579.

18. Richard Rorty, 'The Priority of Democracy to Philosophy', in M. Peterson and K. Vaughan, eds, *The Virginia Statute of Religious Freedom: Two Hundred Years After*, Cambridge: Cambridge University Press 1988, p. 270.

19. I am partly convinced by the answer Rorty himself gives to this question which is that it is literature and not philosophy than can increase our sensitivity to those who are different from ourselves, but I worry that

this is too parochial. See Richard Rorty, *Contingency, Irony and Solidarity*, Cambridge: Cambridge University Press 1989.

20. Carol Gilligan, *In A Different Voice*, Cambridge, Mass: Harvard University Press 1982, pp. 164–5.

21. Seyla Benhabib, 'The Generalized and Concrete Other' in S. Benhabib and D. Cornell, eds, *Feminism As Critique*, Cambridge: Polity Press 1987.

22. Eisenstein, *Female Body*, p. 221.

23. See for example, Diana Coole, *Women In Political Theory*, Brighton: Wheatsheaf 1988.

7

Life Beyond Liberalism?
Individuals, Citizens
and Society

Michael Rustin

One of the dominant issues of economic and political debate of recent years in both West and East European societies has focused on the comparative advantages of state planning and provision on the one hand, and the operations of markets on the other. It seems fair to say that on both sides of Europe, Market has been winning this contest with State rather easily.[1] The outspoken denunciations by Mikhail Gorbachev of the inefficiency and poor quality of goods and services delivered by the Soviet state planning system — so bad, as he has put it, as to threaten the viability of the entire Communist system[2] — have left little else to be said by external critics, and have made Marxist advocacy of command economies in the West an uphill task.

In Britain and the United States (more, it is true, than in some other Western European nations) a major critique and restructuring of our own weaker versions of state planning and provision has been in full swing since the 1970s. Mrs Thatcher's little romance with Mikhail Gorbachev was based in considerable part on her recognition of the parallels between her economic reform programme and his, in their very different contexts. Britain has seen, in the last decade, a large privatization of formerly state-owned industries, reduction in the powers and spending capacities of subordinate state institutions (especially local government), and the mandatory offer-for-sale of a substantial part of the public housing stock to local authority tenants. The latest phase of this programme consists of a restructuring of important areas of state social provision, notably in education and health, with other social services now set to follow with the White Paper on community care. This restructuring, in fields which it is still deemed politically necessary and/or desirable to maintain largely within the public sector, amounts to the introduction of a 'social market'. That is to say, while the systems of education and health remain largely funded from taxation, and are available to citizens free at the point of delivery, they are being reorganized on quasi-market lines, so far as this is practicable.

Whereas formerly, local authorities had power to allocate pupils to schools, and sometimes attempted to use this power to ensure social and educational balance, now parents will have the right to choose schools for their children. Where formerly the education authority allocated funds to schools, now 75 per cent of funding will automatically follow pupil enrolments. School governing bodies, and not local authorities, will control the budgets of their schools. Political party representation on school governing bodies has been reduced, and parent governors put in the majority. In reforms currently proposed for the National Health Service, internal markets are being instituted whereby general practitioners will 'buy' specialist and hospital services for their patients, out of allocations whose size will depend on the number of patients choosing to register with them. Hospitals have the choice either of 'opting out' of Health Authority control and operating entirely in a competitive market for their services (one still largely to be publicly funded, though with incentives for private topping up), or of functioning within a Health Authority-controlled version of an internal market.

The intention of both these reforms is to encourage the benefits of consumer choice between competing service providers, to subject providers to the discipline of 'consumer sovereignty', and to require internal markets, competitive tendering, and so on, to operate wherever feasible. Critics of these reforms fear that some classes of consumers will prove much more effective than others in acquiring high quality services, and that the power of public providers to protect the weak will be greatly reduced. If general practitioners have to work within a fixed budget, won't they have an incentive to minimize the number of costly old and chronically sick patients on their caseloads? If schools are going to be judged in competition with one another by the compulsory publication of examination and test results, won't their main interest be to attract the best pupils, as the surest means of improving their outcomes, rather than trying to do the best for *all* pupils, and especially, as some authorities have tried to do, for those with most educational disadvantages? Critics of these reforms fear that whatever gains may be achieved in terms of efficiency and consumer choice, will be more than offset by losses in terms of equality and justice.[3]

One might view this as an unexpected, Conservative-led version of 'market socialism' in the welfare sector, given the continued commitment (for the time being) to public funding and social entitlement to services. There are attractions in allowing for greater institutional autonomy, consumer choice, and internal trading, in the state welfare sector, just as there appear to be for the production of goods and services in the East. The problem is that institutions such as schools, medical practices, hospitals and universities which have adapted to operate in a quasi-market system, will also in so doing have equipped themselves to operate in a full, privatized market system. Some of those responsible for the Thatcherite re-structurings clearly do not regard the 'social market', still less 'market socialism', as their final goal, but merely as a transitional stage towards what one might describe as 'full capitalism' in all spheres.

In England, anyway, the main response of socialists to the rise of the New Right has been in philosophical terms a defensive one. The left has had to face up to the apparent successes of an ideology of self-enrichment, of programmes of state assistance for the private purchase of public assets, and of the paradoxical deployment of state power to strengthen the rights of individual choice against those of collective decision, in the spheres of trade unionism, local government and education. This has led socialists to think hard about their own values and assumptions, and to question some core beliefs and practices. Some of this rethinking — about planning, public ownership, or the importance of consumption — is motivated by considerations of expediency: the problem of how to construct an electable programme. But it goes deeper than this. *Marxism Today*, which takes very revisionist positions these days, has been vehement in its critique of old-style welfarism and state bureaucracy, and positively enthusiastic about consumption, style, and identity.[4] A recent hard-hitting Fabian pamphlet,[5] returning to the tradition of the Webbs, recommends respect for merit and efficiency as necessary socialist virtues. Above all, the debate about market socialism, or in philosophical terms, about the need to reconcile the core socialist value of equality with the liberal value of individual freedom,[6] shows the influence of liberalism and market theories on current socialist debates. These concerns provide the driving force of the Labour Party's 'new realism' and policy review process.

Other oppositional reactions to Thatcherism, such as that expressed in the well-received Charter 88 programme for constitutional reform,[7] also take up their position on a radicalized version of liberal ground. Here it is the rights of individual against the state, the need for a fair voting system, the reform of the hereditary House of Lords, freedom of expression, and a written constitution to guarantee these rights, which are the main demands. But these are pre-socialist claims, which would in most cases have been hardly unfamiliar to middle-class radicals of the nineteenth century. Indeed, one theory behind this programme is that Britain never achieved the proper bourgeois revolution which would have found expression in a written, republican constitution, and that this is now the belated precondition for any renewal of the socialist project.[8] Related ideas of 'civic republicanism' have recently become current in the United States.

Coming to terms with liberal individualism and seeking to give the most universal and radical force to its claims is all very well, and I don't wish to argue directly against this position.

However, a political position which starts from the value of the individual, and from the aim of making the satisfaction of (reasonable) individual rights and desires attainable for all, is far from a definition of the socialist project. A contrast needs to be drawn between concepts of man which begin with the pre-formed individual, and those whose basic building block is a social idea of man, as constituted through relations with others. This idea of a 'social' root of socialism is what is mostly absent from the various attempts now current to find a workable compromise with, or countervailing force to modern capitalism. The socialist movement was founded in the communitarian experiences of the working class, and on ideas of the social constitution of humanity. If no equivalent social density or 'thickness' can be retained or renewed in modern socialist thought and practice, socialism as a tradition will wither and die, leaving only hard and soft variants of individualist liberalism to compete with each other.

Alternatives to State and Market

This discovery or rediscovery of the virtues of market systems is obviously of great importance. The critique of state and bureaucratic systems is to be taken no less seriously than the critiques of free markets dominant in an earlier social democratic era. There are non-market imperfections as well as market imperfections.[9] 'Public goods' do not become public in their benefits merely because they are described by their advocates as such, and the vested interests embodied in bureaucracies, political power-holders, and even trade unions can and do take unfair shares of resources and power just as private monopoly suppliers may do. All systems of power and organization, whether based on property ownership or state power, have their specific beneficiaries and their particular costs. The existence of opposed critical discourses addressed to the limitations of both state and market systems at least provides intellectual resources for rational choice between alternative systems, in different contexts.

165

I want to argue however that neither pole of this state–market antithesis is adequate for the design of good social institutions. State-based forms of organization are inherently coercive. In societies lacking formal democracy, the coercive basis of power is self-evident, whatever claims to legitimacy are made on its behalf. But even in formally democratic systems, majority power involves the coercion of minorities, and the elitist and minority forms of representation which mostly prevail in them concentrate power among rather small numbers of decision-makers, usually offering populations little more than opportunities to express their consent, or to choose between highly restricted and often poorly clarified options. This is in part a function of the size of many modern nation-states, in which political decisions are made in the name of tens of millions of people. Coercive powers are exercised on behalf of various collective entities, in particular those of nation or class, which each reduce and subjugate to their own claims the many more differentiated social identities and memberships which make up a modern society. The difficulty of the system of government and the present party political system in representing this variety of social identities is particularly marked in modern Britain. The Greens will have much greater problems in gaining a serious political foothold in Britain than they have had in Germany and Italy, for example.

Market-based systems are by contrast largely interest-based and individualistic in their basic operation. They tend to define society as an aggregate of self-interested individuals — in Mrs Thatcher's notorious phrase, 'There is no such thing as society; only individuals and families.' They encourage and rely on the motives of acquisition, either for purpose of pleasure or power. Many Western capitalist societies currently seem to be almost obsessed with consumption. Most of their newest and most lavish public (or semi-public) spaces are designed for the celebration and encouragement of shopping — I am thinking of the new-style shopping malls and city centre regenerations. Their television is dominated, both in its advertising and even in the content of many of its programmes, with images of consumption. And their streets, especially in London, are filled with the disgusting rubbish of thrown-away remains and packaging of so-called fast food, truly the substitution of the mere *consumption* of food by mobile individuals over its shared enjoyment in contexts of sociability. As a result of the primacy of values of possessive individualism over the claims of social membership or citizenship, visitors to New York are approached for money by beggars in every subway car, and in London visitors can walk through communities of people living literally in cardboard boxes right next to London's main cultural complex on the South Bank.

Market systems are self-evidently interest-based, though of course all of them depend on a substructure of altruistic and moral motivation (for example those obligations to others which sustain families, or which ensure customary respect for persons and contracts), since the coercive powers of the law are rarely immediately at hand.[10] Collectivist, state-based systems depend on a mixture of citizen motives: the fear of punishment or pain as the direct inverse of the love of reward or pleasure; opportunities to obtain money or power as rewards within the apparatus; a measure of altruism expressed in the general principles and objectives of these systems. In the case of institutions such as the National Health Service in Britain (or in Solzhenitsyn's description of the work of some doctors in a Soviet hospital in *Cancer Ward*), it is clear that such 'social' motivations can count for a lot.

But the existence of this actual mixture of motivational principles in state systems, the role of altruistic and social motivations — those based on social identification, one might say, rather than individual interest — have been largely neglected in these recent debates. In Britain, such is the retreat of socialists in the face of the onward march of the market that political choice is effectively represented as that between unregulated and regulated markets. The dominant social identity has become that of the 'consumer', whether of public or private goods; but the danger is that if larger social identities are fragmented or neglected, there will be no social force or moral sentiment powerful enough to ensure even the regulation of markets, still less a morally defensible distribution of goods and services.

Even the important debate on the theme of civil society, now given a wide hearing in Britain through the publications of John Keane,[11] among others, threatens to remain caught within a predominantly individualist and interest-based definition of the problem. This is for two reasons. In the East, the antithesis of civil society versus the state is vital in the critique of overweening state power. The institutions of private property and the market are relatively so weak in these systems that their inclusion, consistent with the earlier liberal tradition, as central elements of civil society, carries little immediate risk of substituting one form of domination for another. But in the West, differences within 'civil society', between the concentrated powers of private property, organized in huge corporations on the one hand, and voluntary or civic institutions like trade unions or churches on the other, are of great importance. Advocates of 'civil society' in the West have to identify the power of private property as well as the power of the state as a potential enemy of democracy and participation, and be careful not to assume an identity of interest between market and society.

The second reason for this concern is the emphasis that is given to political life and participation, in much of this debate, as the crucial means of democratization. In Britain this has taken the form of demands for more democratic (that is, decentralized, accountable, and representative) institutions, in contrast to the latently authoritarian forms of state power which have survived centuries of gradualist extension of the franchise. But it is all too easy for the political process to be construed simply as another form of market — this is indeed the working assumption of most politicians in the capitalist democracies. The strengthening of political life offers to substitute one field of competition between individuals and interests for another, without doing much for social bonds or identifications. The political life of the United States is a case in point.

The Dimension of the Social

In contrast to the coercive and interest-based forms of social organization, and the state- and market-dominated systems which broadly correspond to them, there is a third principle, that of normative order, based on identification, shared membership, and consensus.[12] An active 'civil society' depends on this motivating principle, as well as on political choices by majorities and the coercive decisions they imply, and on the self-interested motives of economic actors. I shall argue for the values of social attachment and density against those of individualism. I suggest that there are (at least) two major systems of ideas from which support for this 'social' conception of man can be drawn, and from which I will seek to draw some political and policy conclusions. These are firstly, the communitarian philosophical tradition now enjoying some revival in Anglo-American philosophy, and secondly the distinctive contributions of sociology and also anthropology as social science disciplines, each founded on a rejection of atomistic individualism, and on the priority of social and normative forms of explanation.

Organicism as a philosophical tradition was for a period largely identified with traditionalist conservatism. (This identification incidentally remains important on the right of British political and cultural debate.)[13] It is conservatives who tend to celebrate the links between generations, the importance of kinship ties, the historical continuity of institutions, and the sense of place. They argue these positions against what they see, with some reason, as an insatiable and restless individualism, which celebrates desire, mobility, iconoclasm, and the ceaseless innovations of 'the modern'. Because many radical individualists stand on the left in politics, and most organicists on the right, socialists most often find themselves allied with the former on matters of current ethics and politics, though in terms of their founding assumptions about individuals, societies and states one would expect their own position to be clearly distinct from both.

In recent years a number of philosophers and political theorists, such as Alasdair MacIntyre, Charles Taylor, Michael Sandel and Michael Walzer, have sought to develop a critique of liberal individualism and utilitarianism from positions which might be characterized as organicisms or philosophical idealisms of the left.[14] Taylor has argued that what is missing from liberalism is the idea of a moral discourse which enables rational deliberation about human ends to take place. Walzer has developed the idea that different human activities and callings are framed by distinct systems of meaning and value, and are violated in their specific essences when these are overridden by such one-dimensional values as the ends of profit, or reasons of state or party. MacIntyre argues, in his recent *Whose Justice? Which Rationality?* that pre-modern societies, in particular those reflected and theorized in the writings of Aristotle and medieval Catholicism, located human ends in a structured world of roles and memberships, each with its appropriate virtues and obligations. The idea of justice and human good is not abstract and universal, generalizing the values of individual desire or choice, but is always necessarily located in a particular tradition, which selects among possible desires and choices, and makes rational debate possible only because of the prior existence of such shared substantive understandings about the goals and textures of human lives. MacIntyre in all his work has been exceptionally critical of what he sees as the thinness of liberal accounts of the self, and its relation to society as merely the object or instrument of its desires.

A Burkean version of organicism seems to link the idea of the social rootedness of identity inextricably to conservative ideas of hierarchy and tradition. But from Hegel a more liberal view of the social can be derived, in which self-fulfilment depends on a variety of social bonds, defined by difference rather than inequality.[15] An evolutionary view of social development from this perspective might lead not to a Hegelian hypertrophy of the state, but to a model of the increasing differentiation of civil society. This is also the liberal perspective of both classical economic theories of the division of labour, and of Durkheimian sociology. The increasing weight being given to the idea of 'difference' in contemporary social theory can thus be related both to philosophical and sociological traditions. I

have argued elsewhere that it is possible to defend the value
of social differentiation without abandoning universalistic and
egalitarian claims as a foundation for a beneficial diversity of
values and lifestyle.[16]

It is necessary to develop more descriptive and substantive
versions of these philosophical ideas of the social. Walzer in
particular has done this through his very particularistic style of
philosophical writing, in which he has given vivid and eloquent
accounts of the assumptions and values of various spheres of life,
in the course of defending the autonomous claims of various
forms of life against various kinds of universalist claims, notably
those of political ideology or money-values.

The defence of the social needs to be made in terms of
institutions and practices, as well as in the terms of a critique of
the basic assumptions of individualism or abstract universalism,
central to the work of anti-utilitarians such as Taylor and
MacIntyre. The major scientific resource for this work is to
be found in the disciplines of sociology and anthropology,
fundamentally 'social' as at least large parts of them are in their
constituting definitions, in contrast to the atomistic individualism of classical economics, most psychology, and most political science, whose more empirical branches in the West follow
political practice in thinking of politics as behaviour in a
specialized kind of market. Mrs Thatcher's denunciation of
the idea of society per se, already referred to, implied of course
the dismissal of the whole object of study of sociology, to which
her administration had already expressed its hostility in several
ways. The theorists of the New Right regard this discipline as
having been a major source of legitimation for institutions of
the welfare state — welfare dependency as they would see it
— which they are committed to abolishing, or at least radically
diminishing.

Sociology provides conceptual resources for descriptively
mapping the social bases of individual identity. For example,
individuals' dependence on family relationship, on a sense
of ethnic and/or religious membership, on the values and
satisfactions of work or calling, on affiliation to specific traditions of value and meaning such as those of various art forms,

171

physical sports, or the sciences. What we find when we map lives in these ways (through the methods of ethnography, life history, or case study) is the importance of social memberships and boundaries to nearly all individuals, even in the most atomistic societies.

The family member makes a different moral claim on us, for friendship, help, or support in need, than members of other families. The obligation we feel towards someone who arrives in trouble at our door will depend on our relationship to them, direct or indirect. It is impossible to feel equal obligations towards every other human being, if we are to feel significant obligations towards any individuals linked to us by specific relationship. Our commitments in the present will be formed by the memory of our experiences in the past — we may wish to follow, or avoid, the example of our parents or teachers, when it is our turn to take up roles that they have earlier taken in relation to us. We may wish to honour a calling, whether it take the form of paid work, like science or medicine, or unpaid activity like coaching a football team, by which we have been formed, and without whose tradition we could not do what we do.

The social activity and identity which was central for Marx was that which came from work, and the self-expression which properly took place through it, and this emphasis has heavily shaped the socialist tradition. But other spheres of life are also formed around values, gathering around them communities, shared memory, and a sense of traditions to be perpetuated and renewed. We need a wider sense of human life than that which is found in the workplace, but these dimensions amount to more than the activities of buying and consuming commodities, the so-called 'consumption' so dominant in advanced capitalism. Indeed, even commodities gain most of their meaning from social context and relationships — who eats alone for preference, or dresses simply for their own eyes?[17]

The feminist movement, for example, has brought into being new positive identifications of gender, not only as abstract claims of right, but through identifying new social spaces in which particular relationships can be formed, of friendship and solidarity. Elsewhere[18] I have argued that psychoanalytic thinking, especially in its Kleinian and post-Kleinian forms, also provides an essential model of social relatedness from infancy, as the root of individual identity. The concepts of internalization and identification in psychoanalysis describe how the self is constituted through the real and phantasy experience of others. This approach also helps to illuminate the role of other social institutions in helping, or otherwise, individual development.

We can do more than descriptively fill out our sense of the social, with a richer sense of its texture and density. The social can also be a critical category, a criterion, following the method of Emile Durkheim, of contrasting and measuring one form of society or way of life against another. Some societies are more dense than others — we can say some have richer cultures in an anthropological as well as an aristocratic or elitist sense. In some societies, or parts of societies, families are weak institutions — both young and old may be poorly cared for by their close kin.[19] An ideology of personal self-fulfilment may legitimize merely contractual or limited-liability attitudes to relationships, even with marriage partners. A low value can be placed on the fulfilling role of work, especially for majorities without economic privilege. Institutions committed to the care or development of others — nurseries, schools, hospitals, old people's homes — may or may not be organized in ways which respect persons and their social relationships, both as actual ties to be protected, and as states of mind to be respected. The management of key life-transitions in a society — childbirth, school-leaving, retirement, illness, death and bereavement — illuminate in innumerable individual moments of life what a society's relational qualities really are, how numerous, dependable, or strong are the social ties available to support individuals in times of crisis. A commitment to the value of the social implies a preference for institutions and practices which value continuity and intensity of attachment and relationship, in contrast to more limited, contractual and impersonal ties.[20]

This has critical implications for the spheres of work, welfare, and politics. In all of these a critical sociology potentially provides a language for the evaluation and transformation of social practices. In the sphere of politics, the valuing of social density implies a preference for deliberative, participatory practices, over market choice or bureaucratic methods — for 'voice' over 'exit'. Programmes for decentralization and more direct neighbourhood control of welfare and education services now gaining some support in Britain give effect to this preference. (The USA has always been more actively democratic in some of these respects.) Social solidarity within institutions, and collectivistic competition between them, can channel aggressive impulses in less socially damaging ways than unrestrained competition between unsupported and mobile individuals. Different dominant conceptions of social order will tend to generate different strategies for decision-making, management and control.

Societies with dense social ties, and the moral norms which these generate, will be able to depend more on consensus and negotiated agreement to settle their differences. Individuals will in such societies be restrained in their actions by norms which they share with others. The sense of identity, and the psychological and social security which derive from membership in a community may support positive social motivations, and inhibit the expression of negative and destructive feelings. In societies which enjoy numerous social bonds, moral sanctions are more prominent, and material rewards and coercive sanctions less necessary as modes of control and motivation. Such societies are more restrictive of individual freedom, but they may also offer individuals a richer array of possible identities and goals to choose from. The crazed individuals who now periodically run amock with guns in both America and Britain seem usually to have cut loose from social bonds, living in their own mental bubble of media-derived images and psychotic delusions. Their appearance seems significantly more frequent in ultra-individualist societies, which also give easy access to weapons of destruction as a matter of principle. But they occur widely also in Third World societies experiencing the acute social disorganization and rapid urbanization associated with the early stages of modernization.[21] Societies which provide a firmer moral and cultural containment of individual impulse might be less free, from the point of view of individual rights. But the rights of individuals to express themselves are not the only positive value to be considered.

The organization of mass communications is one institutional sphere where these conflicts of principle are obvious in their effects. Where mass media are organized largely on market principles, dominated by consumer advertising, choice and quality are restricted by the one-dimensional profit-seeking aims of the system. On the other hand, monolithic definitions of public cultural goods by state or party are even worse in their effects. Here is a sphere where a more 'social' form of provision, based on the knowledge and skill of professionals, seeking to communicate with specific audiences who share tacit understandings and interests, is a much better source of both choice and quality than either pure state or market systems, as the 'Channel 4' and to some degree public service model of British broadcasting shows. The images and definitions offered by broadcasting media are now an important element of the relation between individuals and society, and its impoverishment is a serious lack, most obviously but by no means only in the domain of political debate.

High levels of violence, addiction, armed policing, rootless mobility, family breakdown, and indifference to avoidable suffering, indicate a society defective and depleted in its social texture. The most capitalist and individualist societies — the United States, par excellence — display these signs of social unbondedness, or negative social bondedness, to an exceptional degree. All modern societies seem to show some deterioration in these respects, to be offset against the material improvements and lengthening of average lifespans which they have achieved. We have developed concepts of material rights, and of rights against the state, deployed vigorously in criticism of state socialist societies which patently fail woefully to fulfil them. But we have hardly any comparable concept of social rights, so that epidemic levels of murder, drug addiction, imprisonment, and homelessness, because they are supposed to derive from the actions of individuals, not from the conscious decisions of states, are treated as misfortunes rather than as intolerable forms of social injustice. Political imprisonment and murder are counted as offences against human rights, while execution for crimes, or draconian levels of imprisonment (since they are responses to fearful levels of crime) are deemed to have nothing to do with civil rights at all. It does not seem to be widely interpreted as an abuse of human rights for the largest cause of death for young black males in the United States to be murder. If we had an adequately social concept of human rights, it would be.

Traditionalist conservatives defend a social definition of human life, but attach it exclusively to a particular set of institutions, usually hierarchic, patriarchal, and hostile to the changes associated with democracy, equality, and freedom. Liberals attack the claims made on behalf of such institutions as reactionary, arguing usually from the claims of individual rights and aggregated individual interests. Both positions should be rejected as insufficient by socialists, though of course one might expect Americans and Europeans, given the formation of their societies, generally to have different scales of preference in this respect. Commitment to the worth of social institutions, as bearers of meaning, value, transmitted understanding and skill, does not need to imply allegiance to the power of the privileged, or the idea that change is undesirable or threatening. The rights and obligations of kinship or its surrogates, membership of communities located imaginatively in space and time, attachment to an occupational culture, access through the chance to learn to the expressive traditions of music, writing, sport, craft, or natural history, should be seen as universal goods, no less than material wealth or political liberty.

A socialism adequate to our times would appropriate these aspects of organicist thought, and universalize and democratize their implications. Just as Marx saw Greek tragedies, although products of slave-owning societies, as emblematic of human possibility, so today we should see in the best public spaces, craftsmanship, music, or literature of the past, examples of the diversity and density of social lives that should be possible in a society of equal citizens. The central issue is to see that ways of life of such complexity and richness depend not just on individuals, but on the various kinds of community which make

176

human accomplishment, even the everyday accomplishments of parenthood, craftsmanship, or good citizenship, possible.

Dominant traditions of radical thought now attach most importance to the spheres of political rights and material wellbeing. Liberals define a universal sphere of rights, enforced by law, which limit the coercive powers over individuals of the state, and of lesser institutions. Social democrats usually stress by contrast the material preconditions of existence — living standards, education, social security — as 'positive freedoms' and preconditions of social life. But whilst these each define necessary spheres of entitlement, they also lack adequate social and cultural specifications of good societies and good lives. This is the sphere to which socialist theory now needs to address itself.

Choices of Institutional Type

The above argument has posited a 'third way' or type of social organization, alternate both to coercive or bureaucratic forms of state power, and to the contractual–utilitarian arrangements of the market. What are likely to be the benefits of this form of organization, and what evidence is there that motivations of identification and normative commitment have any more than a subordinate role in the functioning of social institutions in practice?

The point can be demonstrated by example. Consider the possibility of setting up a major new social service, or form of social provision — a rare occurrence at the present time in Britain. Imagine the case of funding a system of universally available provision for pre-school children, now provided for only a very small proportion of under-fives. Suppose that the state wanted to make such provision, and not merely leave it to the initiative of private consumers. What institutional choices would it have, and what would their probable consequences be?

The choices appear to amount to three. The customary social democratic method would be to establish a state service,

177

possibly under the control of local authorities but funded in part from national government resources. Such a service would be organized bureaucratically and professionally, and to judge from other institutions would be likely to retain most power in the hands of elected politicians and salaried employees, excluding the general public from much say or participation in service delivery. Such a system would be operated in a formally universalist way (though with many practical variations associated with the neighbourhoods and degrees of privilege of the client populations), and would be subjected to inspection and quality control. The main limitation of this form of provision would be its difficulty in establishing genuine relations of partnership with citizens, and its tendency to define service consumers (in this case the families as much as the nursery children themselves) in a largely passive and subordinate role.

A second strategy would be to offer vouchers or sums of money to eligible parents, and allow the market to generate the supply of nursery school services. The service that emerged would be likely to have very wide variations of standards and resources, since families would be likely to 'top up' their allocation if by doing so they could obtain measurably better services for only a fraction of their total cost. Considerable problems of inspection and quality control would arise, since some of those who would offer to provide nursery care would have scant interest in the intrinsic values of the service. Some clients would also have few resources of any kind to exert pressure on service providers to give a good service.

An alternative both to services organized bureaucratically by the state, and to the contractual arrangements that develop in a voucher-based market, would be to licence or accredit voluntary providers, so long as they met certain acceptable standards. The state would function as a funding, accrediting, and licensing body, and probably as the provider of central resources such as professional advice, inspection or capital resources, since such services might most efficiently be provided for the system as a whole.

The advantage of a system of accreditation or licensing would be to allow greater autonomy to institutions, since the initiative in setting them up would come from communities and groups (neighbourhood, church, educational cooperatives and so on) not from an elected authority with a monopoly of provision in its district. The role of the authority would be to fund, to enable, and to ensure minimum comparable standards, not to operate a universal service. One would expect to see greater diversity in this model, but also stronger attachment between pre-school nurseries and their communities, on whom they would depend. Whereas a market system requires mainly paying customers, and a bureaucratic/political system mainly passive beneficiaries or clients, a system of licensing and accreditation requires more active self-determination and support by those who use it, in order to survive. This system should produce institutions of greater social density and variety, though to be sure with the possible cost of more variable standards. (But the standards of service achieved under supposedly universalistic bureaucratic systems are also very far from equal in practice.)

Morale and Institutional Success

It is sometimes argued that institutions cannot depend on altruistic motives of identification, and that coercion and reward are far more effective means of motivation and compliance.

Evidence to the contrary is found in the literature on school evaluation in Britain and America.[22] Here, the primary predictors of *relative* success by schools (that is, taking into account disparities in the social composition of intakes) on a variety of measures of performance, appear to be the morale of teachers, the quality of leadership, agreement on institutional goals, the existence of explicit forms of deliberation and planning of purposes. The complexity of educational organizations is such that it does not seem easy to break down tasks into measurable components, separable from the properties of the whole. Merely contractual relations between members, whether pupils or teachers, seem to produce less satisfactory outcomes than relations of mutual commitment, and identification with the aims of the whole school.

179

A distinction may be made between forms of work where the wellbeing of the whole person is essential to the definition of the task or the 'output' of an institution, and those forms of production or distribution where such intrinsic considerations do not seem so essential. In the former case of 'people-processing' work, goals are inherently complex and difficult to define. Whilst concentration on specific aspects of the task may bring benefits, there is always the risk of losing sight of some other relevant attribute of the person, especially since what counts as 'relevant' depends on the subject's own definition of the situation. The problem of reconciling the advantages of scientific specialization and division of labour with holistic awareness of the needs of the person are often seen in medicine, where considerations of personal wellbeing understood in psycho-social terms can be ignored or denied in the pursuit of technical excellence.

In work concerned with the production of commodities or other impersonal outputs, there may be relatively few costs in relying on extrinsic or utilitarian motivations. But the more complex and multi-dimensional are the interrelations of persons and roles, the less likely it is that this will be so. Thus forms of activity, such as education, production in the arts, care of dependants, and health care — where goals are inherently diffuse and multi-dimensional — seem to require deep-level identifications by practitioners if their tasks are to be done well. There may thus be a functional fit between the kinds of institutions which can function most effectively in coercive, instrumental, or normative ways and different spheres of activity. The goal of enhancing the meaning of work has always been an important one to the socialist tradition, inspired equally by Marx and William Morris. The central concern has usually been with industrial labour, as the core of the capitalist mode of production, and as the cause of the destruction of what were seen as previously more integral labour processes. The sphere of 'welfare' has been viewed in this tradition less as a form of labour in its own right (since much welfare work was undertaken by women, outside of the labour market), and more as a field of reparation or compensation for the damage caused by industrial labour. But what is striking about 'welfare work' in all its various forms (for example, education, health care, child care) is that it has inherently complex goals, and is difficult to detach from intrinsic values (the preservation of life, prevention of suffering, alleviation of psychic pain, personal development). These forms of work may be naturally less 'alienable', less easily separated from intrinsic normative commitments, than commodity production. The complexity of the work task, and difficulty of fragmenting it without damage, may also generate more participatory and democratic forms of organization than follow from routine industrial tasks. Just as William Morris saw the production of material objects as a potential source of self-expression and fulfilment, so attention should be given to the fields of work based on relationship with persons as a different source of inherent satisfaction. Since in 'post-industrial' economies the 'production' of persons and symbols gains in importance relative to the production of material objects, this attention to the field of welfare may be an increasingly relevant one.

However, a case could be made for saying that the importance of normative identifications and social morale — after all, morale is originally a military expression — extend well beyond these limits. Both military organizations and economic enterprises also give large attention to these factors as means of motivating performance. Some modern industrial firms recognize the disadvantages of alienation and low morale and adopt styles of organization and work sharing which try to involve workers more holistically in the task. Social ties, not confined to contractual advantage, seem to underlie most institutions, not merely a specialized variety of more enlightened ones, and may make the difference between their success and failure.

In practice, of course, the fields of health, welfare and education have been far from immune from powerful pressures to commodify and discipline which have come from the belated 'bourgeois revolution' (or counter-revolution) of the New Right. Whilst those who work in those fields certainly have different and more intrinsic discourses on which to draw in defending their institutional territories, they are certainly being forced to adapt themselves to a new climate in which the differences between their activities and those of other 'industries' or 'businesses' are minimized.

How to respond to the creation of 'social markets' in the welfare sectors is the main issue now facing practitioners. It is here that the contest between normative versus instrumental forms of organization and motivation has in practice to be fought out. The best way of illustrating what is meant by a 'normative' model of social relationship and organization, in opposition to coercive and instrumental ones, may be by means of a detailed example from one sector. What therefore follows is a proposal for evaluation of a specific service — education — at the level of a borough, in the context of the government's Education Reform Act. This Act attempts to extend the role of markets or quasi-markets in this field, as the proposed *Working for Patients* White Paper does for the health service, and as we have already seen with other local government-provided services. (It now seems likely that social services are the next major target for restructuring on quasi-market principles.)

It is necessary to find a way of responding to these market-led reforms which does not merely reiterate the virtues of centralized bureaucratic control. A potential space has been created for more decentralized management, and wider 'consumer' (i.e. citizens') participation. The aim must be to develop this space to enlarge participation, the field of effective democracy near to the level of immediate decision-making, and to encourage rational deliberation. What is proposed here is a methodology which tries to create a larger space for dialogue and debate about the aims and methods of delivering a service (in this case education). The purpose is to enlarge the area available for what Habermas[23] calls 'communicative action' or 'undistorted communication'. A society in which normative concerns — the sphere of ends — are more explicit, will be one in which there is more 'social space' available for thought and the exercise of reason. This conception is what this local example is intended to illustrate.[24]

The Evaluation of Schools: A Participatory Approach

A new emphasis is being given to testing and appraisal both in the education service, after the Baker Act, and elsewhere in the public sector following comparable reform proposals in the National Health Service, and in higher education.[25] The idea of bringing about higher quality in public services, and making them more responsive to people's needs and desires, is important, and vital to the future of the public sector. However, the philosophy of appraisal implicit or explicit in most of the new government proposals is business-oriented and managerialist. Economic incentives both for individuals and institutions are to be prominent. There are to be budget-centres encouraged to operate at the public sector equivalents of 'profit', and personnel appraisal tied to individually negotiated contracts. The main instrument of improvement in services is to be the freedom of consumers to choose a different supplier — to change schools or general practices. This is the power Albert Hirschman has called 'exit', in contrast to the democratic power of 'voice'.

In education, this stress on efficiency and individual merit is to be accompanied by the introduction of standard measures of pupil attainment which by aggregating them become measures of institutional success and failure. Institutions are to be subject to public comparison in terms of the test results they achieve, and parents and pupils are to be encouraged to choose for or against schools mainly by these criteria. Since these measures are likely to be both narrow in their definition of educational goals, and, unless carefully adjusted and interpreted, severely biased by the social intakes of schools, they are likely to reinforce both traditional academic definitions of success, and social divisions within the education system. There is a danger that they will also, in conjunction with the national curriculum, distort the teaching process, since schools will have powerful incentives to teach to the requirements of the tests even when these may be limited or undesirable in terms of broader educational goals. (This however depends on the outcome of debates now in progress about the appropriate forms of attainment testing.) Such quantitative measures have their legitimate place, in providing objective benchmarks of attainments for both individuals and schools. Their introduction may even prove to have some benefit. But the risk is that they will become too powerful, and will reinforce one-dimensional educational values, and social and educational inequalities within the school system. These forms of measurement and appraisal need complementing by others which recognize the plurality of legitimate educational goals, and which can encourage and help all schools, and not merely the most advantaged, to improve their performance over time.

The traditional alternative form of inspection and appraisal in English education is that provided by HMI (Her Majesty's Inspectorate) and its local equivalents. This system relies on the professional knowledge of former teachers of great experience, and depends on informed, qualitative judgements, formed as a result of personal observation, and communicated in the form of written reports and personal advice to senior staff. This system depends on experience and craft knowledge, whereas the performance indicator approach depends on utilitarian concepts of hard fact and measurement. Each reflects particular currents of English social thinking and practice: the one humanistic and literary in its basic outlook (the tradition of Matthew Arnold, former Inspector of Schools), the other empiricist and scientific. The limitations of the HMI approach are on the one hand its failure to make full use of statistical resources (in ILEA the inspectorate and the research and statistics branch were separate institutions making little or no reference to each other's findings); and on the other hand, the location of 'inspection and evaluation' in a separate profession and role, making judgements on those being evaluated, but not directly or actively involving them in the process of self-evaluation and self-reflection. The basic premise of this proposal is that a radical departure is needed from both these methodologies.

The first assumption of this proposal is that schools need to be active participants in the process of evaluation in order for it to become a means of enhancing performance and morale. Evaluation must be a process of self-reflection and self-appraisal, and not merely the obligatory subjection of one group of professional workers to the judgements of another group placed in authority over them. If schools and their staffs are not involved as participants and partners in the appraisal process, they are likely to find many overt or covert ways of ignoring it and of taking little notice of its recommendations.

The mainly punitive or deterrent concept of appraisal implied in the obligations to publish test results (failure to meet standards is to be punished by publicity and loss of clientele) is likely to demoralize as much as it mobilizes positive efforts. Furthermore its negative and latently competitive approach is likely to work against the positive and hopeful spirit which we should wish to see informing the public education system. Public services should have their own positive values which all concerned in them should wish to fulfil. The object of appraisal systems should be to encourage this motivation, not substitute the competitive calculations of the market place for the values of public service.

A second main assumption is that the goals of the education system are or need to be many and complex, not reducible to a few simple measures of skill, and that systems of evaluation and appraisal must be designed to take account of this diversity. The Education Reform Act wishes to enforce a uniformity of educational aims, whilst tolerating inequality in their realization; but we should wish to encourage the recognition of a plurality of legitimate goals and strategies for achieving them (within a basic framework of common objectives) whilst minimizing stratification and inequalities of outcomes.

Acknowledging a plurality of ends requires encouraging schools to reflect on and make explicit choices about their objectives. An important element of appraisal therefore needs to be a process by which schools formulate their own purposes and the means by which they intend to realize them. Schools' objectives will have to be formulated with regard to national and local educational goals, but like all other aspects of the education process, they should be a subject for rational reflection and debate, not be imposed by administrative or political *force majeure*. Objectives having been clarified in a process of discussion, schools can then be held accountable for

185

how far they succeed in attaining them. What is thus proposed is a methodology whereby schools will be encouraged to reflect on and formulate objectives and strategies for realizing them, and be assessed in part by reference to norms they have themselves proposed.

The evaluation process should take the form of a dialogue between those given responsibility for evaluation, and those subjected to it. It should involve the full range of participants in the education process — teaching staff of all levels, non-teaching staff, pupils, and parents. On different occasions, the same individuals may find themselves working either as members of evaluation teams, or among those whose work is being evaluated. The purpose of a democratic evaluation process should be to help schools to function as 'learning communities', devoted to learning from their shared experience as institutions. The idea of involving schools as active partners in evaluation is consistent with the philosophy of teacher-designed and monitored assessment (embodied now in GCSE), and with the participation of pupils in evaluation of their progress, as in the London Record of Achievement.

Professional inspectors have a central role to play in evaluation because of their experience and knowledge. But roles are envisaged also for independent educational consultants (who might be experts in areas of the curriculum, in educational psychology, or in organizational processes), for specialists in statistical measures of achievement (without them such measures are certain to be crudely misused) and also for practising teachers able to bring their professional experience to bear as members of evaluation teams, in a process of peer review. The involvement of practising teachers in the appraisal process, both from within and without the local education authority conducting the evaluation, should serve not only to improve the quality and the acceptability of appraisal, but should also facilitate the transmission of good practices throughout the system, an objective highlighted in the Hargreaves Report, *Improving Secondary Schools* (ILEA, 1984).

Evaluation teams should have a much wider membership. This should include parent governors, those concerned with teacher education (who have contact with a wider range of schools than many practising teachers), and (in secondary schools) senior pupils themselves, who would have their own contribution to make in discerning the real qualities of a school, and who would certainly learn from their involvement. Our objective is to make 'evaluation and appraisal' — that is, reflection on the quality of educational performance and practice — a concern of the entire educational community.

What is proposed is a comparably wide and active involvement in the process of evaluation on the part of the school community being evaluated. By active involvement is meant involvement in definition of a school's aims and methods, and in dialogue with evaluation teams about them. One has in mind the involvement of the whole teaching staff of a school, under the leadership of senior staff and department heads, but also participation in some parts of the process by some parents and pupils. The experience of such a process of evaluation could be a significant one in the life of a school, and it should be stimulating, challenging and creative for those concerned, not merely traumatic or alienating.

A Possible Procedure

One would like initially to see a pilot project to test out possible procedures for Participatory School Assessment, to be practised with a small number of schools over a period of about three years. The intention would be to develop a methodology which if it were successful could then be employed on a wider basis, for example for all the schools in a local authority's field of jurisdiction. Because of the aim of finding a method which could be made common practice, it would be important even in the conduct of the pilot scheme to pay regard to the costs of evaluation in time and money, as well as giving attention to its educational consequences.

The essence of the proposal is that this should be a periodic review process, undertaken not more frequently than once every three years per school, though with some limited annual monitoring in the intervening period. It would be based on a combination of documentation submitted by the school and face-to-face discussions between a visiting evaluation group and members of the school itself. This pattern has some similarities to that developed by the Council for National Academic Awards (CNAA) in the evaluation of courses in polytechnics and colleges, and subsequently taken over by the colleges themselves as internal evaluation procedures.

Schools would be required to prepare a set of documents as the basis for the evaluation process, in which they would identify their educational aims and their strategies, would report their own successes and difficulties in attaining them, and would provide a description and critical justification of their work. The documentation should follow a fairly standard format, to make its preparation easier and to help comparison between schools, and the Borough Education Office and its Inspectors would be available to advise in the preparation of these submissions and to provide schools with particular information, for example relevant statistics.

Such documentation could not of course give a comprehensive account of all of the work of a school. It should however provide certain basic information (measures of attainment, attendance, staying-on rates, and so on), evidence of critical self-appraisal being conducted within the school, and discussion both of particular areas of priority and of any difficulties. Recognition of problems, and evidence of willingness to face up to them, should be a source of credit in this process. Statistical indicators should be designed to show changes over time, since in this evaluation process evidence of improvement or of problems being successfully addressed should be assigned at least as much importance as absolute measures, and probably more. The purpose of the process is to support improvement and development, not simply reward the successful and punish the unsuccessful (or disadvantaged), which might be the effect of over-reliance on judgement by reference to national norms.

After the submission of documentation, a review visit (probably of one full day) should be made to a school by an evaluation team to discuss the school's work. (This will be prepared by shorter informal discussions with inspectors and other members of the evaluation team.) During this visit (for at least part of which normal school work would have to be suspended) discussions will take place between the evaluation team and various groups of staff, pupils, governors and parents at the school. The whole evaluation team would need to meet with the headteacher and senior staff, but for other parts of the visit smaller subgroups of the visiting panel would meet with smaller groups of teachers, and also small groups of pupils and parents. The object of these discussions would be to explore significant aspects of the school's work, both to gain a clear impression of the school's strengths and weaknesses, but also to focus on possible improvements and developments. Smaller group meetings of course allow much wider participation in the process, and a more informal and exploratory approach on both sides.

At the end of the visit, a short concluding meeting would take place at which the evaluation team would give its initial impressions of the visit. Subsequently a written report would be submitted, which could then be the subject of further discussions, especially where it made recommendations for changes or for specific action to be taken.

It would be necessary to develop a clear format for the documentation, to make it simpler to complete, and to ensure comparability of approach between schools. One section would consist of essential statistical data on pupil performance and characteristics, which could give a preliminary impression of the work of the school. Test scores, examination passes (in secondary schools), staying-on rates (in secondary schools), attendance of pupils, participation in extra-curricular activities, are among relevant indices to be considered. Considerable thought would need to be given to what 'performance indicators' are appropriate, and what help schools would need to collect appropriate information on them. Information on pupil recruitment, in regard to ability and social background, would be important contextual background in considering the level of achievement which it is reasonable to expect of a school.

Information should also be provided on various topics concerned with school management. For example, personnel issues, providing data on staff qualification, staff turnover, sickness and absence, and staff development activity, would be an additional indicator of the wellbeing and problems faced by a school. Resource issues, concerning quality of buildings, equipment, teaching materials, should be reported on in the documentation, which should also provide opportunity for schools to make their material and other needs known to the education authority in this fairly public way.

Under the new arrangements for the financial autonomy of schools, the question of what if any budgetary information should be provided would also need to be considered.

Schools would be expected to formulate a statement of their objectives (sometimes referred to as a 'mission statement') in which they identify their priorities. They should be encouraged to do this candidly, and to seek to be explicit and self-aware about their particular concerns and attributes as schools. A set of headings might be developed (including, for example, organization, curriculum, discipline, pastoral care, extra-curricular activity, relations with parents, activities or methods of special merit or interest) under which submissions would be made. These would be related to the overall objectives of the school set out at the beginning.

Clearly, it would be especially difficult to make such reports for the first time, and before any precedents have been established. It would be easier (though not necessarily as thought-provoking) when some routines have already been set. Some firm limits on length of documentation would need to be set, to avoid undue time being spent in preparation, and the provision of more information than can be digested in this process. In any case, the capacity of a school to put together or improvise a lucid and coherent document is likely to be one significant index of its quality of functioning as an institution.[26]

It is obvious that no feasible documentation or visit can hope to be comprehensive in its coverage of a school's work. So long as essential issues are covered, and there is scope to explore problems that emerge (for example from statistical measures) such selectiveness is not a serious problem. The preparation of a report and its discussion is intended to function as a sample or indicative snapshot of the work of a school, helping the school to focus its own attention on the conscious improvement of its work.

An important assumption of our approach, which is supported by much recent 'effective schools' literature, is that the success or failure of schools commonly derives above all from factors of morale and common culture. Whilst specific objectives can and should be set, the work of a school amounts to more than pursuit of a set of disparate goals. Unless a school is working as an institution, in terms of leadership, common goals, shared commitments, and concern for its members, it is unlikely to work well at all. It is because of the diffuse and interconnected qualities of a school's activities that a collective and holistic method of school evaluation seems appropriate. This approach to evaluation is intended above all to address the social and cultural conditions of effectiveness. Thus it is vital that schools should find the process of evaluation in the last resort stimulating and helpful, even if at times it is bound to be challenging and even threatening. Schools will need to enter into the spirit of this process with positive commitment.

The methods of evaluation proposed would require wide consent and participation in the statements of aim made on behalf of a school. These cannot be devised solely by the headteacher and senior staff, without reference to the wider staff group who have to implement them. Dialogue about aspects of a school's work, in small groups of staff, pupils, and teachers, will only be a success from the school's point of view if it demonstrates a capacity for members to work in reasonable harmony with one another. While leadership (in its many different modes) is vitally important in this process, interactive methods of evaluation across a wide range of issues and participants is intended to encourage relatively democratic and consultative methods of leadership within the schools, and also within the local education authority.

What is most important in this conception of evaluation is not its products in terms of documents, statistics, or judgements, but the process of learning, reflection and self-criticism it is intended to set in train within the schools. In this respect it is intended to match our conception of education itself, in which assignments and assessments are a means to a developmental end, not ends in themselves. Those engaged in evaluation should see themselves as agents of positive change, not as judges or regulators.

The atmosphere in which evaluation visits are prepared and conducted are thus of vital importance. Schools must be given proper support in preparing themselves for evaluation, and those engaged in evaluation should be collegial, friendly, and supportive, while being firmly committed to good educational practice. There is a difficult balance to be struck in many kinds of inspection between relationships which are so supportive that they are in danger of being collusive, and confrontations so hostile that they inhibit thinking and change. The right balance of supportiveness and objectivity has to be worked for.

The relatively public nature of an evaluation visit, with its meetings of different kinds and the sense of a school's work being 'on show', has potential advantages over more private observations and discussions in focusing a school's attention on its work. Issues and comments can gain a different status through being raised in public settings. Among other purposes, therefore, we wish to explore the possible role of evaluation visits as a strengthening of the shared or public life of the school.

Consideration will need to be given to the possible outcomes of the evaluation process from the point of view of the schools. What will follow if a school is found to be doing exceptionally well, or exceptionally badly? Should any rewards or sanctions, implicit or explicit, be built into this process? Should schools ultimately be accredited by such a process, as colleges and their courses have been by CNAA? (One logical concomitant of the greater administrative autonomy of schools is their more formal accountability in terms of standards and objectives, and accreditation is one feasible interpretation of this. This is a model that has also been developed for health services in other countries.)[27] How public would the final written report on an evaluation process be? These issues will need to be considered by the education authority.

The education authority will want to find ways of monitoring the outcomes of its evaluations, both in regard to particular schools and as a method. The pilot evaluations would therefore be undertaken as a form of action research, in which careful attention would be given to the meaning and effects of the experience on the schools themselves. The aim must be to set in train a process of improvement in schools, in relation in large part to their own chosen objectives. The statistical data-base underpinning the evaluation process should enable tangible evidence of changes to be collected over a period of years.

It might be possible to engender some special enthusiasm for the initial testing out of this method, as a pioneering experiment by whichever authority first undertook it. In the first stages it might be helpful to involve an interesting and wide-ranging group of participants in evaluation teams, together with teachers and permanent inspectors from the borough concerned. It should also be possible to seek external funding support for a pilot scheme, undertaken as a form of action research. Whilst the positive feedback to performance which sometimes results from being studied ('Hawthorne effects') may qualify the validity of research findings, they may have some practical benefits nevertheless.

The Hargreaves Report rightly laid great stress on the importance of transmitting good practice throughout the system. The involvement of experienced teachers as members of evaluation teams would give them experience of schools other than their own in conditions which encourage concentrated thought about differences of method. This could have benefit in transmitting good ideas throughout the system. The authority might want to give some formal recognition to teachers asked to join evaluation teams. It might want to consider setting up a standing advisory committee to receive and consider reports on specific evaluations, and to monitor the whole process, on the lines of CNAA's higher-level committees by which evaluation panels are appointed and to which they report.

This of course should also include serving teachers among its members.

It is proposed that participants in the evaluation process should consist of inspectors, teachers, and other professionals in education, taking part in evaluation teams as only one aspect of their larger work-roles in education. The fact that many participants would be selected in this way (to take part on a peer-review/consultancy basis) is more appropriate to the joint-evaluation, interactive ethos of this process than the appointment of a staff of professional evaluators. It also means that the procedure could be funded mainly by sessional payments for participation in specific evaluations, or by small additional payments for existing salaried staff, or by part-time secondment. There would however need to be high-quality secretaries/registrars able to keep high-quality written records of evaluations, a statistics department able to assist schools with data collection, and inspectors who would have a key role both in advising schools as they prepare for evaluation and in the evaluation process itself. It is possible that the evidence of classroom observation might be one input into the formal evaluation, as a specific form of report to be considered together with the school's own documentation. But in any case this proposed form of evaluation may best be seen as complementary to those normally used by HMI and local inspectorates.

It is consistent with the broad ethos of this proposal that one suggests resourcing neither by recruiting a large permanent bureaucracy, nor by recourse to private firms of consultants. One hopes instead to make use of the resources both of the professional communities of public education, and of the energies of governors, parents, and pupils involved in it as citizens.

It follows from the ethos and procedure set out above that the Education Department responsible for school evaluation should create an evaluation process for itself, in which its own performance would be periodically assessed against the criteria set out by its Education Development Plan. It would thus be made clear that evaluation is for everyone. An appropriate procedure can readily be inferred from the above proposals, translated to the different scale of the Department.

Summary of Evaluation Proposal

This method of collective, participatory evaluation of schools is intended to fulfil the following aims:

(a) To involve schools themselves in the definition of their own educational objectives, and in considering how to achieve them;

(b) To involve a wide range of participants — senior and other teaching staff, non-teaching staff, pupils and parents — in the definition of the school's tasks, and in reflection on how well it fulfils them. It thus encourages a participatory and consultative approach to school organization;

(c) To provide a basic framework of comparative statistical data to enable objective judgements to be made about how well schools are performing;

(d) To recognize at the same time the variety of different aims schools have, and to find ways of appraising schools' success of terms of goals they themselves set;

(e) To encourage communication and reflection about good educational practices across the authority;

(f) To create a procedure of report-writing and evaluation visits which will strengthen the idea that evaluation is a central function of the education system;

(g) To find a form of appraisal which recognizes the collective qualities of school functioning, and which does not rely mainly on coercive or individually competitive strategies to motivate performance.

Existing educational administration has tended to be bureaucratic in its approach. The present government seeks to impose on this traditional system the alternative ethos of the competitive market. Our approach by contrast stresses the social and cultural preconditions of successful educational performance. Our commitment is thus to develop a form of practice which will be both pluralistic and democratic. The form of institutional evaluation proposed here may have application to other fields of public and voluntary service provision, which share with education a diversity of intrinsic goals.

Conclusion

The argument of this essay as a whole is that the antithesis of state versus market forms of organization provides an insufficient vocabulary with which to make choices between institutions or social systems. This framing of the alternative threatens to replace one alienated form of social organization by another, now that it is the market which is in the ascendant. By undermining moral obligations and identifications, the market by itself produces atomized and somewhat destructive societies, where even individual choice is impoverished by the erosion of social differences and commitments.

This essay argues for the importance of a third normative dimension of social life, and the diversity and differentiation of social forms and choices which become possible when this is respected. From communitarian philosophical argument has been taken the view that identity is developed through social relations, and that life goals and values are the subjects of choice, deliberation, and cultivation, not fixed attributes or consequences of human nature. From sociological and anthropological perspectives is taken a view of the density of social relations and social structure, which is seen as itself one important measure of the quality of social life. Consistent with Habermas's argument for a deliberative rational community to which all have equal access, is the proposal developed above for a participatory mode of goal-setting and performance evaluation in educational institutions.

The underlying contention is that the best conditions for human fulfilment, whether in families, workshops, studios or laboratories, occur where there is a rich network of social relations within which both individual and social goals can be pursued.

Notes

1. There is a large and growing literature advocating various versions of 'market socialism'. Seminal was Alec Nove, *The Economics of Feasible Socialism*, London: Allen and Unwin 1983. More recent articles appear in Jon Elster and Karl Ove Moene, eds, *Alternatives to Capitalism*, Cambridge: Cambridge University Press 1989; also Julian Le Grand and Saul Estrin, eds, *Market Socialism*, Oxford: Oxford University Press 1989.

2. See the collection of speeches by Mikhail Gorbachev, published as *Perestroika*, London: Fontana 1988.

3. These issues were briefly explored in two previous articles: 'Beyond the Fragments' (with L. Fullick), *New Statesman and Society*, 10 February 1989; 'New Model Service', *New Statesman and Society*, 30 March 1989.

4. See the 'New Times' symposium in *Marxism Today*, October 1988, and subsequent articles in the issue for January 1988. See also a critique of these arguments by M. J. Rustin, 'The Politics of Post-Fordism', in *New Left Review* 175, June–July 1989.

5. Paul Corrigan, Trevor Jones, John Lloyd, Jock Young, *Socialism, Merit and Efficiency*, Fabian Society 1988.

6. Roy Hattersley, *Choose Freedom: The Future of Democratic Socialism*, London: Michael Joseph 1986; and Bryan Gould, *Socialism and Freedom*, London: Macmillan 1985, are both concerned with the problems of reconciling equality and freedom.

7. Charter 88 originated in the autumn of 1988 from a group close to the *New Statesman and Society*, where its ideas have been discussed extensively.

8. For a recent development of this thesis, see Tom Nairn, *The Enchanted Glass*, London: Radius 1988.

9. On the theory of non-market imperfections, see Charles Wolf, Jnr., *Markets or Governments: Choosing between Imperfect Alternatives*, Cambridge, Mass: MIT Press 1988.

10. The individualist presuppositions of neo-classical theories have however recently been subjected to renewed critique, which draws attention to the importance of normative underpinnings of market arrangements, and the limited explanatory power of idealized market models in a world where motivation is substantially social and multi-dimensional. See especially Amitai Etzioni, *The Moral Dimension: Towards a New Economics*, New York: Free Press 1988, and also Mark Granovetter, 'Economic Action and Social Structure: The Problem of Embeddedness', *American Journal of Sociology*, vol. 91, 3, November 1985; David Marsden, *The End of Economic Man? Custom and Competition in Labour Markets*, Brighton: Wheatsheaf 1986. I am indebted to Martin Kohli for drawing my attention to this literature.

11. See John Keane, *Democracy and Civil Society*, London: Verso 1988; John Keane, ed., *Civil Society and the State: New European Perspectives*, London:

Verso 1988. See also the article by Michael Walzer, 'Civil Society', in *New Statesman and Society*, 11 August 1989, and shorter contributions by M.J. Rustin et al. in the same issue.

12. Amitai Etzioni, *A Comparative Analysis of Complex Organizations*, New York: Free Press 1961, classified organizations by the dimensions of instrumental, coercive, or normative forms of compliance, in a way which remains relevant to the present argument. His *The Moral Dimension* makes further use of these categories.

13. Roger Scruton is a prime modern example of such a traditionalist conservative. See his *The Meaning of Conservatism*, London: Macmillan 1980; and *The Aesthetics of Architecture*, London: Methuen 1979.

14. Alasdair MacIntyre, *Whose Justice? Which Rationality?*, London: Duckworth 1985; Michael J. Sandel, *Liberalism and the Limits of Justice*, Cambridge: Cambridge University Press 1982; Charles Taylor, *Hegel*, Cambridge: Cambridge University Press 1975, and *Philosophy and the Human Sciences (Philosophical Papers 2)*, Cambridge: Cambridge University Press 1985; Michael Walzer, *Spheres of Justice*, London: Basic Books 1983.

15. On this view of Hegel see Charles Taylor, *Hegel*; and Stephen B. Smith, *Hegel's Critique of Liberalism*. Chicago: Chicago University Press 1989.

16. In various essays, including 'A Theory of Complex Equality', in *For a Pluralist Socialism*, London: Verso 1985; 'Absolute Voluntarism: Critique of a Post-Marxist Concept of Hegemony', in *New German Critique* 42, Winter 1988; and 'The Politics of Post-Fordism — or the Trouble with "New Times"', *New Left Review* 175, May–June 1989.

17. On the social meanings of different kinds of 'consumption', see Mary Douglas and Baron Isherwood, *The World of Goods: Towards an Anthropology of Consumption*, Harmondsworth: Penguin 1980; Mary Douglas, 'Deciphering a Meal', in *Implicit Meanings*, London: Routledge & Kegan Paul 1975.

18. In M.J. Rustin, 'A Socialist Consideration of Kleinian Psychoanalysis', *New Left Review* 132, Jan–Feb 1982; see also M. E. and M.J. Rustin, 'The Relational Preconditions of Socialism', in B. Richards, ed., *Capitalism and Infancy*, London: Free Association Books 1982. A later development of this argument is in M.J. Rustin, 'Post-Kleinian Psychoanalysis and the Post-Modern', *New Left Review* 173, Jan–Feb 1989.

19. Examples of negative indices in the sphere of family care are proportions of single-parent households, or segregated residential communities for the elderly.

20. Isabel Menzies Lyth, *Containing Anxieties in Institutions*, and *The Dynamics of the Social, Selected Essays*, vols. 1 and 2, London: Free Association Books 1988, drawing on psychoanalytical and systems approaches, discusses a number of care settings from the point of view of the quality of human attention they provide. The importance of intense teaching or apprenticeship relationships for creative development are often referred to in writing about the performing arts, the sciences, and sport.

21. Evidence of high levels of violence and social disorganization in Third World societies is to be found in D. Archer and R. Gartner, *Violence and Crime in Cross-National Perspective*, New Haven: Yale University Press 1984.

22. For this literature see M. Rutter et al., *Fifteen Thousand Hours*, Open Books, 1979; Peter Mortimore et al., *School Matters*, Berkeley: University of

California Press, 1988; and from the United States, Bruce Wilson and Thomas B. Corcoran, *Successful Secondary Schools*, Brighton: Falmer Press 1988. David H. Hargreaves, *The Challenge for the Comprehensive School*, London: Routledge & Kegan Paul 1982, incorporates assumptions about the primacy of normative and moral factors into a Durkheimian view of the school community. The Inner London Education Authority's remarkable guide to good practices, *Improving Secondary Schools: Report of the Committee on the Curriculum and Organisation of Secondary Schools*, 1984, brought many of these ideas into the domain of mainstream education policy.

23. Useful collections of articles on Habermas's work are James B. Thompson and David Held, ed., *Habermas: Critical Debates*, London: Macmillan 1982, and Richard J. Bernstein, ed., *Habermas and Modernity*, London: Blackwell 1985.

24. These ideas arose from discussion of the problems of improving educational standards in inner London schools post-ILEA, with Leisha Fullick, now Director of Education in the London Borough of Lewisham. I have also benefited from discussions of issues of inspection and accreditation with students on the MA course in Social Policy and Research at the Polytechnic of East London.

25. A useful collection of articles reviewing the broad field of evaluation in schools is to be found in Robert McCormick, ed., *Calling Education to Account*, London: Heinemann, Open University Press 1982.

26. The programme for national recognition of unusually successful secondary schools in the United States since 1983 (reported in Wilson and Corcoran, 1988), provides some relevant guidelines for the preparation of written documentation. But there are also important differences of aim from what is proposed here, arising mainly from the competitive nature of the American process (designed to establish rankings) and from the absence of the idea of interactive dialogue which is central to this proposal.

27. On accreditation in health service settings, see Ingrid Sketris, *Health Service Accreditation — an International Overview*, King's Fund Centre 1988.

8

Radicalism Without Limit? Discourse, Democracy and the Politics of Identity

Peter Osborne

The place of Marxism within the current crisis of the left in Britain is a peculiar one. At once central to it, insofar as it is disillusionment with the politics and prospects of a revolutionary socialism which has led so many back into a reconsideration of the merits of liberalism, it is at the same time strangely distanced from it. For the terms of this reconsideration have derived less from an engagement with Marxism than from its simple rejection. The identification of 'Marxism', as an intellectual and political tradition, with the programmes and perspectives of Communist and Trotskyist parties has projected the crisis of the latter onto the former, without any sense of the complexity of the mediations through which their association became an historical reality. To the extent that it has found a home in the academy, on the other hand, Marxism lives on almost without connection to the tradition of political practice in relation to which it was founded.

Of the work currently being undertaken to renew the socialist project through a redefinition of both its ends and means, that of Ernesto Laclau and Chantal Mouffe is distinctive, not for its accommodation to the values of liberal democracy, nor for its assertion that 'we are now situated in a post-Marxist terrain',[1] but rather for its dual claim: firstly, to have entered this terrain through an immanent critique and development of the Marxist political tradition; and secondly, to occupy a position in it which not only sustains the radicalism of that tradition but deepens it, by extending its emancipatory potential beyond class to a seemingly unlimited political field, through the idea of radical democracy. 'Post-Marxism without apologies' is in this case 'post-modern Marxism' as well.[2] Whether this amounts to anything more than an 'ex-Marxism without substance' has been the matter of some heated debate.[3]

The problem with this debate, however, has been its pre-dominantly negative, reactive character. In the rush to reaffirm certain truths, critics have tended to lose sight of some of the wider issues involved. In their determination to demonstrate the vacuity of Laclau and Mouffe's theoretical ideas, they have failed to attend sufficiently closely to what it is about them which gives them their political resonance. Neither the sociology of intellectuals, nor the grudging concession that they 'exploit the proper concern there is today about socialist agency'[4] is explanation enough, although both are enlightening. And while it is certainly true, as Geras has argued, that 'intellectual work has not yet become so easy that just addressing serious problems suffices to vindicate whatever they are addressed *with*',[5] actually grappling with such problems does give an edge to those who do so over those who, whilst formally acknowledging them, manifestly do not. Nor is this failure unconnected to certain theoretical failings in the interpretation of Laclau and Mouffe's work by some of its critics. It is not just that they are addressing serious problems. They are doing so in a way which, however theoretically problematic, converges at key points with recent political history. If criticism is to get a proper grip on its object, it must at some point address it here — at the point of this convergence.

Hegemony and Socialist Strategy stands at the endpoint of a process of development marked by the confluence of a number of disparate theoretical and political streams. Theoretically, it marks the point at which the Althusserian project to map the 'specificity of the political' within Marxist theory, transformed by an increasing awareness of the theoretical import of the Gramscian concept of hegemony, gives rise to a new conception of politics as the discursive 'definition and articulation of social relations', when placed in the context of post-structuralist theories of meaning and a political theory indebted to the later work of Merleau-Ponty.[6] Politically, it marks the point at which an interest in the articulation of class to the non-class dimensions of political struggles in Latin America, and during the period of fascism in Europe, understood in terms of the idea of populism, is extended into a critique of class politics as such in the name of the 'new political subjects — women, national, racial and sexual minorities, anti-nuclear and anti-institutional movements, etc.'[7] Epistemological 'radicalism' and political history intertwine and reinforce one another to produce an alleged 'Copernican revolution' in Marxist theory.

Central to this 'revolution' are the concepts of *discourse*, as the medium of all social identities and struggles, and *democracy*, as a historically specific 'institution of the social', in terms of which, it is argued, all emancipatory struggles must henceforth locate themselves. It is the expansion of the domain of the political, and thereby of both the possibilities for and modality of political action, which is affected here, that provides the background to the 'politics of identity' with which Laclau and Mouffe's work has become so closely associated.[8] Their position is presented as the result of a working out of the immanent logic of the concept of hegemony beyond the confines of the class essentialism of an orthodox Marxism. Yet, like Althusser before them, Laclau and Mouffe rely upon the introduction of concepts from quite different theoretical traditions in order to construct their view. A resumé of these concepts, and the problems to which they give rise, will serve as an introduction to their thought. I will then go on to consider the politics with which it is associated (radical democracy as a politics of identity), before concluding with some general remarks on the current state of debate on the left.

The problem of identity for a socialist politics, it will be argued, is not so much that of the 're-articulation' of demands stemming from a radical plurality of existing social identities, as the construction of substantial socialist identities through an *explanatory unification* of demands, which would enrich the concept of socialism while transforming social into political identities. The polarization of left politics into the 'old' and the 'new' with which the debate over Laclau and Mouffe's work has been associated is both politically destructive and theoretically misconceived. Neither the older forms of thought and organization on the left, nor more recent innovations and movements are, by themselves, adequate to the character of the task ahead. Only the creative exploration of new relations and combinations between the 'old' and the 'new' has any hope of reconstituting the socialist project in such a way as to transform it into a viable alternative to the existing order. To approach this problem through the tangled thicket of Laclau and Mouffe's work, however, it is necessary first to rid ourselves of a certain amount of theoretical baggage.

Discourse

The idea of discourse adopted by Laclau and Mouffe is without doubt the single most controversial and perplexing concept of recent theoretical debates. Derived in part from Althusser's concept of ideology ('there is no practice except by and in an ideology'),[9] in part from the Wittgensteinian notion of a language-game (language and action form an integral semantic whole),[10] and in part from Foucault (the unity of a discourse is that of 'regularity in dispersion'),[11] it takes ideas originally developed in the context of quite different, clearly defined theoretical projects, and yokes them together to produce a general account of the 'discursivity' of the real. For Laclau and Mouffe, 'discourse' is the generic term for a *productivist* and *differential* or *relational* conception of meaning, according to which all meaning is produced as the result of practices which establish relations between signs. On this conception, the meaning of a sign is (1) always relative to the totality of signs to which it is related, and hence (2) subject to transformation through the transformation of the relations constitutive of the totality or 'discourse' of which it is a part. All meaning is 'discursive', and all discourse is socially produced through 'articulatory practices' which establish the relations between

its constitutive elements. On the other hand, all social relations
and practices are themselves meaningful, and are thus as such
discursively produced. 'Discourse' thereby becomes a general
term for the medium of the 'being of objects', within which
social objects (relations and practices) possess a privileged status,
since it is they which articulate the discourses through which
all 'being' is constituted. The discursive, it is maintained, is
'coterminous with the being of objects'.[12] 'Every object is
constituted as an object of discourse', and articulation is 'a
discursive practice which does not have a plane of constitution
prior to, or outside, the dispersion of the articulated elements'
of the discourse it articulates. *All* practices are discursive
practices.[13]

Laclau and Mouffe are careful to indicate what, in their view,
this does not imply. It does *not* mean that there is nothing
external to consciousness, that there is nothing outside of
language, or even that there is nothing external to discourse.
A discursive structure 'is not a merely "cognitive" or "contem-
plative" entity; it is an *articulatory practice* which constitutes
and organizes social relations.'[14] Discourse is the structured
totality which results from the sum of all such practices.[15] It
is 'a totality which includes within itself the linguistic and the
non-linguistic'.[16] Actions can speak louder than words. What *is*
implied though is (1) that the distinctions between consciousness
and what is external to it, between language and what is
outside of it, and between discourse and the extra-discursive,
are all discursively produced; and (2) that the extra-discursive
(whatever falls outside the field of meaning, and hence outside
the distinction between the meaningful and the meaningless)
can be defined only negatively, not as 'objectivity', but as mere
and sheer *undifferentiated* 'existence'. 'What is denied is not that
. . . objects exist externally to thought, but the rather different
assertion that they could constitute themselves as objects outside
any discursive conditions.'[17] It is in the ambiguity or 'discursive
instability' of this statement that the mystery of Laclau and
Mouffe's thought lies.

Before we turn to this mystery, however, it will be useful
to summarize what Laclau and Mouffe themselves take to be

the implications and value of this discursive construal of the 'being' of objects. There are two main points. The first is that since all identities or points of reference are purely relationally or differentially defined, they are in principle 'precarious' — subject to the possibility of discursive transformation — insofar as the elements in relation to which they are constituted are open to re-articulation. The second point is that since the 'field of discursivity' (the field of meaning) everywhere exceeds the partial fixation of meaning achieved within any particular discourse, the possibility of re-articulation is always present. A relational conception of the 'being' of objects is in this respect also an historical one.

> There is no . . . identity fully protected from a discursive exterior that deforms it and prevents it becoming fully sutured. . . . As a systematic structural ensemble, the relations are unable to absorb the identities; but as the identities are purely relational, this is but another way of saying that there is no identity which can be fully constituted.[18]

Every identity is 'incomplete, open and [hence] politically negotiable'.[19] Every discourse 'is constituted as an attempt to dominate the field of discursivity, to arrest the flow of difference, to construct a centre'.[20] But its success can only ever be partial. 'Necessity' exists only as 'a *partial* limitation of the field of contingency', practically imposed, through articulations which attempt, but never fully succeed, to totalize a field of differences.[21] All relations are 'socially constructed' and are as such contingent. Their 'basic instability and precariousness' is their 'most essential possibility'.[22] This is not, however, to say that they are *random*. There is a 'logic', a discursive logic, of contingency: a political 'logic of spontaneism'.[23] The only difference between 'natural' and 'social' objects would seem to be that while both are discursively produced, and hence fall within the basic sociality of the discursive, those discourses through which objects are constituted as 'natural' make up a 'naturalist paradigm' within which the discursivity of such objects is effectively denied.[24]

Such is the formal or 'philosophical' structure of Laclau and Mouffe's thought. But this is not the whole story. Clearly, very little of concrete social or political significance follows from an account of such generality. To derive anything of more direct relevance to political debate, it is necessary for them to supplement the above with an historical account of the precise character, form and degree of stability/instability of those discourses through which the social relations of advanced capitalist countries have been, and continue to be, defined and transformed. It is at this point that we are introduced to the twin theses of the 'democratic revolution' and the 'proliferation of sites of antagonism', a re-reading of two centuries of political struggle which, while it may be framed within the terms of the discursive logic of contingency, is nonetheless in important respects quite independent of it. Before turning to this account, though, it will be as well to confront some of the more strictly philosophical problems associated with the concept of discourse. For these spill over into, and vitiate, the political perspective which the idea of discourse is deployed to sustain.

Discursive Constitution/Constitutive Ambiguity

The central problem here concerns the way in which the concept of discourse is constructed through the ontological generalization of a category from the theory of meaning into one descriptive of the medium of objectivity as such. For while it may be true that all 'objective' relations and practices fall within the field of meaning, in the sense that they must be constituted as 'objects' within discourse if they are to acquire an intelligible reality beyond their mere facticity, it does not follow from this that they are exhausted, ontologically, by the duality of meaning and existence. There is a discourse, and an astonishingly prevalent one at that, within which it is maintained that discourse itself may serve not merely to constitute objects within the field of meaning, but also to represent structures of existence which have an effective determinacy independent of the forms through which they are 'constituted as objects' within discourse: the discourse of a minimal epistemological realism in natural science. Laclau and Mouffe do not present a single argument against this position. Yet it is both extremely widely held (practically, some would say, it is *universally* held) and incompatible with their purely discursive construal of the 'being' of objects. It is, of course, the specific claim of the Marxist tradition to ground its politics upon some such notion of social being, rather than to rely upon merely 'moral' exhortation, projection and action. But I will come back to this.

Laclau and Mouffe *think* that they have dealt with the issue by identifying themselves with a general anti-positivist argument to the effect that 'no object is *given* outside every discursive condition of emergence': 'There is no fact that allows its meaning to be *read* transparently'.[25] But such claims, whilst true, are irrelevant here. There is no need to be naive about representation. Representation is the medium of thought, and all representation is misrepresentation *if* by representation we mean the literal (and mythical) re-presentation of an object in some self-constituted original state. However, it is precisely the inevitable failure of any such notion of representation as this which makes a representation a representation — something, that is, which is constituted through a *relation* between itself and something else, independent of it, which it claims to re-present. The issue is not the possibility/impossibility of a 'pure' or pre-discursive access to objects, but what criteria of 'truthfulness' are suitable for which forms of representation and for what purposes, and how they are related to those forms of *extra*-discursive determinacy which impose themselves upon us practically, as limits, in all our dealings with the world. Laclau and Mouffe cannot even begin to discuss this, *the* substantial epistemological issue, since they have placed themselves outside its terms of reference by denying the intelligibility of the idea of extra-discursive 'objects', beyond the acknowledgement of some underlying but indeterminate 'existence'. As we shall see, this is not without consequences for their conception of politics.[26]

The plausibility of their position depends, ironically, on the exploitation of an ambiguity or 'discursive instability' in the term 'object'. It is not, we are told, that objects do not 'exist' externally to discourse, but they cannot 'constitute themselves as objects' outside any discursive conditions.[27] Objects 'exist' beyond discourse, but they do not exist there 'as objects'. What are we to make of this? There are, I think, two possible interpretations. Either it is true by definition, a restrictive, quasi-phenomenological definition imposed upon the use of the term 'object' to limit it to the realm of discursivity, as the result of some kind of methodological reduction or *epoché*; or an extremely strong and highly implausible philosophical claim is being made against the use of discourse in a referential way: namely, that the extra-discursive does not just exceed the determinacy of its representations within discourse, but has in principle no determinacy of its own at all. The first interpretation sidesteps the ontological issue by bracketing it. Yet we can question the usefulness of such a procedure for anything but the most restricted of philosophical enterprises. The second *approaches* idealism in its emptying of 'existence' of all determinate content. Its compatibility with some notion of materialism can be sustained only by a surplus of meaning within the term 'object', whereby the determinacy attributed to it by its place within the discourse of 'discursive constitution' secretly spills over into the idea of it as a mere 'existent', while nonetheless being denied. Speaking strictly, on Laclau and Mouffe's view, 'objects' do *not* 'exist'. On the other hand, the existential connotation of the term 'object' is secretly exploited within its application to the discursive realm, to compensate for the fact that it is there denied any extra-discursive reference *qua* 'object'. For Laclau and Mouffe, 'objects' oscillate between determinacy and existence. What they are categorically denied is the possibility of determinate existence.

It is hard to interpret this position in any other way than as a form of neo-Kantian nominalism wherein the relation between consciousness and its objects has been replaced by that between discourse and its objects. The latter position may be more sophisticated (and less straightforwardly 'idealist'), but it is a sophisticated variant of an old and notoriously antinomic structure of thought. Its problematic character is confirmed when Laclau and Mouffe draw out the consequences of their

209

view. 'If the discursive is coterminous with the being of every object — the horizon . . . of the constitution of the being of every object', they argue, 'the question about the conditions of possibility of the being of discourse is meaningless.'[28] Yet it manifestly is not. Indeed, it is the object of a specific enquiry: the historical emergence of 'social' out of 'natural' being. The philosophical history of such claims of 'meaninglessness' should be warning enough. Ontology is not so easily avoided as the apparently self-contained epistemological formalism of discourse theory would have us believe.

All practices may be discursive practices, but they are also always more than this. Not only do they have an extra-discursive dimension, but this dimension is itself a determinate part of their 'being'. The fact that it can only be *represented* discursively is neither here nor there from the standpoint of the ontological issue at stake; although it is, of course, the starting point for other, epistemological and political, debates. It is, I would suggest, the tension between the irreducible dimension of extra-discursive determinacy in the object and the plurality of its possible discursive constitutions that is the site of ideological struggle. To reduce this struggle to a *pure* discursivity is to rob it of its human (that is, its existential) significance.

Discourse and Democracy

It is the issue of what defines the parameters of political practice within any particular society, at any particular time, which is the subject of Laclau and Mouffe's speculative reconstruction of two hundred years of European political history in terms of the idea of the 'democratic revolution'. The element of extra-discursive determinacy in the object, lacking from their discursive construal of 'being', is replaced here by the relative closure imposed by the (contingent) historical dominance of a particular political discourse. Paradoxically, however, it will turn out that this is a discourse within which almost anything is possible.

Laclau and Mouffe's historical thesis is a simple one, breathtakingly simple in fact:[29] namely, that all political struggles in

Europe since the French Revolution are to be located within the discursive field of the 'democratic revolution': a 'decisive mutation within the political imaginary of Western societies' wherein the 'logic of equivalence' became 'the fundamental instance of production of the social'. 'Democracy' is understood neither as a specific set of institutional arrangements, nor as a particular political ideology (with its own internal discursive instabilities), but as 'a new mode of institution of the social': a *foundational* break in the discursive history of the West which has set the terms for all future emancipatory struggles.[30] It is the 'discursive exterior' which makes possible the 'interruption' of all relations of subordination by providing the terms for their transformation into 'relations of oppression' ('sites of antagonism') through a principle of equivalence (equality) which 'impedes the stabilisation of subordination as difference'.[31] As such, it is understood to open up the social to the 'irreducible plurality' of its inherent discursivity. Sites of antagonism proliferate without limit.

The political logic of this thesis is twofold. In the first place, it allows Laclau and Mouffe to reinterpret class struggles as a particular instance of democratic struggle: the application of the 'logic of equivalence' to the relations between classes. Secondly, it provides them with a unitary conceptualization of the new social movements, in terms of the extension of the logic of equivalence to ever more areas of social life, which brings them under the same conceptual framework as the understanding of class. All outstanding theoretical problems about the unity and direction of left politics can, it seems, be resolved at one fell swoop. The task of the left, it is argued, 'cannot be to renounce liberal-democratic ideology, but on the contrary, to deepen and expand it in the direction of a radical and plural democracy . . . [by] expanding the chain of equivalents between the different struggles against oppression.'[32] Such a task is 'hegemonic' insofar as it posits a unity between struggles which must be *constructed*, rather than 'discovered', and which will modify the *identities* of the agents in struggle, rather than simply establish new relations between subjects whose identities are already fixed (as, for example, in the classical notion of a Popular

211

Front). At the same time, however, it is argued that this is only possible on the basis of *separate* struggles, since these can only exercise their 'equivalential and overdetermining effects' within their own specific social spheres. The discursive specificity of different relations of oppression must be maintained. We are thus confronted with an argument for the 'autonomisation of spheres of struggle' and the 'multiplication of political spaces' as the condition for a hegemonic unity of oppressed groups at another level, all of which are understood to be made possible by the 'logic of equivalence' of the discourse of democracy. All that is needed to complete the picture, to transform the negative, counter-hegemonic character of the project into a positive, fully hegemonic one, is 'a set of proposals for the positive organisation of the social', a 'strategy of construction of a new order'.[33] Symptomatically, Laclau and Mouffe have nothing to say about this beyond the recognition of its necessity, except for the general maxim that it must not violate the irreducible 'plurality and indeterminacy' of the social.

As an analysis of the meaning of 'democracy' in Western capitalist societies over the last two hundred years, this picture is hardly plausible enough to merit further comment; except to note, as Rustin does, its deeply Tocquevillean, mid-Atlantic tones.[34] Yet its political resonance is a strong one within various parts of the left in Britain and elsewhere, and the programme to which it gives rise retains a significance beyond the tendentiousness of the history from which it derives. The model has four main parts:

1. The general thesis of the discursivity of the social.
2. The idea of politics as the 'institution of the social'.
3. An account of democracy as a specific institution of the social which opens it up to the full potential of its own discursivity.
4. The idea of a hegemonic radical democratic 'politics of identity' capable of redeeming this potential through its recognition of the irreducible plurality and indeterminacy of the social.

We have already considered the thesis of the discursivity of 'being', and pointed to some of its more central problems. The thesis of the discursivity of social space suffers from all the same problems, but poses, for us, the additional problem of the way in which extra-discursive determinants impose limits upon the discursive forms of social relations. This problem is reflected in *Hegemony and Socialist Strategy* only in the form of an absence: an absence of institutional analysis and a failure to account for why certain articulatory practices 'are more central than others and are therefore more likely to succeed in hegemonising a political space'.[35] The gap is covered by an expansion in the concept of the political to make it coterminous with the social itself. The problem of the political, it is argued, is that of the 'institution' (in Castoriadis's sense of an active instituting) of social relations.[36] The trouble with this position, as Mouzelis has pointed out, is that it ignores the existence of

> a differentiated set of institutional structures which have a *predominantly* political character: i.e., which are geared to the production and reproduction of the overall system of domination. . . . The fact that we often use the term politics to refer both to a differentiated institutional sphere and to the 'political' as an inherent dimension of all social situations is no good reason for rejecting the former in favour of the latter.[37]

Once more, the semantic wealth of a particular term, in this case 'institution', is exploited to compensate for a *loss* of meaning which, if apparent, would undermine the credibility of the position proposed. Laclau and Mouffe acknowledge the relative durability and stability of some sets of relations and practice over others, but they are unable to begin to explain why this should be so. The connotation of stability within the term 'institution' steps in to paste over the gap.[38]

The social specificity of predominantly political institutions in capitalist societies, to which Mouzelis refers, is central to the issue of democracy, since, as Wood has pointed out, it is only on the basis of the *separation* of economic from juridical and political power that the expansion of democratic citizenship within capitalist societies has taken place.[39] The expansion of democracy within capitalism has involved, as its necessary correlate, both its 'devaluation' as a form of power and a transformation in its theoretical meaning. The new democracy, Wood argues, 'has certainly meant great advances in representative institutions, civil liberties, and so on, but it has not redistributed social power . . . between appropriators and producers';[40] at least, not in any *fundamental* way. Clearly, the extension of the franchise *has* increased the social power of producers in crucial respects, by placing electoral constraints on the state's management of economic crises and providing a political forum for the articulation of economic demands. Such changes cannot be written off as superficial modifications of the system. Insofar as they represent a form of socialization of political power within capitalist societies, they contribute to the dialectic of its deeper historical transformation. The point, however, is that the *form* of liberal democracy places structural limits on this redistribution of power, while serving at the same time to *legitimate* class inequalities through the ideology of the 'free society'. It is because of this that we have recently seen such a fetishized defence of this form against the threat of its further socialization (the welfare state). It is at this point that we can begin to see both the fallacy of the idea of the democratic revolution as an 'institution of the social', and the formalism of the idea of a radical plurality of democratic subjects.

Within capitalist societies, democracy is and has always been restricted to highly specific social spheres, and identified with a correspondingly narrow range of formal procedures. On this basis, and on this basis alone, is it compatible with private property in the means of production. 'Liberal-democratic ideology', with its abstract, possessive individualism and its correspondingly procedural definitions of democratic norms, reflects this situation. There is no democratic imaginary other than a *liberal* one which 'institutes' the social in Western societies. To suggest that there is — that there is a dominant democratic discourse which is independent of a quite particular (liberal) specification of the character of democratic subjects — is to misrepresent the political structures and ideological self-understanding of these societies in a quite dramatic way. It is not even clear that the democratic component of liberalism is its most important one; or that liberal democracy is capable of 'instituting the social' within capitalist societies without the supplement of nationalist, ethnic, patriarchal and other 'discursive elements'.[41] This is not to say that things cannot change, that there are not important progressive elements within liberal–democratic ideology, or that there are not other democratic traditions. But it does point to a dilemma for Laclau and Mouffe's idea of radical democracy. Either, as they explicitly claim, it is to be understood to involve a 'deepening and expansion' of liberal–democratic ideology, in which case it suggests an expansion of democratic practices into those social spaces which remain insulated from the sources of economic power; or, as they also suggest, it represents something else entirely: a principle of radical plurality which goes beyond liberalism *in principle* without recourse to the allegedly 'essentialist' structures of traditional forms of socialist thought. In this case, though, it is not at all clear that it does not represent a politics of 'collective self-assertion in antagonism' which is open to the most reactionary forms of particularism.[42] Everything hangs upon how we understand the idea of a 'politics of identity'.

Hegemony Without a Hegemonizer: The Politics of Identity

The 'politics of identity' has become a flag of convenience for a variety of often widely differing political positions. At its most general, it signifies little more than an awareness of the existence of a subjective dimension to political practice: an awareness that political activity 'involves a continuous process of making and re-making ourselves — and ourselves in relation to others'.[43] This consciousness of the subjective dimension of political action is associated with the movement politics of the 1960s and early 1970s. The expression 'identity politics' may thus be understood to refer to what has become in the 1980s of that politics which, in an earlier period, marched under the banner 'The Personal is Political'; movements which, by attending to the subjective moment of social oppression, contested the borders between the 'public' and the 'private', 'challenged the existing scope of political issues and presented an alternative kind of political process'.[44] Laclau and Mouffe are clearly attempting to provide a theoretical form adequate to this kind of politics.[45]

The problem is that once the original impulse of these movements was first diffused and then turned back, in the changed political climate of the 1980s, two quite different interpretations of their significance emerged, each of which claims for itself the legitimating mantle of the earlier period. For some, the distinctive feature of these movements was the way in which they broadened the scope of a *socialist* politics, enriched it with new agendas, dynamized it with libertarian impulses, and thereby transformed it at a fundamental level.[46] 'However fierce our criticisms of the traditional left and labour movement', Lynne Segal argues, 'the strength of the "fragments" in the 1970s came precisely from our sense that we were part of a united socialist struggle'.[47] For others, however, it was the critique of the very idea of a 'united socialist struggle' which was the most important thing. Claiming an 'identity' on the basis of the experience of a specific oppression is seen here as the ground for a wholly new kind of politics, for which the affirmation and validation of experiences of 'difference' are at least as important as the analysis of the basis of oppression and its location within the perspective of a wider oppositional movement — if not more so.[48] On this model, oppressed social identities are transformed *directly* into oppositional political identities through a celebration of difference which inverts the prevailing structure of value but leaves the structure of differences untouched. The original movements undoubtedly contained elements of each approach, in a creative but unresolved tension. More recently, however, it is the latter model which has become predominant.

If the problem with the first position is that it aspires to a unity the conditions for which it has yet to theorize, the problem with the second position is that it tends to reduce radical politics to the expression of oppressed subjectivities, and thereby to lead to the construction of moralistic, and

often simply additive, 'hierarchies of oppression', whereby
the political significance attributed to the views of particular
individuals is proportional to the sum of their oppressions.[49]
Such a tendency both positively encourages a fragmentation
of political agency and harbours the danger of exacerbating
conflicts between oppressed groups. It also makes group
demands readily recuperable by the competitive interest-group
politics of a liberal pluralism, especially at the level of the
local state.[50] Laclau and Mouffe aim to provide an antidote
to these problems without reducing the specificity of the
demands of different groups or threatening their organizational
autonomy. They can only do this, however, by reverting
to a level of abstraction which leaves all the real problems
untouched.

The distinctive feature of the version of identity politics
associated with Laclau and Mouffe's work is that it is resolutely
opposed to all notions of fixed social identities. The implication
of the discursivity of the social for the category of the subject
is that it can be retained only in the sense of '"subject
positions" within a discursive structure'.[51] This has two main
consequences. The first is that while it provides that fluidity in
social identity which is a prerequisite for a radically hegemonic
project (a project, that is, in which the identity of *all* the groups
involved is transformed by the articulation of their respective
constitutive discourses), it does so at a level of abstraction
which suggests that *any* form of political subjectivity can
be conjured up at any time provided one has the right
discourse. The second is that in removing from the category
of the subject all remnants of the idea of it as an 'origin' or
'ground', it cuts it off, in principle, from the category of
agency.

Laclau and Mouffe are highly selective in their application
of the logic of discourse to political analysis. They assume
sufficient *stability* in the discursive construction of relations
of subordination for them to be converted, via the logic of
equivalence, into relations of oppression, and thereby to become
the basis for political organization around oppressed identities.
Yet they assume sufficient *fluidity* both for such a conversion,

and for the converted relations to become articulated with one another in a chain of democratic equivalents. This chain, in turn, must transform identities in the direction of an expansive hegemony, but without undermining the specificity of each group's demands. We are given no account of the conditions of possibility for this extraordinarily convenient distribution of stability and fluidity. Nor does such an account seem possible, other than in the form of the kind of explanatory theory that Laclau and Mouffe rule out of order as 'essentialist' because of the extra-discursive closure it would posit as the ground of successful articulations. Without some such theory, however, the whole project looks dangerously close to wishful thinking. The trick is supposed to be performed by the equivalential logic of the discourse of democracy. But this logic has no social content. It is pure form. Only thus is it capable of respecting the 'irreducible plurality and indeterminacy' of the social.

The radicalization of the concept of hegemony beyond its Gramscian frame posits the idea of a 'democratic' hegemony, in which no particular group or organization has the role of hegemonizer, yet each is united with the others through a chain of equivalence linking emancipatory struggles on the basis of their common use of the logic of equivalence to convert relations of subordination into relations of oppression. The discourse of democracy thus acts as a kind of invisible hand, regulating and totalizing the effects of autonomous struggles behind the backs of their participants to produce a hegemony without a hegemonizer, within which the twin discursive principles of 'autonomy' and 'equivalence' alone provide the conditions for a unity of struggles. If, as Laclau and Mouffe suggest, Hindess and Hirst moved from 'an essentialism of the totality to an essentialism of the elements' and thereby 'replaced Spinoza with Leibniz, except that the role of God is no longer to establish harmony among the elements, but simply to secure their independence',[52] it is hard to avoid the conclusion that they have themselves returned to a more orthodox Leibnizianism. The possibility of a *unified* discourse of the left, we are told, is 'erased' by the radical plurality of democratic subjects. In its place, there is a 'polyphony of voices', each of which is to contribute its own 'irreducible discursive identity' to the democratic programme.[53] But should all identities be treated equally, politically, irrespective of their specific character, and its implications for issues of power and resources? Is it even coherent to suggest that they could? And if so, are we not more likely to get a Tower of Babel than a 'strategy of construction of a new order'?

Laclau and Mouffe lack a sufficiently differentiated set of analytical tools to embrace the complexity of identity formation and transformation. Their analysis *looks* sophisticated — at first glance — but it only operates on one level. The expansion of the political throughout the social promises to open up new dimensions of political analysis, but it ends up *reducing* political to social identities. The specifically political, the moment of hegemony, appears only as a bare logical form (equivalence) in libertarian mimicry of the formalism of classical liberal thought. The creative tension between the ideas of *discovering* and *making* an identity is lost; whilst the exploration and transformation of the boundaries between the social and the political — the idea of politics as the redefinition of the political — is suppressed, by the peremptory and indiscriminate declaration of the social to be always already political. Yet it is precisely here, on the issue of where we are to locate the boundary between the social and the political, and how it is to be transformed, that the history of the new social movements must itself be subjected to critical scrutiny.

It is ironic that these movements should have come to be lionized by sections of the 'old' left (primarily the Communist Party) at precisely the moment at which their original organizational forms were being dissolved and their broader political impact diffused; at precisely the moment, in fact, that a consolidation and defence of earlier gains involved the modification of their politics to fit the interest-group structure of a liberal pluralism. The problematic character of this shift is increasingly recognized by socialists within the movements themselves.[54] It is the product, in part, of the general downturn of left politics in Western capitalist societies which followed the economic recession of the mid 1970s, and in part of problems inherent in the political form of the movements themselves. The former points to the extent to which the force of their radicalism was based in certain more general social and economic conditions; while the latter suggests that whatever the form of their unity it was ultimately insufficient to change the existing framework of political power. The *redefinition* of politics in terms of personal relations, social identities and the ideals of a global humanism (peace, ecology, economic development), however mobilizing and transformative in its own right, turned out to be inadequate when not combined with a common strategy specifically addressed to transforming the existing centres of power. In fixating on the issue of identity, and its capacity for discursive transformation, while neglecting questions of *power*, *strategy* and *agency*, Laclau and Mouffe reproduce those very weaknesses of the politics of the 1970s that it is increasingly important to confront.

At this point, the importance of *distinguishing* social from political identities, whilst nonetheless recognizing and developing the connections between them, comes more clearly into view. Divisions between the 'social' and the 'political' (and the 'public' and the 'private') are the outcome of the existing balance of power and interest; definitions imposed, institutionally, by politically dominant social forces. To be transformed, they must first be recognized for what they are: materially embedded structures of interest with an inbuilt resistance to change. It is not necessarily those who suffer most from the effects of particular institutions and practices who are alone most strategically located to challenge them effectively; although they may possess a privileged relation to the definition of the form of their oppression. It is the structural centrality of waged labour to the reproduction of capital, for example, which gives it its centrality to the struggle for socialism (human emancipation on the basis of the collective determination of the pattern of economic life), not some *a priori* moral privilege. The struggle for socialism, for the abolition of all oppression, transcends particular interests; not in the direction of an abstract humanism, but in the concrete unity of oppressed groups. This unity can only be built if the recognition of the strategic dependence of different struggles and identities upon each other leads to the formation of specifically political *socialist* identities: identities which transcend the social bases from which they derive and feed back into them, in an ongoing *socialization of the political* and *politicization of the social*. This is a quite different process from a unity grounded in 'equivalence'. It derives its possibility from both the common sources of different forms of oppression, and the experience of multiple oppressions. To counterpose the labour movement to other movements ignores the fact that workers are women as well as men; black as well as white; gay as well as straight. The oppressions associated with these differences are generally experienced most intensely within the working class itself. Only some coming together of the universalism of traditional socialist aspirations, with the emphasis on subjectivity, identity and specific differences of the movements, which recognizes this fact, can hope to achieve the political synthesis necessary to pose a serious challenge to existing centres of power. The reduction of subjectivity to the articulation of discrete and free-floating 'subject positions' negates the experiential basis from which such a synthesis must set out.

It is no longer possible to pretend that the old organizational forms of socialist politics are adequate to the realization of its goals. Nor however is it possible to pretend that all the problems we face can be laid at the door of the older forms of socialism. A sustained process of *mutual* criticism and interaction between these forms and the new movements is necessary. To oppose them to one another as exclusive alternatives is both unnecessary and divisive. It does not so much open up new political spaces as further reduce 'the beleaguered space which exists for combining newer sources of discontent with older organisational and theoretical strengths'.[55] Such combinations will not be easy to produce, and they will need more than 'democratic equivalence' to keep them together. But then socialism was never going to be that easy.

221

Notes

1. Ernesto Laclau and Chantal Mouffe, *Hegemony and Socialist Strategy: Towards a Radical Democratic Politics* (hereafter *HSS*), London: Verso 1985, p. 4.

2. Ernesto Laclau and Chantal Mouffe, 'Post-Marxism Without Apologies', *New Left Review* 166, November/December 1987, pp. 79–106; Ernesto Laclau, 'Politics and the Limits of Modernity', in Andrew Ross, ed., *Universal Abandon? The Politics of Postmodernism*, Edinburgh: Edinburgh University Press 1989, p. 72.

3. Norman Geras, 'Ex-Marxism Without Substance: Being a Real Reply to Laclau and Mouffe', *New Left Review* 169, May/June 1988, pp. 34–61. See also Ralph Miliband, 'The New Revisionism in Britain', *New Left Review* 150, March/April 1985, pp. 5–26; Ellen Meiksins Wood, *The Retreat From Class: A New 'True' Socialism*, London: Verso 1986; Geras's initial critique, 'Post-Marxism?', *New Left Review* 163, May/June 1987, pp. 40–82; Nicos Mouzelis, 'Marxism or Postmarxism?', *New Left Review* 167, January/February 1988, pp. 107–23; and Michael Rustin, 'Absolute Voluntarism: Critique of a Post-Marxist Concept of Hegemony', *New German Critique* 43, Winter 1988, pp. 147–73. The weight of argument against Laclau and Mouffe's characterization of the theoretical structure of Marxism is overwhelming. I shall not rehearse it here. What is at issue is whether or not there is anything in their work of value to the further development of the tradition.

4. Geras, 'Ex-Marxism Without Substance', p. 61.

5. Ibid.

6. Ernesto Laclau, *Politics and Ideology in Marxist Theory*, London: Verso 1977; Chantal Mouffe, 'Hegemony and Ideology in Gramsci', in Chantal Mouffe, ed., *Gramsci and Marxist Theory*, London 1979, pp. 168–204. The definition of the problem of the political as the 'definition and articulation of social relations in a field criss-crossed with antagonisms' appears in *HSS*, p. 153. Laclau's reception of post-structuralism is well known. Less attention has been paid to the role within his thought of categories derived from that tendency within French political theory which grows out of Merleau-Ponty's later work. See in particular, Cornelius Castoriadis, *The Imaginary Institution of Society* (1975) translated by Kathleen Blamey, Cambridge: Polity 1988, and Claude Lefort, *Political Forms of Modern Society*, Cambridge: Polity 1986.

7. Ernesto Laclau and Chantal Mouffe, 'Socialist Strategy, Where Next?', *Marxism Today*, January 1981, p. 17. For Laclau's earlier work on the articulation of class to non-class ideological elements, see 'Fascism and Ideology' and 'Towards a Theory of Populism' in *Politics and Ideology in Marxist Theory*, pp. 81–142, 143–99.

8. See in particular, Stuart Hall, *The Hard Road to Renewal: Thatcherism and the Crisis of the Left*, London: Verso 1988, a collection of essays written over the previous decade, and the Communist Party of Great Britain's *Manifesto For New Times*. For Laclau's endorsement of the latter, see his 'Roads From Socialism', *Marxism Today*, October 1989, p. 41.

9. Louis Althusser, 'Ideology and Ideological State Apparatuses (Notes Towards an Investigation)' (1969), translated by Ben Brewster in *Lenin and*

Philosophy and Other Essays, London: New Left Books 1971, p. 159.

10. Ludwig Wittgenstein, *Philosophical Investigations* (1953), translated by G.E.M. Anscombe, Oxford: Basil Blackwell 1976.

11. Michel Foucault, *The Archaeology of Knowledge*, translated by A.M. Sheridan Smith, London: Tavistock 1972, Part II.

12. 'Post-Marxism Without Apologies', p. 86.

13. *HSS*, pp. 107, 109. The move parallels that made by Barry Hindess and Paul Hirst on a similar post-Althusserian trajectory, between their works *Pre-Capitalist Modes of Production*, London: Routledge & Kegan Paul 1975, and *Mode of Production and Social Formation*, London: Macmillan 1977. There are, however, theoretical differences between the two moves. For Laclau and Mouffe's account of these differences, see *HSS*, pp. 100–104. For an overall view of Hirst's theoretical and political trajectory, see Gregory Elliott, 'The Odyssey of Paul Hirst', *New Left Review* 159, September/October 1986. The differences at stake — over the stability of the identity of discursive elements — are mirrored in the difference between Hirst's Labour Party reformism and Laclau and Mouffe's quasi-libertarian radical pluralism.

14. *HSS*, p. 96.

15. *HSS*, p. 105.

16. 'Post-Marxism Without Apologies', p. 82.

17. *HSS*, p. 108.

18. *HSS*, p. 111.

19. *HSS*, p. 104.

20. *HSS*, p. 112.

21. *HSS*, p. 111.

22. 'Post-Marxism Without Apologies', p. 89.

23. For the conflation of contingency with randomness, see Wood, *The Retreat From Class*, chapter 5, 'The Randomisation of History'; an account which derives from Perry Anderson, *In the Tracks of Historical Materialism*, London: Verso 1983, pp. 48–55. The problem is not randomness but, as both Geras and Rustin have seen, the *arbitrariness* which follows from the conjunction of an account of the essential instability of meaning with a reduction of reality to meaning. Randomness is a red herring which allows Laclau and Mouffe to escape the consequences of their position by charging their opponents with a misunderstanding of the concept of contingency.

24. *HSS*, p. 110. Cf. the discussion of stones in 'Post-Marxism Without Apologies', p. 54.

25. *HSS*, p. 107; 'Post-Marxism Without Apologies', p. 84, emphasis added.

26. The *irrealism* of Laclau and Mouffe's position ('idealism' is too contested and in certain ways too strong a term to be useful here) attests to the continuing influence of an Husserlian phenomenology within post-structuralist theories of meaning. It is interesting in this respect that when they move on from their account of discursivity to discuss political change they are forced to supplement it with the explicitly *ontological* category of 'institution', in Merleau-Ponty's sense of an active 'instituting'. As Sartre saw very early on, you can't discuss action without opening the phenomenological brackets. Similar problems arose within Laclau's earlier work with regard to the issue of how to conceptualize empirical controls on theory, within the Althusserian

223

problematic, and how to account for the relation of theory to practice. For a useful criticism of the first of these aspects of Laclau's earlier work, see Nicos Mouzelis, 'Ideology and Class Politics: A Critique of Ernesto Laclau', *New Left Review* 112, November/December 1978, pp. 45–61, pp. 59–61.

27. See note 13 above.

28. 'Post-Marxism Without Apologies', p. 86.

29. Geras, 'Post-Marxism?', p. 80. Cf. Wood, *The Retreat from Class*, pp. 64–71, and Rustin, 'Absolute Voluntarism', pp. 162–73.

30. *HSS*, p. 155. The slip back into a quasi-foundationalist discourse of historical dominance here is symptomatic of the limits of the attempt directly to extend anti-foundationalist arguments from philosophical to social analysis.

31. *HSS*, pp. 154, 159. Relations of subordination are those in which 'an agent is subjected to the decisions of another'. Relations of oppression are those relations of subordination 'which have transformed themselves [sic] into sites of antagonism'.

32. *HSS*, p. 176.

33. *HSS*, p. 189.

34. 'Absolute Voluntarism', p. 172.

35. Mouzelis, 'Marxism or Post-Marxism?', p. 115. Cf. Geras, 'Post-Marxism?', pp. 79–80.

36. *HSS*, p. 153.

37. 'Marxism or Post-Marxism?', pp. 119–20.

38. It is interesting to note that Stuart Hall, the most influential political thinker to have been influenced by Laclau, is somewhat at sea with the philosophical issues underlying the application of discourse theory to politics. In the Introduction to *The Hard Road to Renewal* (pp. 10–11), he claims to 'stop short before what is sometimes called a "fully discursive" position', having 'not always follow[ed] to their logical conclusion' the extension of Laclau's earlier arguments which takes place in *HSS*. At the same time, however, he declares himself 'much more in agreement' with the formulation of the concept of discourse outlined in 'Post-Marxism Without Apologies', which he sees as a reformulation of their position. The problem is that the position is the same one. If anything, its defects are clearer in the later article. Hall, it seems, wants to follow Laclau's extension of his earlier position, but not to its logical conclusion. It is hard to see how this could be justifiable. What it leads to in practice is the deployment of the Laclau/Mouffe conceptual framework, with a kind of philosophical waiver clause attached. The result is ideological analyses which appear, immanently, to totalize the political field, but which are then (retrospectively) attributed a more limited significance. The dynamics of this process can be seen at work in Hall's 'Authoritarian Populism: A Reply to Jessop et al', *New Left Review* 151, May/June 1985; reprinted as chapter 9 of *The Hard Road to Renewal*. See also the response by Bob Jessop et al, 'Thatcherism and the Politics of Hegemony: A reply to Stuart Hall', *New Left Review* 153, September/October 1985. Hall's lack of clarity on this issue has had significant political effects on the left, not just via his overly ideological analysis of Thatcherism as a hegemonic project, but primarily through his use of this analysis as a stick with which to beat purportedly 'outdated' forms of left politics.

39. Ellen Meiksins Wood, 'Capitalism and Human Emancipation', *New Left Review* 167, January/February 1988, pp. 8–14. See also Ralph Miliband, *Capitalist Democracy in Britain*, Oxford: Oxford University Press 1985.

40. Miliband, p. 13.

41. Cf. Rustin, 'Absolute Voluntarism', p. 165.

42. This is Rustin's ultimate charge, 'Absolute Voluntarism', p. 173.

43. Rosalind Brunt, 'The Politics of Identity', *Marxism Today*, October 1988; reprinted in Stuart Hall and Martin Jacques, eds, *New Times: The Changing Face of Politics in the 1990s*, London: Lawrence and Wishart 1989, pp. 150–59, p. 151.

44. Sheila Rowbotham, *The Past is Before Us: Feminism in Action Since the 1960s*, London: Pandora 1989, p. 246.

45. See, for example, Laclau and Mouffe, 'Socialist Strategy, Where Next?', p. 22 and 'Post-Marxism Without Apologies', p. 106.

46. Sheila Rowbotham, Lynne Segal and Hilary Wainwright, *Beyond the Fragments: Feminism and the Making of Socialism*, London: Merlin 1979; Lynne Segal, *Is The Future Female? Troubled Thoughts on Contemporary Feminism*, London: Virago 1987, chapters 2 and 6; Angela Weir and Elizabeth Wilson, 'The British Women's Movement', *New Left Review* 148, November/December 1984.

47. Lynne Segal, 'Still Seeking a Union', *Interlink*, February/March 1989, p. 27.

48. Mary Louise Adams, 'There's No Place Like Home: On the Place of Identity in Feminist Politics', *Feminist Review* 31, Spring 1989, pp. 22–33, p. 25.

49. For an account of the dynamics of such a process in a particular case, see Susan Ardill and Sue O'Sullivan, 'Upsetting An Applecart: Difference, Desire and Lesbian Sadomasochism', *Feminist Review* 23, Summer 1986, pp. 31–58.

50. Kathryn Harris, 'New Alliances: Socialist-Feminism in the Eighties', *Feminist Review* 31, Spring 1989, p. 51.

51. *HSS*, p. 115. Cf. Stuart Hall, 'Minimal Selves', *ICA Documents* 6, 1987.

52. *HSS*, p. 103.

53. *HSS*, pp. 191–2.

54. See, for example, the special issue of *Feminist Review*, 'Twenty Years of Feminism', in which the essays cited in notes 48 and 51 appear; and Rowbotham, *The Past is Before Us*, pp. 243–302. For a wider selection of views from the same period, see Amanda Sebestyen, ed., *'68, '78, '88: From Women's Liberation to Feminism*, Bridport: Prism Press 1988. The movement from women's liberation to feminism is characteristic of the contradictory process of advancing in some areas while retreating in others, which has marked the history of the social movements more generally.

55. Sheila Rowbotham, 'Twiddling Our Toes in Backwaters', *Zita Magazine*, December 1989, p. 25.

9

Remembering the Limits: Difference, Identity and Practice

A Transcript

Gayatri Chakravorty Spivak

I will confine myself, first, to the apparent contradiction within liberal ideas of universal humanism, and second, to the nature of the master/slave dialectic, in a general way. There is a third thing that interests me, although I'm not yet prepared to speak of it: a new conception of history as violence which would perhaps ask us to reconsider our terms altogether. But I think that had better be deferred.

First, then, the apparent contradiction within ideas of universal humanism. It has appeared to some of my readers recently that I seem to be moving towards some notion of universal humanity, and this has surprised them — I am expected to emphasize difference. On the other hand, there are those who think that one of the specious effects of *that* discourse is that the emphasis seems to fall completely on difference. I would like to bring universal humanism and difference together. Contrary to the received assumption, it seems to me that the non-foundationalist thinkers are suggesting that you cannot have any kind of emancipatory project *without* some notion of the ways in which human beings are similar, but that there are practical-philosophical problems that attend on that assumption. Historically, the people who have been involved in emancipatory projects from above — slave-holders and proponents of Christianizing the natives, and so on — are the ones who have produced the discourse. This contradiction can be avoided only if the principles of a universal humanism — the place where indeed all human beings are similar — is seen to be lodged in their being different. So that difference itself becomes a name for the place where we are all the same — a '*name for*', because difference is not something that can be articulated, or should be articulated, as a monolithic concept. But if difference becomes a name for the place where we are all the same — if difference becomes the name for that — then it stands as a kind of warning against the fact that we *cannot not* propose identity when we engage in actual emancipatory projects. No more than that. But it is a great deal. No more than that, but also no less than that.

When Kant, in the *Critique of Teleological Judgement*, starts speaking of the greatest antinomy and says that the biggest mistake that the philosopher can make is to confuse the reflective and the determinant judgements,[1] he gives us one example — and it is not a throwaway example — at the end of the eighteenth century. It goes as follows: the reason why we cannot base the project of *cosmopolithea* on the determinant judgement, which is heteronomous, is because it will lead us factually to the wrong kinds of conclusions. And, says Kant, for example, if you think of the inhabitant of New Holland, or of Tierra del Fuego, then you will be right in thinking that man need not exist. Now, this is the absolutely crucial example, from which the reflective judgement must begin to disengage in order to base the notion of the noumenon on that concept of the subject on which one *can* base ethical programmes. In fact, Kant chooses these people not because he's particularly interested in the New Hollander or the Fuegan — he chooses them because as Jakobsen says in that very famous essay included in *Style in Language*, there is a sort of poetic principle where equivalence takes over.[2] The two names rhyme in German — *Neuholländer* and *Feuerländer*.

That's why, on the back of a rhyme and with the backing from recent voyages, these two names crop up as proofs that man need not exist. The philosopher must not make this confusion. (I know I'm making a category mistake here. I'm anthropomorphizing by talking about philosophy in this way. But that's exactly the mistake that we must make in order to suggest that the great doctrines of identity of the ethical universal, in terms of which liberalism thought out its ethical programmes, played history false, because the identity was disengaged in terms of who was and who was not human. That's why all these projects, the justification of slavery, as well as the justification of Christianization, seemed to be alright: because, after all, these people had not graduated into humanhood, as it were.) It is from such reminders that the notion of difference is useful on the most practical level, even when it serves as a reminder that the *absolutely* other cannot enter into *any* kind of foundational emancipatory project. Even granting these limits, there is some virtue in notions of difference rather than notions of identity as the basis of universal humanism. One doesn't have to jettison the idea — that very strong idea — that I must think of the other as a self. But one has to maintain a very strong kind of vigilance right there. Because to think of the self as a self may be simply a survival technique. This would lead us into more mysterious thickets. But I think that I have covered the first point for our present purposes.

The other thing that I want to speak about is what Blackburn says about the master/slave dialectic. Genevieve Lloyd is of course quite right in saying that in Hegel the agenda is not just master/slave, but is also quite deeply involved with gendering.[3] That is, however, not the only way in which the master/slave dialectic misses the point in trying to understand the relationship between liberalism, colonialism and decolonization. In his book *The Overthrow of Colonial Slavery*, Blackburn says that the dialectic of the subject also fails to address the problem of how intersubjectivity could develop between slaves in different situations and of different extraction. And he goes on to speak about what Sartre had said about many masters.[4] Now this is, I think, a very good, strong point: many different kinds of slaves and many different kinds of masters; and also third groups, such as free people of colour and non-slave-holding whites. But I'm going to make a point which is more like me and less like Blackburn, when I say that the problem with the master/slave dialectic is also that the master and the slave are not continuous; just as, let us say, consciousness and the unconscious are not continuous. The unconscious is not just that part of consciousness which is not yet available to consciousness. The two are discontinuous; they are on two different planes. You can't make them actually come together by moving one into the other. The real problem with the master/slave dialectic is that the master and the slave do not inhabit a continuous space. (I believe Marx's early treatment of Hegel can produce this critique.) It is only when they begin to do so — and this relates to what I was saying about difference — that the dialectic can play. But what is much more interesting is the area where they *cannot* begin to play together, and don't feed into each other in a dialectical way. Here I want to give two examples.

Recently I have written about a novel by the Afrikaaner novelist J.M. Coetzee, a novel called *Foe*, which is a rewriting of Daniel Defoe's *Robinson Crusoe* and *Roxana*; the two together in a very slim novel.[5] One of the most wonderful things that Coetzee does there is to make a distinction between Defoe's Friday and the Friday of Africa. Robinson Crusoe, the mercantile capitalist, trains a Friday, who is represented in Defoe's novel as the *willing* proto-colonial subject. Coetzee makes a distinction between the two Fridays and stitches in a woman called Susan Barton from Defoe's *Roxana* as the narrator of his own novel. She is an anachronistic eighteenth-century Englishwoman who longs to give the muted racial other a voice — but in this novel Friday's tongue has been cut out. And so you have these two different representations — one representation within the master/slave, master/servant dialectic (Crusoe's Friday); and one where the dialectic won't begin to play (the Friday of Africa).

The play between Friday and Crusoe is dialectical. One of them is becoming the other in certain ways; and validating the other in certain other ways. But in Coetzee's novel, the white woman — that is to say, the metropolitan, neo-colonial anti-colonialist, as it were — her effort to give Friday a voice doesn't come through, and in interesting ways. Susan Barton is extremely anxious to get to father her story, her own story. She was the one who was on the island, Robinson's island. Robinson died. So to an extent she is putting her story into history. That's one story. But she also wants to give the muted racial other a voice. At the very end of the novel, there is an allegory of reading which violates the narrative. There she is dead, bloated: Defoe's novel has not been written. These are the remains of the dream of continuity. This discontinuity is something which we in the present conjuncture should be thinking about more and more as the failure of the master/slave, or master/servant dialectic.

The dream of continuity, the lack of attention to the possible failure of the master/slave dialectic, is related to the failure of many projects — which certainly we in the United States see — where extremely strong and good feminist workers, who are capable of doing brilliant work in redressing the patriarchal muting of women within their own cultural script, go with the same passion into anti-imperialist studies without ever thinking that there they are dealing with a cultural script which they do not inhabit. And even if they think it, they think that they can manage it by modelling the Other on US national migrancy, multi-raciality or multi-ethnicity where the dialectic is in play — although the question of who plays in the dialectic is up for grabs: a reversal. It's quite different to try to redress a wrong from within a cultural script that you inhabit yourself, and that actively writes you, and to try to do a critique within a cultural script that you do not inhabit. This is another way of talking about the failure of a dialectical vision of master/slave or master/servant.

Lest I seem to be relating only to my colleagues in the United States, I will end with an example from my own life.

As you may know, I'm forty-six years old and I come from the bosom of the middle class. In that context — in a labour-intensive situation in the 1940s and 50s — there were domestic servants, even for this class. (Kalapana Bardham and Geraldine Heng have, by the way, worked on the relationship between feminists and the exploitation of female servants in India and Singapore, but that's something else.[6]) In my family we were not bad: we were exemplary masters. The woman I'm going to speak about, our servant whose name was Swadeshi (she was named after the 1906 Swadeshi independence movement) was never called by her first name. She was called Gita's mother, because that's how you called servants. They don't have real names, especially female servants: they are mothers of other characters. But anyway, according to the script of good masters, she was able to really tyrannize us, the children, especially me, the third child, second daughter. She felt she was a 'member of the family'. But all three sisters, myself included, went on slowly through school, through college, to get our PhDs. (All three of us are professors.) We never thought about the fact that she was illiterate, but she was.

At that time, menstruation for my class was a heavily shaming event. You used to have to wear these diapers that you fabricated out of old torn saris and bedsheets, and the like. For my class there were no sanitary napkins or Tampax. There was a whole incredible event of menstruation, and in that extraordinarily hot weather with the damp, she must have menstruated too. We wore these clothes with petticoats and long saris. She on the other hand, her sari came down to her knee, and she wiped the floors. But we never thought about the fact that this woman was also a menstruating woman. Remember, I'm trying to talk about the discontinuity. In terms of the master/servant dialectic, this one was fully in play. Nevertheless, we were very good masters and she felt good about all of this. (I know because she still comes out of retirement to look after my mother — who is herself a brave, social-working proto-feminist woman of seventy-five — when she's in Calcutta.)

In 1979 when I went back, she came to see me at the door, and I was carrying two cases, and she wanted to take my cases. She's very short. I looked at her and I smiled with all of the affection that is generated in a good household between the master's children and the servant. I smiled at her and I said, 'You're crazy. I can carry you in one hand and my two cases in another.' And she drew herself up to her four-foot seven, and looked at me, and she said, 'Gayatri, at last you have become white.'

If you think that the disenfranchised are not capable of speaking about this discontinuity, then you're wrong. They just don't get here to talk about it. So to an extent you can say that I'm representing her in this way. I'm speaking in a slightly dressed-up English here because I'm speaking *here*. But in terms of this particular thing, we don't even have to look at the ways in which the colonial victims actually use the discourse of liberalism and dehegemonize it and organize resistance. It's not even necessary to read about those things. If we keep vigilant we will see that this awareness of the dialectic *not* playing is not unavailable among the disenfranchised.*

To end, I will quote something to demonstrate what happens when one thinks about the other in an identitarian way. Here are some lines from Sartre's *Existentialism and Humanism* (1946). Then I'm going to read you something from Todorov's *The Conquest of America* (1986). Forty years have passed. Here is Sartre: 'And diverse though man's projects may be, at least none of them is wholly foreign to me.' You know what he means: *homo sum: humani nil a me alienum puto*, courtesy of Terence. Rome is imbricated in the history of the subject who speaks here.

> Every project, even that of a Chinese, an Indian or a Negro, can be understood by a European. The European of 1945 can throw [pro-ject] himself out of a situation which he conceives towards his limitations in the same way, and he may re-do [*refaire*] in himself the project of the Chinese, of the Indian or the African. There is always some way of understanding an idiot, a child, a primitive man or a foreigner if one has sufficient information.[7]

---

* It might be of interest to report that, when I gave this paper, during the lunch break a young Indian woman came up to me and said that she had felt exactly the same way when two white male students came up to carry her cases when she had just arrived from an elite university in New Delhi to go to the LSE. I had to explain to her that her feeling, legitimate no doubt in its place, was not 'exactly the same'. Difference, the ungraspable as such, has to be grasped in the coding. In our own space (not so easily when we are migrants) we 'become white' in the unquestioning cathexis of non-interventionist egalitarianism: 'I can carry you and my cases'. Although Gita Ma is, from the metropolitan point of view, the same race, and from an essentialist point of view, the same sex, the dynamics of class/gender/imperialism has made us 'upwardly race mobile' and created a real discontinuity. I am obliged to use all this paraphernalia to explain myself theoretically. Her pleasant words, much more difficult to understand: 'At last you have become white'. And of course in the mother tongue she doesn't invoke colour — but that's another thicket:

"এইবার তুমি সায়েব হইছ ।"

No one can doubt Sartre's benevolence. In many ways he has done much more than many of us. But words are not nothing, and this is the paragraph where he is defending what he is doing. Now Todorov, hegemonic French migrant, forty years later:

Many acts of revenge have been, and are still taken against citizens of the former colonial powers — not just the slave owners — whose sole personal crime is that of belonging to the nation in question. That Europe should in her turn be colonised by the people of Africa, of Asia or of Latin America, we are far from this I know, would be a sweet revenge, but cannot be considered my ideal. This extraordinary success that the colonised peoples have adopted our customs [no talk of discontinuity here] and have put on clothes, is chiefly due to one specific feature of western civilisation which for a long time was regarded as a feature of man himself, its development and prosperity among Europeans thereby becoming proof of their superiority, it is paradoxically the European's capacity to understand the other.[8]

This is in conclusion to his book *The Conquest of America*, where he is trying to understand the Other. These are the kinds of things that remind us that even words are not unimportant. We are a word-making species. It is because of this that it is necessary, though it is not the whole programme, to talk about difference: to remember that when we think that words are just the indispensable motor of deeds, just the servants of the things they mean, it is then that words can identify too quickly.

So these are the two main points that I wanted to make: one was the lesson of non-foundationalism — the importance of difference as a principle of universal humanism; the other was a critique of the master/slave or master/servant dialectic in terms of discontinuity, rather than the avoidance of intersubjectivity or multiplicity. Both of these relate to some of the critiques that Blackburn has made of 'where discourses come from'. The third thing, which I hope to be able to discuss at some future time, is a rethinking of the historical narrative as itself a violence. But that must await another occasion.

Discussion

JAY BERNSTEIN: *Under what conditions do people revolt? Barrington Moore's thesis was that people actually need to see the practices under which they are suffering as unjust, as a necessary but not a sufficient condition. There is a stuttering dialectic here. What I'm unclear about is how a dialectic could ever be other than stuttering in this way. There are discontinuities in the continuity. There are both elements. I take it this discontinuity is one between an actual, existent set of situations and the perception of those situations, which is non-continuous.*

Let me begin by saying that I don't think that discontinuity should be *primarily* argued on the basis of perception and consciousness. When we are speaking of resistance, we must assume agency and even collective agency, but then a step has already been taken.[9] Within that framing, I agree with what you're saying. By that argument, discontinuity does not stop us, and difference marks the moment of vigilance. These non-foundationalist theories, looking out for what's prior to agency, should not tell us what to *do*. They can tell us what not to do. They can tell us where not to stop. If discontinuity stops us, then it does indeed, as we have seen, become language-games.

When a movement coalesces, when points of resistance actually coalesce into some kind of movement, then a dialectic is provisionally established. That is rather different from justifying situational changes on the monumentalized blueprint of the great discourse holders. It doesn't just come from above. The two sides begin to play, *in a certain sense* or direction, when the movements coalesce. One of the strongest examples of this, discussed in the work of the Subaltern Studies Group, is the way in which the Indian tribals, peasants, transformed religion into resistance.[10] Religion can be a most potent lever for the provisional undoing of discontinuity, even as it remains a conservative blueprint. Here for example is Blackburn:

I have suggested that anti-slavery grew in the secular space opened up by the arc of bourgeois revolution. Yet manifestly [anti-]slavery often received strong sponsorship from religious enthusiasts. Quakers, Methodists, radical *abbés*, black deacons, revolutionary deists and voodoo *houngans*. The conclusion I wish to suggest is not that anti-slavery was itself purely secular in inspiration, but that its achievements required a secular setting.[11]

In the Indian context, secularism is discontinuous with the situational subaltern transformation of religion. (It was a liberal alibi within decolonization quickly transformed in the 1970s by Mrs Gandhi from *asampradayikata*, which would have been a kind of secularism, to *sarbadharmasamanvaya*, that is to say, all religions combined; and in a country with an 84 per cent Hindu majority, you know what that means.) The tribal or peasant movements in India never moved into secularism. So that what we are really looking at is a possibility for the liberatory discourse of religion to provide a field for the fabrication of continuity in movements, so that there can be a dialectic between the masters and the slaves. Then we can take the next step, and say that the people from above, the hegemonic planners of 'national identity', were in fact *fabricating* a continuity outside of secularism, by a language-game — Mrs Gandhi's name-changing. As long as we think of secularism as the master word, we won't solve that one, because secularism — that great rational abstraction — has various ways of organizing itself into alibis. In the present context, we see it over and over again.

If arguments coming from the idea of discontinuity stop us from doing anything, then they are useless. When non-foundationalist philosophers dabble with founding politics, the political programmes become dangerous or inane. That stuff is not there for doing, but for the important lesson of remembering the limits of one's powers. Discontinuity is an absolutely crucial reminder: an obstinate remainder from all solutions. The stutter in the dialectic is still within the normative language: those necessary adjustments and justifications that constitute resistance. Resistance is not just the Black Jacobins. The possibility of resistance lies unclaimed in discontinuity —

the rejoinder of my servant to me. It's not only recognizable when you point at it as dialectically matching what is coming from above. There are those mis-matched places which remind us that after those critical events, leading sometimes to a different state-formation, the dust settles, and we come into an everyday world where somehow the results of those critical events don't seem to translate. The discontinuities don't seem to live in a better world.

MADAN SARUP: *One of the things I find difficult to understand about difference is: what is the principle which holds a society together? I'm trying to express a worry about how in many Western industrial countries there seems to be a conflict between indigenous people using the ideology of nationalism and other movements stressing the idea of difference. There's a clash of ideologies, and nationalism seems to win.*

I agree with you that nationalism wins, and here I'm speaking from the Indian context. But the fact that it wins is not something that should make us give up the effort persistently to critique it. I will take an example from the tribal movement in India. As you know, in the 1947 constitution, various sanctions were written for the so-called 'scheduled tribes' (the STs), as they were written for the so-called 'scheduled castes' (the SCs). But what has happened with those sanctions is that since the tribals themselves do not know about them, when they go — if they go — to the petty functionaries to ask for things, they feel they have no right to ask anything, and they are decimated. They're always called for when there is armed struggle because they know how to fight, and they get killed, and they never get anything. The tribes are not only not unified but, ethnographically speaking, these roughly sixty-three million people of three-hundred-odd so-called Austro-Asiatic tribes, they are not the same. At this point it is completely ridiculous to say, as it is at all points: 'Look here, guard your difference and base your society on this wonderful idea of difference.' Nothing can be based on an idea of difference. At this point in the movement, the best part of the movement take the caste Hindus and middle-class, upper-class

Muslims as guarantees. The constitutional sanctions are being published in the tribal languages, distributed to the tribals, and we, the caste Hindus and so on, can stand as guarantees. So if the petty functionaries screw them up, they know that there are people among those who daily qualify as constituting the nation who will make trouble.[12]

Now in this case, the tribals themselves, the very small percentage that is educated, what they are suggesting is unity: a completely spurious unity, but unity. In fact, they are claiming that the name they should be given is *adim jati*, 'original nation'. (*Jati* of course is not quite nation, not *advasi*, original inhabitant, which is how they're written in the sanctions.) Their claim for the word loosely translated as 'original nation' is a catachrestical claim. The name is a catachresis, like most decolonized claims to nationhood. Since the real story of the formation of nations was obviously not written in that space, they are catachrestical claims. They are themselves trying to fabricate a kind of nationhood, a kind of unity which will allow the dialectic to play. With the constitutional sanctions, they will confront the Indians whose religions are written into the constitution, unlike these people. What they are doing is strategically using a notion, the notion of nationhood, *against* a very strongly nationalistic country where nationalism is often identical with the extreme right, and today, with the centralizing power. In that sort of situation, it seems to me, it is important to remember that this nationhood is something that they are constructing in order to get their share, rather than in order to establish a new definition of the tribes as another national liberation movement, which will then freeze into nationalism, if it succeeds. Here is the reminder of difference. Nationalism is not a unified thing. There is a difference which runs through the notion of a nation all over the globe, and it should stand as a reminder.

Notes

1. Immanuel Kant, *The Critique of Judgement* (1790), translated by James Creed Meredith, Oxford: Oxford University Press 1957, Part II, 'Critique of Teleological Judgement', Second Division.

2. Roman Jakobsen, 'Closing Statement: Linguistics and Poetics', in Thomas A. Sebeok, ed., *Style and Language*, Cambridge, Mass: MIT Press 1960, p. 370.

3. Genevieve Lloyd, *The Man of Reason: 'Male' and 'Female' in Western Philosophy*, London: Methuen 1984, Ch. 6.

4. Robin Blackburn, *The Overthrow of Colonial Slavery, 1776–1848*, London: Verso 1988, p. 530.

5. J.M. Coetzee, *Foe*, London 1987.

6. Kalapana Bardham, 'Women: Work, Welfare and Status. Forces of Traditions and Change in India', *South Asia Bulletin*, vol. 6, no. 1, Spring 1986; Geraldine Heng, 'To Govern and to Populate: Sexuality and the State', unpublished paper, Nationalisms and Sexuality Conference, Harvard University, June 1989.

7. Jean-Paul Sartre, *Existentialism and Humanism*, translated by Philip Mairet, New York: Haskell House 1948, pp. 46–7. Translation altered.

8. Tzvetan Todorov, *The Conquest Of America: The Question of the Other*, translated by Richard Howard, New York: Harper and Row 1984, pp. 246, 248.

9. Michel Foucault, *The History of Sexuality Volume 1: An Introduction*, translated by Robert Hurley, London: Allen Lane 1979, p. 96.

10. Ranajit Guha and Gayatri Chakravorty Spivak, eds, *Selected Subaltern Studies*, New York: Oxford University Press 1988.

11. Blackburn, *Overthow of Colonial Slavery*, p. 531.

12. I am referring here to *Aikya Parishad*, of which Mahasireta Devi is a prominent sponsor.

10

The Malthusian Challenge: Ecology, Natural Limits and Human Emancipation

Ted Benton

I have read some of the speculations on the perfectibility of man and of society with great pleasure. I have been warmed and delighted with the enchanting picture which they hold forth. I ardently wish for such improvements. But I see great, and, to my understanding, unconquerable difficulties in the way to them.

MALTHUS

Written just a few years after the French Revolution, these lines epitomize a powerful and pervasive strand of conservative thought. Malthus was here commenting on the wave of utopian and optimistic literature unleashed by the revolution in France. Condorcet and Godwin are the writers he singles out for special mention. He does not directly challenge their (egalitarian, libertarian, communitarian) value-perspectives. On the contrary, he gives some show of a sentimental attachment to them. Sadly, however, he has had to resign himself to a hard–headed recognition that a society infused with such values would be unsustainable.

Traditions of thought which, like Malthus, resist emancipatory projects on broadly cognitive grounds — I call them 'epistemic conservatisms' — make use of two main kinds of argument. One, most famously deployed by Popper, criticizes totalizing projects for social transformation on the grounds that

241

the cognitive basis for such 'utopian social engineering' could not conform to scientific standards. For Popper, 'piecemeal social engineering' was exempt from such epistemological criticism.[1] The second kind of cognitive argument, more familiar and pervasive, takes as its key premise the invulnerability of the world to human intentionality. As Malthus puts it, 'there are unconquerable difficulties' in the way of our realizing our hopes. Emancipatory projects, so the argument goes, leave out of account crucial features of human nature, of external nature, or of social life itself which either are simply unalterable, or if alterable necessarily productive of self-defeating unintended consequences.

Since social and cultural variation and historical change can hardly be denied, most of these epistemic conservatisms take the form of an attempt to specify limits to variation or change, transcendence of which will be self-defeating and/or catastrophic. Such limits are not always thought of as deriving from 'nature' ('external', or 'internal', human nature). Some social theorists, for example, attempt to specify functional requirements of social systems, the fulfilment of which is necessary for 'system-maintenance'. However, my focus in this chapter will be upon natural-limits epistemic conservatism, and on the implications of different ways of defending emancipatory projects from its criticisms. More narrowly than this, I will try to analyse and hopefully transcend some of the dilemmas arising from the widespread tendency on the 'traditional' Marxist left to criticize ecological politics as a form of natural-limits conservatism and yet also to recognize it as an important source of anti-capitalist criticism and action. What are the roots of this mutual suspicion and bad blood between Marxist socialists and many of the advocates of 'green' analytical and political perspectives?

Socialism versus Environmentalism?

The grounds for green hostility to 'traditional' socialist and Marxist perspectives are well rehearsed in the literature. There is a tendency to identify these perspectives directly with the practice of the East European and Asian 'state socialist' societies, with their disastrous environmental record, or, alternatively, with the social democratic parliamentary parties in the West. These have, by and large, abandoned the struggle for fundamental social transformation, so that their strategies for economic amelioration and social welfare have become premised upon an indiscriminate and unqualified commitment to aggregate economic growth, regardless of the ecological consequences. Both strands of the 'traditional' socialist movement, seen from this perspective, share a 'Promethean' view of the historical relations between humanity and its natural environment, see progress in terms of an ever-increasing technological control over and exploitation of nature, and have ceased to view human wellbeing in qualitative and 'spiritual' terms, but rather in more quantitative, materialistic ones. Jonathan Porritt is an eloquent and persuasive advocate of this view. Of the traditional opposition of left and right in politics, he says:

> Both are dedicated to industrial growth, to the expansion of the means of production, to a materialist ethic as the best means of meeting people's needs, and to unimpeded technological development. Both rely on increasing centralization and large-scale bureaucratic control and co-ordination. . . . For an ecologist, the debate between the protagonists of capitalism and communism is about as uplifting as the dialogue between Tweedledum and Tweedledee.[2]

Of course, this is a caricature. There is much both in the Marxian tradition and in non-Marxian socialist writing which anchors its critique of capitalist social and economic forms precisely in the estrangement they impose between humans and their physical and living environment.[3] But, and I shall say more on this later, there does remain a very substantial environmentalist case against the socialist traditions — especially where it really counts, in their 'actually existing' political practice. Nor can these practical failings be written off in terms of simple-minded or sophisticated notions of 'betrayal' of socialist values and objectives. There are well-founded, if partial readings of the socialist classics which do genuinely sustain an ecologically blind, 'Promethean' orientation to the natural environment. These aspects need to be openly recognized and systematically criticized if a truly contemporary and sustainable vision of a socialist future is to be created.

A necessary step in this critical self-renewal on the part of the socialist — and especially Marxist — traditions is, I think, to consider again what is and is not defensible in the 'traditional' Marxist and socialist responses to ecological politics itself. In this response five argumentative themes can be distinguished (they are of course usually intertwined with one another in the practice of debate).[4] First (my above quotation from Jonathan Porritt might serve as a target for this line of argument), 'greens' are accused of a reactionary/utopian opposition to industrialization and technology as such. This allegedly fails to recognize the actual or potential benefits for human welfare that can accrue from properly used technical advance, and naively undervalues the material aspects of wellbeing. Connectedly, in laying the blame for environmental destruction at the door of an abstractly conceived 'industrialism', the greens distract attention from the specifically *capitalist* character of the principal causes of environmental destruction.

Secondly, it is argued that the 'catastrophist', doom-laden tendency in much environmentalist propaganda is liable to induce a sense of human impotence and fatalism, and to play into the hands of conservative forces who benefit from the preservation of the 'status quo'. Thirdly, the environmentalist emphasis on a universal interest in survival, overriding all social and political differences and particularities, can be viewed as, like other 'general interest' ideologies in class societies, a mask, or disguise, for *particular* interests. In this case, the interests are those of an alliance of technocrats and affluent middle-class activists who share vested interests in ecological scaremongering and/or the defence of a privileged minority lifestyle. In effect, this ideology displaces attention from ever-widening class and regional *inequalities* in resource use and environmental destruction, in the name of a proclaimed universal interest in ecological sustainability.

A fourth, closely connected line of argument against environmentalists is that their priorities reflect elite preferences. Environmental preservation is a matter of taste, or of aesthetics, which may be imposed by privileged and powerful minorities upon the rest of a population, many of whom lack fulfilment of their most basic needs:

> A tiny minority of self-appointed arbiters of taste dictates what the living standard of the rest of us shall be . . . the ever present ancient establishment, the landed aristocracy, the products of Oxford and Cambridge, the landowners, the officer class, and, behind them, their hangers-on: the trendy academics with less pretensions to gentility who prove their club-worthiness by espousing these elitist views . . .[5]

This kind of approach — less widespread now, perhaps, than formerly — expresses a still deep-rooted conception of a hierarchy of needs or wants. Environmental preferences may, as in this quotation, be seen as mere matters of 'subjective' taste, or they may, in more sympathetic versions, be acknowledged as genuine components of human wellbeing. Nevertheless, such 'basic' needs as food, clothing, shelter and security are accorded a higher and more urgent priority. Only, it is commonly argued, when these more basic needs have been met for the poorest people on the earth, can we be justified in giving priority to environmental quality. More recent environmentalist arguments which demonstrate a link between the urgency of environmental protection and survival itself have done much to undermine this line of criticism of environmental politics, but the presumed hierarchy of needs remains largely intact. Though I have insufficient space to argue the case here, it is my view that this hierarchy itself will have to be challenged if political strategies which synthesize traditional socialist objectives with environmental sustainability are to be devised.[6]

Finally, and more centrally to the concerns of this paper, ecological politics is often criticized from the left as a form of 'natural-limits' conservatism. The designation 'neo-Malthusianism' captures this well.[7] Just as Malthus invoked natural constraints on human aspirations in order to undermine progressive political projects, so, it is argued, the 'neo-Malthusian' environmentalists use the notion of natural ecological limits to oppose much-needed social and economic development, and to assign endemic poverty, recurrent famine and epidemic disease to 'natural' causes:

> The metaphors used by these writers are striking. Each suggests an image of an *uncontrollable* catastrophe. The growth of human populations is a 'bomb'; the peoples of the developed world live in a 'lifeboat', and can rescue others only at peril to all; the 'carrying capacity' of the planet earth is finite, and will only be damaged by over-use; the only responsible approach to world poverty must follow the military principle of 'triage', denying help not only to those who need none, but to the neediest also, who must be left to starve or survive as best they may while assistance goes only to the 'best risks'; like animal populations, human populations expand to fill available niches and are unavoidably 'culled' by famine.[8]

Of course, this neo-Malthusian perspective is only one among many sources of environmental concern. Its most forceful and influential representative writings appeared between the late 1960s and mid 1970s. The work of P.R. Ehlich and his associates (*The Population Bomb*, 1968, and subsequent writings), Garrett Hardin, E. Goldsmith et al. (*Blueprint for Survival*, 1972), and above all, D.H. Meadows et al. (*The Limits to Growth*, Club of Rome, 1972) have all been characterized as neo-Malthusian, and subjected to sustained criticism. Although work in this tradition is now far more methodologically and theoretically sophisticated, the broad outlines of the approach remain discernible and distinctive and its influence remains undiminished.

With some notable exceptions, Marxian critiques of this tradition of thought have relied, explicitly or implicitly, on characterization of it as a resurrected Malthusianism to which can be applied, more or less unchanged, the terms of Marx and Engels's critique of Malthus himself. A significant event in this re-run of the nineteenth-century intellectual battle was the reprinting in 1971 of R.L. Meek's 1951 edition of *Marx and Engels on Malthus* under the title *Marx and Engels on the Population Bomb*. The foreword by S. Weissman explicitly situated the text in relation to the neo-Malthusian challenge of P.R. Ehrlich's bestseller, *The Population Bomb*. I want to argue here that the project of a thorough and radical critique of this form of technocratic environmentalism remains an urgent necessity. However, this must be a critique which does not merely reject, but which transcends and surpasses its opponent, recognizing, incorporating and further illuminating the positive insights contained in it. Everything turns, then, on *how* 'neo-Malthusian' environmentalism is criticized, and what the Marxian tradition itself can learn in the exercise.

There are three main reasons why a simple reproduction of the terms of the classical Marxian critique of Malthus will not serve our purposes today. First, modern 'neo-Malthusianism' is significantly different from classical Malthusianism; second, there are significant ambiguities and defects in Marx and Engels's critique of Malthus himself; and, third, the historical distance which separates us from the nineteenth-century controversy has rendered far more politically urgent and pressing these limitations in Marx and Engels.

Malthus and Neo-Malthusianism

The broad outlines of Malthus's argument are well known. The tendency of population is to increase geometrically, whilst on the most optimistic estimates food production can rise only arithmetically. There is, then, a constantly operating tendency for population to exceed the available food supply, with consequent malnutrition, disease, and premature death. Malthus's approach is naturalistic in several respects. Methodologically, appeal is made to a 'Newtonian' model of scientific knowledge, in a familiar empiricist and inductivist version. His view of scientific laws as statements of observable regularities in event-sequences, when applied to the domain of human history, rules out sharp qualitative transfomations of the kind envisaged by Condorcet (and later, by Marx and Engels). Expectations about the future can be scientifically grounded only in so far as they can be represented in the form of a quantitative extrapolation of previously observed regularities. Quite apart from his substantive claims about population and food supply, Malthus was predisposed towards a form of natural–limits conservatism by his particular version of epistemological naturalism.

Malthus's approach is also naturalistic in that the law of population as it applies to the human case is, with some limited qualifications, only a special case of a more general law of population which covers all animal and plant species. Throughout the animal and vegetable kingdoms there is a great disproportion between the 'seeds of life' and 'the nourishment necessary to rear them'. Necessity restrains their population, and 'the race of men cannot by any efforts of reason, escape from' this law of nature. 'Among plants and animals its effects are waste of seed, sickness and premature death. Among mankind, misery and vice.'[9] The law of population operates with natural necessity upon humans, no less than animals and plants, but there are two qualifications in its manner of operation. Whereas animals and plants can have no way of increasing their food supply by their own efforts, humans do. However, the rate of increase possible for even humans is subject to strict (natural) limitations. The second qualification is that humans are capable of 'artificially' restraining their fertility. In addition to the general category of 'positive' checks to population (i.e. all causes of premature death, such as disease and starvation, which humans share with other species) Malthus introduces a further category of 'preventive checks', such as 'promiscuous intercourse, unnatural passions, violations of the marriage bed, and improper acts to conceal the consequences of irregular connections'. This category of preventative checks to population is a significant restriction on Malthus's naturalism since, although the practices referred to are all viewed by him as vicious, they do nevertheless indicate a recognition that the rate of increase of population is no simple natural fact, but is potentially vulnerable to human intentionality.

But this partial concession is hedged around, especially in Malthus's 'first *Essay*' by a further strongly naturalistic postulate of the universality and fixity of 'the passion between the sexes'.[10] It is a 'dictate of nature' in men to seek early attachment to one woman, and from this follows the tendency of the population to increase. Not only is restraint of marriage invariably accompanied by vicious practices, which in turn necessarily lead to misery, but so strong is the desire to form 'virtuous' attachments that the pressure towards population increase is but little affected.

In later editions Malthus claimed to have made possible a 'softening of the harshest conclusions of the first *Essay*'[11] by means of an explicit recognition of a further category of preventative check in the form of 'moral restraint' unaccompanied by vicious practices. Though, as a suppression of a natural instinct, this must cause some temporary unhappiness, it is far preferable to the operation of the other checks: misery and vice. It also brings within the power of the lower classes of society some prospect of alleviating their condition. Also the target of Malthus's argument shifts in successive versions of the *Essay*. Whereas the first *Essay* was primarily a polemic against the utopian speculations of Godwin and Condorcet, later editions give more prominence to an extended critical treatment of the poor laws. Throughout, however, the general tendency of Malthus's argument is to demonstrate that well-meaning attempts to ameliorate the condition of the poor, whether through economic redistribution or by institutional reform, can only be self-defeating. Provided with both means and encouragement to increase their families, the poor will be confronted by the positive checks to population in the form of starvation and disease on a new and more terrible scale than before.

As many of Malthus's critics pointed out, the inference from his law of population to his conservative 'laissez-faire' political conclusions could only be sustained if the many causes of both premature death and voluntary reproductive restraint could all be represented as so many mediations of the one ultimate and fundamental case: pressure on the means of subsistence.

Otherwise, the most that can be argued from Malthusian premises is that in the absence of any other limits to population growth, the population would ultimately be limited by the available food supply: not an especially worrying claim from the standpoint of Malthus's critics. Malthus does make some considerable show of demonstrating this interconnectedness of the different causes of premature death. Disease is linked to 'unwholesome occupations' and to overcrowding, and these, in turn, to scarcity of the means of subsistence. In the case of the preventative checks, and moral restraint in particular, the connection is clear: only when the *threat* of poverty and starvation is strongly felt will the necessary self-restraint be forthcoming. The preservation of economic inequality, the family and private property is not only a natural necessity, but also a moral necessity. Where the law of population does not act directly in culling the population, it acts indirectly through social institutions and the rational calculations of human agents in the form of a 'preventative check'. On the basis of this kind of argument, social critics such as Condorcet and Godwin who identify institutions such as private property and the family as the sources of social evil and suffering are seen to have too superficial a view. What they recognize are only secondary immediate causes of a more fundamental, mediate cause: the law of population, whose effects cannot be abrogated.

Now, how much of this conceptual structure is retained in modern 'neo-Malthusian' environmental analysis? My paradigm here will be the immensely influential Club of Rome report *The Limits to Growth*. Commissioned as part of the Club of Rome's Project on the Predicament of Mankind, the centrepiece of the study is a computerized 'world model' which can be used to project future possible states of the world system on various assumptions about past and current trends in key variables. Meadows et al. claim to have identified five major 'factors' (population, industrial production, food production, the use of non-renewable resources, and pollution) whose dynamic interactions are responsible for growth in the world system and ultimate limits to it. The central problem facing human-kind is exponential growth in a complex but finite world.

The world system is currently in a 'growth-phase', which involves exponential growth of both population and industrial production. In both cases negative feedback loops (death rates and capital depreciation) are weak whilst positive ones (birth rates and capital investment) are strong. These are conditions under which growth is exponential — even 'super-exponential' (i.e. magnitudes are increasing with a progressively shorter doubling-time). There are, of course, interconnections between population dynamics and industrialization, which is recognized in the text by the use of the phrase 'population-capital system'. A necessary precondition for population growth is increased food production, whilst both industrial production and agriculture utilize renewable and non-renewable resources, and emit various kinds of pollutant at rates which bear a definite quantifiable relationship to the scale of production itself. This gives us our five basic 'factors' or 'variables' whose interconnections provide the framework for the world-system model.

The central thesis of *The Limits of Growth* is the finitude of the environmental systems which sustain growth in each of these dimensions. Most crucially, agricultural production is limited by the availability of cultivable land, and by the pollution and capital costs of further increases in the intensity of agriculture, whilst industrial growth is dependent on non-renewable energy and raw-material resources which are present in finite quantities. Both industrial and agricultural growth are liable to (as yet imperfectly understood) outer limits to the absorption of pollutants on the part of the hugely complex and delicately balanced world eco-system. Running the model on a range of assumptions — including the most optimistic — about the future growth rates and technological innovations to overcome ecological limits yields a single outcome: growth to and beyond the carrying capacity of the world system, followed by system collapse, with dramatic falls in both industrial production and population. Varying the assumptions has the effect of altering the timescale, but not the general character of the outcome.

Now, there are several points of contact between the approach adopted by Meadows et al. and that of Malthus. Both postulate

outer natural limits which are invulnerable to human intentionality. We may chose to live within these limits — the favoured
option — or we may recklessly proceed as though they did not
exist, in which case they will impose themselves forcibly upon
us. Both draw attention to the 'geometrical', or exponential
character of growth in populations, and the disproportion
between this growth and the potential for sustainable growth
in agricultural production. Both rely on extrapolation of past
trends and empirical relationships for thinking about future
eventualities — both are, in other words, inductive empiricist
in methodology. Both approaches tend to play down qualitative
differences in the organization of societies as of only secondary
causal significance in the face of large-scale natural or quasi-
natural quantitative tendencies and limits. Finally, both forms
of 'natural-limits' analysis appeared in the wake of widespread
popular radicalizations, which traumatized conservative interests. In the case of the Club of Rome — formed from a
meeting of industrialists, civil servants, scientists, economists
and 'educators' in 1968 — a quotation from the preface to *Limits*
is revealing:

> The intent of the project is to examine the complex of problems
> troubling men of all nations: poverty in the midst of plenty;
> degradation of the environment; loss of faith in institutions; un-
> controlled urban spread; insecurity of employment; alienation of
> youth; rejection of traditional values; and inflation and other
> monetary and economic disruptions.[12]

These common features are important, and for many purposes may well justify the epithet 'neo-Malthusianism', but
they must be set against some important differences between
the two approaches. First, Malthus's tendency to represent the
symptoms of scarcity — poverty, starvation, disease and so on —
as a direct or mediated function of the pressure of population on
the food supply is abandoned. Instead Meadows et al. represent
the sources of human pressure on environmental limits as a
combination of population growth and growth in the scale of
industrial production. In the advanced industrial countries,

252

per-capita demands on agricultural and industrial production, consumption of non-renewable resources, and pollution impacts far outweigh comparable per-capita figures for non- and less industrialized countries. These inequalities in both material living standards and environmental pressures are clearly revealed in the data employed by the study.[13] Considered in isolation from industrial growth, population control could not avert the impending environmental catastrophe.[14] However, the method of aggregating data to produce a global dynamic model does have the effect of obscuring the significance of these distributional inequalities, both within and between geographical regions. I'll return to this point.

Secondly, although the argument deployed by Meadows et al. does involve extrapolation of observed growth trends in population and other 'factors', they are quite explicit about the hypothetical and conditional character of the 'predictions' which such extrapolation generates. Malthus oscillated between attempts to ground his 'law' of population growth in available demographic data, and a deductive demonstration of it as a consequence of the fixity of natural sexual desires. Only if the geometrical ratio of increase could be shown, by some such strategy, as the empirical expression of a natural causal power or tendency of populations would the extrapolation be rationally justified as a basis for prediction. Unlike Malthus, Meadows et al. do not attempt to do this. Exponential population growth is taken merely as an *empirical trend*, not a *natural tendency*. The model explicitly builds in a recognition of some of the complex economic, cultural, psychological and technological factors which are known to influence reproductive rates. In particular, Malthus's own model of the considerations which induce voluntary reduction of family size (ability to foresee the difficulty of providing for one's offspring, and fear of the consequent destitution) is abandoned in favour of a more orthodox sociological view of the 'demographic transition'.[15] This is close to a complete inversion of the Malthusian picture.

Third, the world model developed by Meadows et al. attempts to identify a range of distinct respects in which population and capital growth press upon specific environmental limits, and to map the dynamic interactions between them. In addition to food supply they consider renewable and non-renewable energy and mineral resources, thermal and chemical pollution, and so on, as constituting actual or potential limits to growth. This contrasts with Malthus's abstract consideration of 'means of subsistence' as the sole pertinent ecological variable. It is perhaps worth noting here that Darwin's famous reference to the Malthusian population law as a key source for his concept of natural selection is in this respect very misleading. Darwin's own conception of the environmental forces which 'cull' natural populations was much more complex and multi-faceted than the Malthusian one. Darwin says that 'we know not exactly what the checks are in even one single instance', and goes on to speak of the face of nature as 'a yielding surface, with ten thousand wedges packed close together and driven inwards by incessant blows'.[16] It is this Darwinian legacy rather than the Malthusian one which informs the approach adopted in *Limits*, although of course, the specificity of the ecology of the human species is acknowledged.

Finally, the moral and political implications of a recognition of natural limits are profoundly different in the two cases. As we have seen, Malthus's first *Essay* concluded that, in the face of natural limits, attempts at egalitarian and communitarian social transformation would be self-defeating or worse. Though the notion of 'moral restraint' in the later editions gives more space for human intentional regulation of their reproductive rate, the moral and political stance remains unaltered: the social conditions under which this rational capacity could and would be exercised are precisely those (marriage, private property, social and economic inequality) which natural forces would, in the long run, impose in any case.

In sharp contrast, the conclusion of Meadows et al. is that conservatism, simply carrying on as we are, is just not an option.[17] Either we forestall catastrophe by a profound change of institutions, values and practices, or natural forces will impose profound changes of an involuntary kind upon us. Suspending considerations of political plausibility, Meadows et al. use their world model to specify the conditions for long-term sustainability of the world's human population and productive activity. They are:

1. The capital plant and the population are constant in size. The birth rate equals the death rate and the capital investment rate equals the depreciation rate.

2. All input and output rates — births, deaths, investment, and depreciation are kept to a minimum.

3. The levels of capital and population and the ratio of the two are set in accordance with the values of the society. They may be deliberately revised and slowly adjusted as the advance of technology creates new options.[18]

Together these conditions define what the authors call a state of 'global equilibrium'. The authors, understandably enough, duck all of the interesting political and institutional questions about how transitions to such a state might be attained, and set a characteristically technocratic and 'managerialist' priority on improvements in our knowledge of the functioning of socio-economic systems as a precondition for controlling them. But we already do know enough about the dynamics of socio-economic systems to recognize that the state of global equilibrium could not be a condition of society in which capitalist institutions, relations and value perspectives prevailed. The institutions of private property in productive capital and market competition install an economic dynamic in which the progressive expansion of capital must become the overriding priority of that class of economic agents — capitalists of one variety or another — who make investment decisions. Of course, this is only a *tendency* in the system. It is not, as we know, always realized. Capitalist expansion generates its own social-relational and ecological counter-tendencies, but the dispersed and unregulated character of economic decision-making which is intrinsic to the system ensures that such limits are experienced as natural or quasi-natural catastrophes: precisely the pattern which 'global equilibrium' is supposed to avoid. The capacity to regulate and control capital investment in line with socially — even globally — established priorities would require either complete abolition of private property in capital resources, or curtailment of currently recognized property rights on a scale which would presuppose the virtual destruction of the social and political power of capitalist interests. Furthermore, the regulatory capacity to sustain an economic steady state would have to be vested in some authoritative institutional form. This would have either to directly control economic resources, or to have decisive authority over those who (residually) continued to do so. Finally, to globally regulate the pattern and scale of investment in terms of socially established values presupposes the virtually complete abrogation of 'market forces' and profitability, an abolition of what Marx called the 'fetishism of commodities', in favour of a re-socialization of the mechanisms by which productive activity and human needs are adjusted to one another.

But if the conclusions to which Meadows et al. are driven are implicitly anti-capitalist, they are not by this token necessarily socialist. One of the most influential originators of the method of analysis used, Forrester,[19] emphasized the counter-intuitive character of the policy implications of system analysis in a way which favoured an elitist-technocratic form of decision-making as against popular democratic forms. The discussion in *Limits* remains politically indeterminate. Global equilibrium would require a degree of socialization of economic life incompatible with the persistence of capitalist economic relations, but its political preconditions might be met by either an authoritarian-technocratic monopoly of state power, or a popular-democratic and socialist world order.

Marx and Engels on Malthus

Marx and Engels were, along with most other socialist and progressive writers of their time, fiercely critical of Malthus's 'law', and there are numerous references to it throughout their work.[20] Polemics aside, there are two main elements in their critique: a series of arguments purporting to show that the 'law' is neither universal nor necessary in its application to human populations, together with a reconceptualization and alternative explanation of the phenomenon (relative surplus population) which Malthus's law addressed.

Engels, in an early text, argued against Malthus's assumptions about both limitations on agricultural production and the naturalness of population growth. Only one-third of the earth's surface was cultivated as yet. Application of improvements to agricultural technique already known could raise the production of even that third by some sixfold. Moreover, the assumption of an 'at most arithmetical' increase in agricultural production is unjustifiably pessimistic. Scientific knowledge, Engels argued, advances geometrically, so, presumably, does its application in agricultural technique: 'And what is impossible to science?'.[21] As regards population growth, Engels draws upon Malthus's own later concessions to the possibility of intentional regulation through 'moral restraint'. Even if Malthus were right about limits to the increase of agricultural production, then this would only make more urgent still the kind of social transformation which would be needed for moral restraint to be exercised by the mass of the population. Engels, in line with most contemporary critics of Malthus, was here arguing that population growth is not the outcome of a natural tendency, but rather an effect of alterable social conditions. His substantive view of the social conditions under which voluntary family limitation would be encouraged was, of course, very different from Malthus's quasi-naturalistic model, and closer to the conventional wisdom of demographers today.

But Marx and Engels never denied the reality of the phenomena which constituted the empirical basis for Malthus's laws. They rather offered an alternative conceptualization and explanation of them. The contested phenomenon was the persistence of widespread poverty and misery due to lack of availability of means of subsistence for a significant but fluctuating proportion of the population. However, this poverty and misery occurred in the midst of great wealth on the part of some sections of the population, and often in the face of large scale surplus production. Poverty was not a consequence, therefore, of shortage of means of subsistence, but of the means to *purchase* them. The surplus population was surplus relative to the available means of paid employment, rather than means of subsistence as such. In *Capital* Marx explains this 'reserve army of labour' as an effect, *specific to capitalism*, of the long-run tendency for variable capital to decline as a proportion of total capital employed (i.e. in essence, for technological advance to displace labour). This variable 'reserve army of labour' is also functional for capital in producing a source of extra labour in periods of rapid economic expansion, in offsetting the power of organized workers, and in providing competitive downward pressure on the wages and conditions of those in employment.

What Malthus had attributed to the (direct or mediated) effects of a (quasi) natural law of population, Marx and Engels explained as the outcome of a historically specific economic mechanism. Whatever might be said of some hypothetical future, poverty and scarcity as currently (and foreseeably) encountered were the historically transitory consequences of capitalist economic relations: a *socially*, not a *naturally* imposed limit.

Taken together, these arguments are decisive against Malthus. First, in so far as Malthus's law has any validity, its status (properly reformulated) is that of a law of specifically *capitalist* accumulation, not that of a universal regularity affecting human populations at whatever historical stage, or combined in whatever social forms. Second, Malthus's law fails as an explanation of economic insecurity and poverty in capitalist societies. Enough food is, or, at any rate can be, produced to feed everyone. Persistent poverty and malnutrition is an effect of specific economic relations and social forms. Thirdly, the arguments are decisive against Malthus's political conclusions. No law of nature stands in the way of a social transformation aimed at abolishing hunger, poverty and unmet need. Even the restraint of population growth desired by Malthus himself could only be achieved as a result of such a social transformation.

It was, of course, the requirement to defeat Malthus's anti-socialist conclusions which necessitated Marx and Engels's engagement with his population theory, and, in turn, disposed them against this theory as a form of natural-limits epistemic conservatism. Even as late as the 'Critique of the Gotha Programme', Marx continues to make this link:

> But if this theory is correct, then again I can*not* abolish the law even if I abolish wage labour a hundred times over, because the law then governs not only the system of wage labour but *every* social system. Basing themselves directly on this, the economists have been proving for fifty years and more that socialism cannot abolish poverty, which has its basis in nature, but can only make it *general*, distribute it simultaneously over the whole surface of society! [22]

Understandably, then, Marx and Engels were for political reasons strongly disposed against arguments which, like that of Malthus, postulated natural limits to the power of human transformative projects. This predisposition was further buttressed by their experience of the dynamism of modern industrial production: something of which Malthus himself could have had but little comprehension. Albeit in a distorted and estranged form, modern industry demonstrated the seemingly boundless power of human ingenuity and social combination to transcend all natural limits. Finally, the very indifference of capital as self-expanding value to the concrete character of the specific labour, raw materials and use-values in which it was embodied furthered the illusion of a historical movement subject only to the limits imposed by its own inner contradictions.

In line with this idealist, utopian moment in the thinking of Marx and Engels are the most obvious readings of many of their comments on Malthus. Engels, for example, went so far as to say:

> Thanks to this theory, as to economics as a whole, our attention has been drawn to the productive power of the earth and of mankind; and after overcoming this economic despair we have been made *for ever secure against the fear of over-population*. [23]

Often, too, when Marx and Engels wrote about long-term directional processes in human history, and especially about the significance of the eventual transition to a communitarian future, the image of a progressive transcendence of nature-imposed limits and a consequent human mastery over the natural world was invoked. For example, Engels says:

> The whole sphere of the conditions of life which environ man, and which have hitherto ruled man, now comes under the dominion and control of man, who for the first time becomes the real, conscious lord of Nature, because he has now become master of his own social organisation. [24]

In *Capital*, too, Marx speaks of the emancipatory content of the future communist society in terms of a 'realm of freedom' which presupposes the prior historical development of human productive powers, together with the cooperative social regulation of their exercise. [25] Emancipation presupposes transcendence of both natural limits themselves, and the quasi-natural limits imposed by unregulated social powers. In his early writings Marx employs rather different metaphors in characterizing the future relation between nature and humanity: visions of reconciliation, and 'humanization' of nature are prominent. But though these images avoid the 'Promethean' connotations of struggle and domination, the content Marx gives to them has an unmistakably anthropocentric, utopian and idealist moment: nature will be only fully humanized when its surface everywhere bears the imprint of human purposive activity. This is a reconciliation with nature on terms decided by human kind itself. But however arguable the normative content of these ideas, their ontological foundations cannot be reconciled with Marx's more deep-rooted naturalistic and materialistic cast of thought. This notion of the 'humanization' of nature is barely capable of sustaining a view of the reality of the natural world independent of human intentional activity and consciousness. [26]

As I have suggested, these idealist and utopian moments in the thought of Marx and Engels may have been sustained by both the transformative power of nineteenth-century industrial production and the indifference to the concrete, material character of the elements of production of specifically capitalist forms of economic calculation. They were also most prominent in their polemics against 'natural-limits' conservatives, such as Malthus and his followers. Probably for all three reasons, some of the most basic concepts of the 'mature' economic theory of Marx and Engels suffer from a serious under-theorization or misrecognition of the material limits and preconditions of human interaction with nature. These defects, in turn, weaken the explanatory power of Marxism in relation to specifically ecological crisis-tendencies of capitalism, as well as conceptually impoverishing the Marxian view of socialist emancipation itself.

Labour: Intentional Structures and Natural Limits?

I have space here for only a brief and dogmatic exposition of some of these idealist and utopian features of Marxian thought. When, in *Capital*, Marx comes to define the labour-process as 'the everlasting Nature-imposed condition of human existence', his thinking is resolutely naturalistic and materialist. We are and must always remain, dependent upon interaction with non-human nature for the meeting of our needs. Staying at this level of abstraction (i.e. specifying transhistorical necessities consequent upon our status as natural beings, and independently of any *specific* form of human society or stage in the development of our productive powers), Marx distinguishes three 'elementary factors' of the labour-process: the personal activity of man (work), the subject of that work, and its instruments. The process itself is an activity in which these elements are brought into appropriate relationships with one another, and set in motion:

> In the labour-process . . . man's activity, with the help of the instruments of labour, effects an alteration, designed from the commencement, in the material worked upon. The process disappears in the product; the latter is a use-value, Nature's material adapted by a change of form to the wants of man.[27]

Marx's paradigm here is clearly some form of craft-labour, in which instruments are used to transform a raw material into a form appropriate to the meeting of a pre-existing human requirement. It is significant to note that the non-human elements (and sometimes human elements — such as limbs and bodily powers, too) figure in Marx's conceptualization under a principle of classification which relates them to human intentions, i.e. as 'instruments', 'subjects', 'products'. One and the same material, or object, might figure as 'product' of one labour-process, and as 'instrument' in another. The material characteristics and causal powers of these material elements in the labour-process figure in Marx's conceptualization of it *only in so far as* they are involved in the realization of human purposes in the process. It is this which constitutes the principle of their classification, and not their causal powers as such. Marx's account of the labour-process is an attempt to display, therefore, what I call its 'intentional structure'.

Now, there are several important respects in which reliance on *this particular* intentional structure for thinking generally about the forms of human need-meeting interaction with nature is misleading. First, the centrality of the idea of adapting nature to the wants of 'man'. This neglects the significance for human wellbeing of a whole range of technologies which are better characterized as enlarging the capacity of humans to adapt to natural forces and conditions which are themselves not subject to intentional manipulation: shelter, clothing and medicine, though they each, of course, do have transformative moments and presuppositions, nevertheless share this broad character of enlarging our capacity to survive and flourish despite unfavourable environmental conditions, as distinct from enabling us to transform those conditions themselves.

Second, even where nature itself is acted upon with the intention of adjusting its forces and mechanisms to our purposes, Marx's abstract characterization of the labour-process is misleading. Two classes of labour-process, in particular, can be shown to have an entirely different intentional structure. In a whole range of 'primary' labour-processes, materials, objects and living beings already exist in nature in a form appropriate to human uses. To make these available for use as industrial raw materials, building materials, food, and so on does require deliberate human intervention, in the shape of various practices such as hunting, gathering, mining, collecting and transporting. In each case, the intentional structure of the labour process is one of *selectively appropriating*, rather than transforming the subject of labour. Where and when the labour-process is performed is determined by naturally given patterns of distribution of the material and beings appropriated, and also naturally given developmental rhythms in the case of living beings. Effective performance of such labour-processes requires both practical skills and sophisticated knowledge of these naturally given patterns and rhythms. Such conditions enter indispensably into agents' calculations.

A second class of labour-processes, including agriculture, horticulture, forestry and animal husbandry, do centrally involve transformation but in these cases the principal transformations are naturally given organic ones, rather than direct outcomes of human transformative powers. The ripening of seed and fruit, the maturation and fattening of livestock, and so on, are organic processes whose conditions are optimized by effective agricultural and other labour-processes. In these cases, work is performed on the environmental conditions which favour natural developmental processes. These occur and have a dynamic which, beyond definite limits, is insusceptible to human intentional manipulation. Once land is appropriated for agricultural and other uses, subsequent labour-processes upon it are primarily eco-regulative, rather than 'transformative'. Again, these practices are highly dependent upon naturally given conditions, locations and temporal rhythms such as soil properties, climate and seasons. The 'intentional structure' of such labour processes is one of sustaining and optimizing conditions for the organic development of selected species or varieties of organisms, rather than of transforming a raw material into a useful product. Again, such practices are highly dependent on agents' knowledge of the non-manipulable material conditions and contexts of the labour-process, so that such conditions enter indispensably into agents' calculations.

Marx's conceptual focus on productive-transformative intentional structures at the expense of eco-regulatory and primary appropriative ones was understandable given the increasing social, economic and political weight of industrial production in nineteenth-century Europe. But it nevertheless rendered his theoretical system — like that of the Classical Political Economists whom he criticized in other respects — insufficiently sensitive to the permanent dependence of all human interaction with their natural environment on naturally given materials and resources, climatic conditions, chemical cycles, patterns of global energy-flow and so on. Precisely because, by and large, the presence or abundant availability of such conditions and resources (fresh air and water, for example) could be taken as 'given' they did not figure in the intentional structure of industrial labour-processes, nor in the conceptual structure of the economic theories of the period.

Of course, more than a century later, it is now widely recognized that the nature and scale of human interactions with nature have produced unforeseen and/or unintended consequences (exhaustion of non-renewable resources, various categories of pollution and so on) which constitute a progressive destruction of the sustaining conditions of such practices themselves. Such conditions can no longer, in other words, be taken as 'given', but must enter into the calculations of economic agents, even those concerned with industrial production, and into the theoretical structure of the economic theories of our times. This is the main historical reason why the limitations in the classical Marxian critique of Malthus have acquired an importance for us which they did not have for Marx and Engels themselves.

However, these criticisms of Marx and Engels, important though they can now be seen to be, are directed against what is only one moment or tendency in their writing. I now want to indicate, all too briefly, how, appropriately corrected, Marxian political economy provides both the basis for a powerful explanation of the ecological crisis tendencies of specifically capitalist societies, and also the conceptual means for a critical transcendence of the 'neo-Malthusian' tradition of environmental analysis.

First, it is necessary to develop and correct Marx's own

comments on the labour-process, recognizing and elaborating a typology of distinct intentional structures, of which the 'raw materials/instruments/transformative labour/product' structure is only one. Secondly, it has to be recognized as a trans-historically necessary feature of all forms of human socio-economic existence that productive-transformative labour processes presuppose and necessitate primary-appropriative and eco-regulatory ones. These cannot be written off, as Marx and Engels sometimes tend to do when they are thinking schematically of the historical process, as forms of humanity/nature interaction characteristic of earlier, superseded historical phases. Though in modern capitalist societies they may not be the most economically dynamic sectors, and may also be marginal from the standpoint of global class relations and conflicts, from the standpoint of the genesis of environmental contradictions they represent the key 'nodes' at which the tendency of these economic forms to push beyond their conditions of sustainability is most concentrated.

Marx's own account of capitalist production theorizes it as dominated by a dual intentional structure: as *capitalist* production it is dominated by the value-maximizing intentional structure of capital accumulation, with its blindness to material conditions and elements, and as productive *labour-process* it is governed by a means/ends schema of intentional action which is more or less indifferent to 'given' non-manipulable material conditions and contexts. Finally, the dispersed and unregulated character of economic decision-making, intrinsic to capitalism, implies an absence of socialized normative regulation of productive interaction with nature. In the early *Manuscripts* this feature is recognized in the concept of estrangement from nature, and the consequent instrumental character of human labour under regimes of private property. Taking these three features together, capitalism can be characterized as an economic form whose intrinsic expansionary dynamic lacks adequate means of recognizing, monitoring and regulating its own extrinsic conditions and effects.

In itself, this is, however, insufficient for an understanding of the specific liability of capitalism to generate ecological crises. For this, it is necessary to supplement Marx's account of the labour-process (itself suitably qualified, as suggested above) as an intentional structure with a non-anthropocentric conceptualization of the *specific configuration* of material conditions, contexts and systematic environmental interconnections the persistence of which is necessary for the sustainability of the process. This must include a specification of the structure of causal mechanisms and powers of those materials and objects involved in and presupposed by the practice *independently* of those picked out in the conceptualization of its intentional structure. Only if this is done will it be possible to analyse the generation of what might be called 'the naturally mediated unintended consequences' of intentional action upon nature. A full specification of the capitalist mode of production, then, would incorporate both intentional and non-intentional specifications of the labour-process as a form of appropriation of nature, combined with a social relational specification of it as a distinct form of domination and exploitation of labour.[28] Such a theorization *would* be capable of identifying natural limits to specifically capitalist expansion and analysing the consequences of its dynamic tendency to exceed these limits.

Generalizing such an explanatory strategy would involve the construction of concepts of each of the principal economic forms of society, or modes of production, as specific forms of *structured articulation* of a set of systematically interconnected material mechanisms, conditions and contexts *together with* a social-relational form with its intrinsic dynamic tendencies and/or contradictions. Of course, this is an extremely abstract and provisional statement of a point of departure. The crucial work of giving 'flesh and bones' to these proposals, and revising them in ways that may well turn out to be necessary, still remain to be done. In particular, it will be necessary to take into account empirical material on the geographical variations and historical phases in the technical basis of each 'mode of production', so as to arrive at a view of the material/environmental conditions and limits of each social-technical form. Fraught with difficulties though it is, such a project of concept construction is necessary if Marxian economic theory is to be rendered consistent with its own materialist and naturalistic philosophical premises, and with those many broad features of the theory of history advocated by Marx and Engels which give a central place to human need–meeting interaction with nature. It would transcend the sterile opposition between natural–limits conservatisms of the Malthusian kind, on the one hand, and knee-jerk social constructionism, on the other.

As the above analysis of one modern form of neo-Malthusianism has shown, a recognition of natural limits does not necessitate politically conservative conclusions. Expanding the scope and flexibility of human adaptability in the face of natural limits which are invulnerable to intentional manipulation is no less rich in emancipatory possibilities than the Promethean 'transformationist' project, which must now be approaching its close as a phase in human history. But where an appropriately revised Marxian perspective can offer insights unavailable to contemporary neo-Malthusianism is in the clear recognition that natural limits cannot be specified independently of an analysis of the *social-relational dynamics* of each form of appropriation of nature. The authors of the *Limits* acknowledge that their world model lacks any adequate specification of the socio-economic and political limits to growth. They rely for their projections on a notion of outer *physical limits* to the carrying capacity of the planet, considered in abstraction from anything but a globally aggregated quantitative assessment of the dynamics of production and population. But if each form of economic life has its *own* distinctive pattern and dynamic of structured interaction with its *own distinctive* material presuppositions, conditions and contexts then the analytical strategy of the *Limits* cannot be well founded. However, what their analysis does show, against all forms of idealist-utopian would-be radicalism is that any sustainable emancipatory strategy — and this must mean *any* genuinely emancipatory strategy at all — must build a conception of natural limits, of a natural order which is only partially vulnerable to human intentional projects, into the very core of its vision of the future.

Notes

1. Sir K.R. Popper, *The Poverty of Historicism*, London: Routledge & Kegan Paul 1961.

2. J. Porritt, *Seeing Green*, Oxford: Blackwell 1984.

3. A valuable reading of Marx which gives emphasis to these themes is Kate Soper's contribution to this volume (chapter 11). Among the most well-known recent attempts to synthesize socialist and environmentalist perspectives are the writings of A. Gorz and R. Bahro (see especially André Gorz, *Ecology as Politics*, London: Pluto 1980; Rudolf Bahro, *Socialism and Survival*, London: Heretic 1982, and *From Red to Green*, London: Verso 1984). See also M. Ryle, *Ecology and Socialism*, London: Pluto 1988.

4. K.J. Walker 'Ecological Limits and Marxian Thought', *Politics* XIV, 1979, provides a very useful commentary on Marxist responses to environmentalism, whilst H.M. Enzensberger, 'Critique of Political Ecology', *New Left Review*, March/April 1974, pp. 3–31 (reprinted in *Dreamers of the Absolute*, London: Radius 1988) is a classic expression of Marxist ambiguity towards it.

5. D. Eversley, quoted in H. Newby, *Green and Pleasant Land?*, London: Wildwood 1979.

6. A very preliminary sketch for a view of needs which is designed to displace the concept of a hierarchy of needs is given in Ted Benton, 'Humanism = Speciesism? Marx on Humans and Animals', *Radical Philosophy* 50, 1988, especially pp. 14–15.

7. Enzensberger (Dreamers of the Absolute, pp. 267ff.), for example, uses this term to characterize writers such as the Ehrlichs (P.R. Ehrlich, *The Population Bomb*, New York: Ballantine 1968; P.R. and A.H. Ehrlich, *Population, Resources, Environment*, San Francisco: W.H. Freeman 1970). though he is also critical of the irrational 'voluntarism' of those Marxists who reject all forms of population-limitation policy. K.J. Walker also notes the dependence of many modern Marxist criticisms of environmentalism on a presumed identification of modern environmentalism with Malthusianism.

8. O. O'Neil, *Faces of Hunger*, London: Allen and Unwin 1979.

9. T.R. Malthus, *An Essay on the Principle of Population*, ed. A.G.N. Flew, Harmondsworth: Penguin 1970, p. 72.

10. Ibid., p. 70.

11. T.R. Malthus, *An Essay on Population*, 2 vols, London: Everyman 1960.

12. D.H. Meadows et al., *The Limits to Growth*, London: Pan 1972.

13. Ibid. See, for example, table 4 and figure 14.

14. See pp. 160–1.

15. Roughly, that industrialization, with consequent improvements in material living standards, welfare provision and economic security, *encourages* voluntary family limitation.

16. C. Darwin, *The Origin of Species*, ed. J.W. Burrow, Harmondsworth: Penguin 1968.

17. Of course, other modern 'neo-Malthusians' *are* more Malthusian in their political conclusions. Some, such as G. Hardin ('Tragedy of the Commons' in J. Ban, ed., *The Environmental Handbook*, London: Pan 1971;

and 'Lifeboat Ethics: the Case Against Helping the Poor' in W.G. Aiken and H. La Fochette, eds, *World Hunger and Moral Obligations*, New Jersey: Prentice Hall 1977) are very close to the original Malthusian 'do nothing and let nature take its course', whereas others focus on population control in the poorer countries. This latter conclusion is ruled out for Meadows et al. given their recognition of the problem as one of the *combined* effects of economic and population growth.

18. Meadows et al.

19. See J.W. Forrester, *Urban Dynamics*, Cambridge, Mass: MIT Press 1969; and 'Counterintuitive Behaviour of Social Systems', *Technology Review* 83, 1971, pp. 52–68.

20. See R.L. Meek, *Marx and Engels on the Population Bomb*, Berkeley: Ramparts 1971.

21. K. Marx and F. Engels, *Collected Works*, Vol. 3, London: Lawrence and Wishart 1975, pp. 439–40.

22. L.S. Feuer, ed., *Marx and Engels: Basic Writings on Politics and Philosophy*, London: Fontana 1969, p. 165.

23. Marx and Engels, p. 439. Emphasis added.

24. Feuer, pp. 149–50.

25. K. Marx, *Capital*, Vol. 3, London: Lawrence and Wishart 1972, Ch. 48.

26. Benton, pp. 3–18.

27. K. Marx, *Capital*, Vol. 1, London: Lawrence and Wishart, p. 76.

28. There are places where Marx himself does attempt to do this, for example in a remarkable passage in *Capital*, Vol. III, p. 818:

> We have seen that the capitalist process of production is a historically determinate form of the social process of production in general. The latter is as much a production process of the material conditions of human life as a process taking place under specific historical and economic production relations, producing and reproducing these production relations themselves, and thereby also the bearers of this process, their material conditions of existence and their mutual relations, i.e. their particular socio-economic form. For the aggregate of these relations, in which the agents of this production stand with respect to Nature and to one another, and in which they produce, is precisely society, considered from the standpoint of its economic structure.

This is remarkable especially in that Marx clearly intends to include relations between agents of production and their material conditions within the economic structure, as well as to consider the production process as involving production and reproduction of its own material conditions. Where the materialism of this approach is vitiated, it seems to me, is in its failure to include within the conceptualization those material conditions which are presupposed by, and may be unintentionally modified by, the production process, but which are neither produced nor reproduced by it (non-renewable resources, climatic and geological conditions, and so on).

11

Greening Prometheus: Marxism and Ecology

Kate Soper

For the first time in history, ecology is moving to the centre-stage of politics. Its arrival there is long overdue, and may have come too late. But it seems unreasonable now to doubt that so long as a forum for politics remains, it will be deeply involved with matters of ecology. Indeed, it is now clear that the fate of the planet and its various species, including our own, now hangs on the nature and depth of the green revolution we manage to effect.

It is this centre-staging of ecology which has inclined many to herald the green movement as the most important radical force for social change since the development of socialism, and particularly Marxist socialism, in the nineteenth century.[1] The comparison is telling insofar as it captures the here-to-stay quality of ecological pressure: just as nothing was ever quite the same again after the *Communist Manifesto*, so we can safely assume that no politics in future will be able to ignore the greens. It also brings out the contrast between the attention now being paid to ecological arguments and hedonist projections, and the almost total neglect in the past of green alarms and utopias.[2]

However, the counterposing of socialism to ecology which is implied in this approach to the coming of the greens is very misleading. For just as socialism can only hope to remain a radical and benign pressure for social change if it takes on the

271

ecological dimension, so the ecological concern will remain largely ineffective (and certainly incapable of reversing the current trends in the manner required) if it is not associated in a very integral way with many traditional socialist demands, such as assaulting the global stranglehold of multinational capital.

Obviously, there are now many avowed 'eco-socialists' who recognize this truth and are committed to the 'red–green' synthesis. Some would even insist that the 'socialism' in question here should be given a strongly Marxian interpretation (which does not at all mean asociating it with the practices of 'actually existing socialism'). Others, I think, would prefer simply to make clear that the 'socialism' they are advocating is neither the labourism or social democratic reformism associated with the European socialist parties, nor Soviet-style Communism. But there are many 'greens', both in and out of the Green Parties, who are very suspicious of any socialist, let alone Marxist, vocabulary; and some too, I believe, among the 'eco-socialists' who remain very uncomfortable with an explicitly Marxian form of argument. It is this sense, fairly pervasive in green circles, that even if socialism and ecology might recognize a kinship, Marxism and ecology are much harder to splice and may even belong to hostile tribes, which sets the agenda for this article. I am not attempting here to deal with the range of issues raised under the broader 'eco-socialist' concept, but proposing to confine myself to the narrower task of considering the relations between ecological and specifically *Marxist* argument. In what follows, then, I shall discuss the reasons behind the resistance among green thinkers to Marxism, consider how far they are justified, and put forward some themes of Marxist argument which need to be weighed in the balance before any final judgement is delivered on Marx's ecological credentials.

Why the Marx Allergy?

There are three main reasons why Marxism has been thought to be no friend of ecology. Of these, the most important is probably not primarily intellectual but political. It derives from the association of Marxism with the societies of 'actual existing socialism' and their Communist Party support. It derives, that is, from the link between Marxism and the politics (until very lately) of Stalinism and neo-Stalinism and the economic practice which has brought some of the worst pollution and environmental degradation in the industrial world to the countries of central and eastern Europe.[3] Large parts of Poland and Czechoslovakia are now designated ecological disaster zones, and the situation is not greatly better in the other Soviet bloc countries, including some parts of the USSR itself (especially post-Chernobyl). The problem, here, of course, does not stem in some abstract fashion from the imposition of socialist methods of economic organization, but from their use in a 'catch-up-and-overtake' pursuit of capitalist styles and levels of consumption.[4] Nevertheless, it was this particular use of the powers of socialist planning together with its totalitarian political integument, which was foisted upon the peoples of central and eastern Europe in the name of 'Marxism-Leninism' and the association between the practice and its supposed 'theory' is one that is understandable, even if Marx and Engels would have been amazed and dismayed by the 'socialism' to which their names have been annexed.

The second main reason for ecological suspicion of Marxism is more theoretical. It relates to the argument of historical materialism itself, which seems to accord priority to the 'development of the productive forces' as a criterion and goal of social progress, which makes appeals to an era of communist 'abundance', and attaches importance to the advanced technological infrastructure which capitalism will bequeath to the socialist post-revolutionary forces of renewal. The 'productivist' dynamics of this portrayal of human development, the associated faith in the virtues of technical growth, the implied anthropocentric and instrumental attitudes to the rest of nature: all this is more or less diametrically opposed, it seems, to the green emphases on sustainability, on *re*productive rather than growth economies, on *de*-industrialization, on sober consumption and on a more humble and holistic approach to world ecological balance.

Of course, as we shall see in what follows, the 'productivist' and 'technocratic' Marx is not the only Marx. Moreover, even those texts (the 1859 Preface to the 'Critique of Political Economy', for example) which lend themselves most directly to a 'technological determinist' reading of historical materialism,[5] demand a more qualified and sceptical appraisal as guides to the 'true' Marxist theory when placed in the context of Marx's work as a whole. Nonetheless, although it may be a caricature in certain respects, the 'green' perception of historical materialism as anti-ecological is not entirely without justification; there are even some self-styled Marxists who would defend the less green aspects of Marxism as distinguishing its own point of view from the Arcadian nostalgias of the socialist utopians. By the same token, greens find, unsurprisingly, a deep vein of incompatibility between their own and the Marxist projections of progress and its means of achievement. Some of these points have been brought together in Rudolf Bahro's argument:

> Our customary idea of the transition to socialism is the abolition of the capitalist order within the basic conditions European civilisation has created in the field of technique and technology — and not in Europe alone. Even in this century, a thinker as profound as Antonio Gramsci was still able to view technique, industrialisation, Americanism, the Ford system in its existing form as by and large an inescapable necessity, and thus depict socialism as the genuine executor of human adaptation to modern machinery and technology. Marxists have so far rarely considered that humanity has not only to transform its relations of production, but must also fundamentally transform the entire character of its mode of production, i.e. the productive forces, the so-called technostructure. It must not see its perspective as bound up with any historically transmitted form of the development of needs and their satisfaction, or of the world of products designed for that purpose. The commodity world that we find around us is not in its present form a necessary condition of human existence. It does not have to look the way it does in order for human beings to develop both intellectually and emotionally as far as we would like.[6]

In addition, and thirdly, many greens would challenge the

adequacy and relevance today of the Marxist class-based analysis and revolutionary strategy.[7] How, it is asked, when we are dealing with such universal, trans-class problems as those of resource attrition, the depletion of the ozone layer, Arctic pollution, the greenhouse effect, and so forth, can it be thought appropriate to approach them purely in class terms or to suggest that we must see through the class struggle to its goal of proletarian emancipation before we can hope for any satisfactory resolution of the ecological crisis? In any case, if emancipation is conceived — as it often has been in Communist Party circles — in terms of increased productivity and expanded consumption, it must exacerbate rather than counter resource-exhaustion and pollution. Indeed, even when it comes to the management of the ecological crisis within any nation-state, and the adjustment of its social inequalities, the Marxist recipe of 'working-class victory' is regarded as increasingly unconvincing given the fragmentation of the traditional proletarian class, the economic advancement of many of its members relative to those occupying traditional petty-bourgeois and middle-class jobs, and the political impotence of all the most economically and socially deprived sectors of contemporary capitalist society. Industrial workers, moreover, driven by the logic of capital into putting job security before every other consideration, are by no means the first constituency to which one looks for protection of the environment — a point brought home rather forcefully by the posting of an unofficial blacklist at the Trawsfynydd power station by which union members were advised which local shops had put up posters for an anti-nuclear meeting.[8] Not all greens would agree that these developments have rendered any form of class politics obsolete. Many would accept, in fact, that ours is still very much a class society, and that the capitalists are, as ever, firmly in control and having the best of everything. But even the more eco-socialist vein within the green movement would insist that the orthodoxy of 'class struggle' needs considerable re-thinking if it is to be anything more than a ritual response to the grotesque exploitations — both human and ecological — of our times.

275

Of Alienation and Fetishism

I shall in a moment suggest some reasons for qualifying the picture of Marxism as inherently unfriendly to green arguments. Nonetheless, I think it would be doing a disservice to Marx and Marxism to attempt to claim that there is really no target at all for the green attack. The Marxist corpus is a large one, and it is always possible to bend the stick of interpretation, dispute the meanings placed on various texts, and so on, and come up with a somewhat different picture. But that is not the point. The point is rather that there are without doubt significant elements of the Marxist argument which either directly conflict with much green thinking, or are too under-elaborated for us to claim definitively that they do not. Inversely, however, I would argue that a disservice is done to the green cause by all those who refuse to recognize these ambiguities in Marxism or to admit that there are any aspects at all of its outlook which are more consonant with their own position. For there certainly are themes in Marx which are not only congruent with current ecological critique, but which powerfully reinforce it. They are also of some importance in what they imply for the economic and political strategies essential to its progress.

In the first place, there is the definite green slant of the arguments around the concept of 'alienation' (and the related notions of 'reification' and 'fetishism'). When green critics make use of the term 'alienation' to describe the bleak environments and impersonal relations resulting from industrialization they may acknowledge a debt to Marxist theory. But the deeper pertinence of the theory of alienation is seldom recognized. For what Marx meant by alienation (and his usage of the term is here formally consistent with Hegel's)[9] is a process whereby a 'subject' conceives 'itself' as subservient to an external and supposedly quite independent objectivity of which 'it' is 'itself', in reality, the creative source. If we think of the 'subject' here as the contemporary market society, then there is no doubt of the extent to which 'it' assumes 'itself' to be held in thrall to those very same economic determinations (financial investments, interest rates, inflationary tendencies, and the like) which 'it' is 'itself' — through the cumulative acts of its various individual members — responsible for setting in motion. When green critics, for example, challenge the rhetoric which speaks of the 'critical condition' of the pound as if it were a patient in a hospital bed (now rallying and able to take some nourishment from the decline of the dollar, now falling back, and so on); when they denounce the perversion of a society which needs to export more Cindy dolls before it can afford the luxury of child kidney dialysis; when they point out how far economic forces are in the saddle and riding us — what else are they doing if not exposing what Marx referred to as capitalist 'alienation'?[10]

Let us not forget, either, that the attack on alienation goes together with a most passionate denunciation of the fetishism of money and of the subordination through the 'cash-nexus' of all other values to those of commercial profit. 'Money', thunders Marx in the *1844 Manuscripts* is the 'general distorting of all individualities and conversion of them into their opposites'; it

> transforms fidelity into infidelity, love into hate, virtue into vice, vice into virtue, servant into master, master into servant, idiocy into intelligence and intelligence into idiocy . . . it is the world upside-down — the confounding of all natural and human qualities . . .

These, and other similar polemics against the inverted values of bourgeois society may not be green in the strict sense of relating explicitly to the destruction of the natural environment. But they are certainly fired with the same sense of revolt against the philistine and mercenary tendencies of the market society which moves so much of the green critique at the present time.

There is also, at the very least, a family resemblance between much contemporary green argument and Marx's more theoretical discussion around the notion of fetishism in the chapter on 'commodity fetishism' at the beginning of *Capital*. Jeremy Seabrook, for example, has recently drawn attention to the 'magic of the markets' through which the 'blood and filth and pain' which attend the creation of the products of Western affluence are miraculously washed away by the money which can afford to buy them:

One of the most extraordinary by-products of the information-rich society is the creation of a kind of un-knowing, even ignorance, that is strangely at odds with the profuse means of communication that they have at their command. Indeed, some observers have seen in this process a human-made replica of older patterns of natural ignorance, whereby people today have become as unaware of the origin, the violence, the exploitation involved in the production of everyday articles and necessities as the peasantry was unaware of the forces that governed the rhythm of lives in bondage to the vagaries of the seasons and to the owners of the earth they cultivated. A new and artificial techno-peasantry is in the making: it is to this version of pauperizing people in the rich countries that the advertising industry is dedicated.[12]

If we think of the central thesis of the theory of 'commodity fetishism' as consisting in the claim that the exchange economy masks the source of value creation in human labouring, then there are obvious parallels between it and Seabrook's arguments about the ingenuity with which the global market cultivates a modern consumer ignorance of the productive context of the commodity. Where the emphases differ, it is not so much because of any major theoretical incompatibility but in virtue of the specific conditions of modern capitalist production on which Seabrook is focusing — in particular, the relegation of so much of the Dickensian world of suffering and exploitation to the Third World 'perimeter'. The 'veil of ignorance' about the source of the commodity is today that much easier to draw because the pre-packaged item on the supermarket shelf is often enough remote by several continents from the misery and pollution of its production, not merely by the distance between high street and local factory. Or as Seabrook himself puts it, 'the separation of consumers from producers has been one of the greatest triumphs of the global capitalist market. . . . The de-industrialization of Britain has been accompanied by a loss both of consciousness and memory'.[13] And the further effect of this separation, of course, is that it obscures not only the source of value of the commodity, but also the environmental damage which so often accompanies its production.

Of Fish and Men

Underlying these Marxist arguments on alienation and fetishism there is an ontological thesis of particular relevance to current green debates. This is to the effect that the human species is self-creating through its productive and labouring activity. Marx depicts this as a process simultaneously involving a 'humanization' of nature and a 'naturalization' of the human. By the technologies whereby we extract and utilize resources in the satisfaction of human requirements, we 'transform' the natural world, and the environment itself thus comes to bear the imprint (whether sealed in the field pattern or the cement of the airstrip) of our particular patterning of need. At the same time, since we are creatures dependent upon an objective environment for becoming the subjects that we are, we thereby create our own 'nature': we are returned to ourselves, so to speak, through the objective products of our industry, since these provide the context for all our aesthetic, moral and cognitive experience. This in turn implies that such experience must itself be viewed as the outcome of dialectical mediation: our subjective needs and senses (of sight, taste, and so on) acquire their objective existence in the products we create for their satisfaction, and these then condition our subjective sensibility and mould our future needs, aesthetic sense, and so forth.

Marx regards this 'ontology of labour' as distinctive to the human species: humanity, he claims, differs from other animal species in producing in the form of an objective accumulation of cultural artefacts, languages, knowledges and institutions: a stock pre-existing the individual and determining upon social life in general, but acting as an external matrix of behaviour rather than in the manner of a biological inheritance. It is this contrast between the objective store of skills and knowledges available to humankind, and the restriction of other animals to those aptitudes which are genetically transmitted, which explains the ever-widening gap between animal and human capacities (whether to do good or ill) and it is associated in the Marxist argument with the possession of reflexive consciousness, and this in turn with our capacity to value:

> Man freely confronts his product. An animal forms objects only in accordance with the standard and the need of the species to which it belongs, while man knows how to produce in accordance with the standard of every species and knows how to apply everywhere the highest standard to the object. Man therefore also forms objects in accordance with the laws of beauty.[14]

Now this last is obviously an anthropocentric and somewhat dubious claim. It is not at all clear that man *does* know how to produce 'in accordance with the standard of every species', or even what that might mean. If it means, for example, that we can produce the honeycomb or spider's web, then it is simply untrue — though we might, perhaps, be able to produce to bee or spider standards in the sense of making artificial replicas of combs or webs.[15] Nor is it clear what Marx means by saying that man knows 'how to apply everywhere the highest standard to the object' given that the one thing that 'man' seems everywhere given to quarrelling about is what constitutes the 'highest standard'.

That said, Marx is surely right to direct attention to *valuing*, and the associated symbolic and aesthetic capacities, as distinctive to humanity, since it would seem true that we alone of organic nature are able to stand back to applaud or condemn the effects of our activities on the rest of nature. Indeed, ecological or any other form of social critique only makes sense in the light of the acceptance of our distinguishing powers of self-evaluation and self-change.[16] The ecologists do not address themselves to the AIDS virus, the musk-rat, the Dutch elm beetle, the garden weed, or any other of nature's seemingly less eco-friendly species, precisely because it is assumed they lack the capacity to mend their ways or even to perceive the evil of them.[17] (This, incidentally, is not to say the human species *will* manage to mend its ways but only to point out that the potentiality for it to do so is presupposed by any critical attack on its existing practice.)

Marx is also surely right to direct attention, through his 'ontology of labour', not only to the ways we change the rest of nature, but to the ways in which our own nature is thereby changed. This is an important dialectic to sustain against the opposing essentialisms of both crude Enlightenment and 'deep ecology' outlooks. Neither the picture of a rational humanity locked in struggle with an essentially 'hostile' nature, nor its inversion in the idea of an essentially benevolent and blameless nature victimized by an instrumental and self-aggrandizing humanity is helpful to the green cause. For both pictures in their differing ways tend to an unscientific denial of natural and human capacities for renewal and readjustment — a denial which in the end must undermine the cardinal green point about the *limits* on the possibilities of adaptation. They also tend to abstract from the positive impact humanity has had on the natural environment, and vice-versa, and from the role this interaction has played in developing the love and respect for nature which will be an essential stimulus to future checks on ecological degradation. But, finally, it is only the more dialectical approach of Marxism which captures the truth that human beings, like other species, are creatures of their environment in the sense that their structure of needs and affectivity — their overall sensibilities — are formed in relation to their social and material situation and bear its imprint. Overcrowded, car-dense, high-rise, noisy, concrete-ridden environments have long been related empirically to crime, depression, drug abuse, apathy and low expectations of life. The point here, is that the need for improved environments is stimulated in their provision. Understanding this dialectic whereby in changing our policies on the use of nature we also enrich ourselves, will be crucial to mobilizing the political forces for any green revolution.[18]

I have suggested that we should avoid the essentialist picture of the humanity–nature relationship in part because it fails to acknowledge sufficiently the capacity for ecological adjustment. On the other hand, there is also a risk that in stressing the dialectical quality of the humanity–nature interaction, one understates the limits on change. Felix Guattari has recently drawn our attention to the octopus from the port of Marseilles which instantly collapsed and died on being placed in unpolluted water.[19] But should we conclude from this that all is well with the Mediterranean, or even with the quality of octopus life therein? No indeed. For not all species are likely to prove so accommodating, least of all those — like human bathers — who do not live in its waters but rely on them for less essential purposes. And as for the octopus, who can say what kind of a life this is for it, but one might speculate that it was nearer to that of the drug addict or alcoholic than to that of the healthy individual. In any case, even if most species were to prove as adaptive as the octopus — which is far from being the case — the main limits on ecological viability would still remain. For these include physical limits on natural resources — fossil fuels, minerals — which of their nature cannot 'adjust' to their growing scarcity and are, quite simply, non-renewable and irreplaceable.[20] Or else they derive from the physical-chemical properties of things in conjunction with the physiology of organic species, including our own. The biology of humans, seals, salmon, and so on is such that there is no withstanding certain forms of toxicity (most of them humanly produced) such as radiation, chemical poisons, oil slicks and the like. In fact, the whole history of planetary life suggests that adaptation to these kinds of poisons and pollutions is simply out of the question, so that any appeal to nature's wondrous powers of self-renewal is grossly misleading as to the true nature of our current crisis.

Now if we ask at this point where Marx stands in regard to all this, then I think the answer is that he stands ambiguously with a foot in both camps, but mainly weighted, I shall argue, on the side of sustaining a humanity–nature dialectic which is also cognizant of limits on nature. For example, if we look at the closest he comes to commenting on the octopus, he certainly seems biased in this direction. The proletariat, he tells Feuerbach in the *German Ideology*, will take as kindly to the idea that its 'essence' is realized in the living conditions of its capitalist 'existence' as the fish to the idea that its 'essence' is equally realized whether it swims in clean or polluted water.[21] Against Feuerbach's abstract essentialism (which finds the 'essence' of every species everywhere realized in interaction with its conditions of existence), Marx is here pointing out that the real, as opposed to 'philosophical' essence, of things is not so elastic: that just as 'man' is incapable of realizing his essence or truth in capitalist conditions, so fish nature is such as to rule out any realization of its essence in the port of Marseilles. The emphasis here is clearly on the *limits* imposed by the intrinsic nature of any entity or species on the forms in which the potentialities inherent in that nature can be actualized.[22] It is of the nature of the tulip bulb to require an uncontaminated soil, a sufficiency of warmth and water, etc., if it is ever to actualize its potentiality to become a fully grown, blossoming plant; and so on.

Of Limits, Presuppositions and Nature

It is true that in the later discussion of alienation in the *Grundrisse* we are offerred an account of human development which is seemingly less congruent with the recognition of natural limits implied in the earlier argument around 'species-being'. Alienation in the *Grundrisse* is presented less in terms of the loss or lack of actualization of an essential species-being under capitalism, and more in terms of the latter's destruction of all natural ties relating the individual to a given environment, and providing him or her with what Marx describes as a 'direct extension of self in the inorganic'. In virtue of the impersonality and generality of capitalist society (where the worker figures as an exchangeable unit of labouring capacity, rather than as occupant of a particular role) the individual is deprived of the 'objective presuppositions' of selfhood which come from being tied to a specific place and community: the worker under capitalism, says Marx, is 'objectless' and 'naked in his subjectivity'.[23] But Marx also insists that this same process is that which frees the worker of all 'presuppositions' and bonds with the 'inorganic conditions of life' and thus, in principle, places the individual in a position to break out from any limited and predefined selfhood. Pure subjectivity is here conceived as the condition of escape into any and every possible mode of objectification. Capitalist production may create 'objectlessness', but it also drives labour 'beyond the limits of natural paltriness'; and whereas previous stages of production represented 'mere local developments of humanity' and 'nature idolatry', under the spur of capitalist industry, nature

> ceases to be recognised as a power for itself and the theoretical discovery of its autonomous laws appears merely as a ruse to subjugate it under human needs, whether as an object of consumption or as a means of production. In accordance with this tendency, capital drives beyond the national barriers and prejudices as much as beyond nature worship, as well as all traditional, confined, complacent, encrusted satisfactions of present needs, and reproductions of old ways of life.[24]

And associated with this line of argument goes the well-known salute to the 'universality of individual needs, capacities, pleasures, productive forces, etc.' which are to be made available through universal exchange once 'the limited bourgeois form' has been stripped away and the human individual no longer 'strives to remain something he has become, but is in the absolute movement of becoming'.[25]

Against, then, the recognition of limits on human fulfilment and gratification implicit in the *German Ideology*'s approach to the realization of the essence of species-being, we must set these more Promethean aspirations to break loose from all natural limitations and essential presuppositions into a utopia of hedonistic insatiability. Nonetheless, Marx is aware of the tensions in the Promethean position:

> In bourgeois economics — and in the epoch of production to which it corresponds — this complete working-out of the human content appears as a complete emptying-out, this universal objectification as total alienation, and the tearing down of all limited, one-sided aims as a sacrifice of the human end-in-itself to an entirely external end.

This is why the childish world of antiquity *appears on the one side as loftier*. On the other side, *it really is loftier* in all matters where closed shapes, forms and given limits are sought for. It is satisfaction from a limited standpoint; while the modern gives no satisfaction; or where it appears satisfied with itself, it is vulgar.[26]

He is very aware, too, I suggest, of exactly how much blame must be attached precisely to the 'limited bourgeois form', in particular to the subordination of bourgeois society to the quest for profit, for diverting the potentialities opened up by modern industry into rapacious and destructive channels. Indeed, in several pronouncements, it is precisely the *contrariness* of the 'bourgeois form' from the point of view of human and natural wellbeing which is emphasized. Thus, for example, having compared progress in exploiting societies to that 'hideous pagan idol who would not drink the nectar but from the skulls of the slain', he goes on:

> In our days everything seems pregnant with its contrary. Machinery gifted with the wonderful power of shortening and fructifying human labour, we behold starving and over-working it. The new-fangled sources of wealth by some strange weird spell, are turned into sources of want, the victories of art seem bought by the loss of character. At the same pace that mankind masters nature, man seems to become enslaved to other men or to his own infamy. Even the pure light of science seems unable to shine but on the dark background of ignorance. All our inventions and progress seem to result in endowing material forces with intellectual life, and in stultifying human life into a material force.[27]

Admittedly, this passage speaks of 'mastering' nature and is clearly committed to the idea that technology and science are in principle benevolent forces: Marx's position is in no sense nostalgic, Luddite or irrationalist. But that in itself need not make it un-green. One may argue, on the contrary, I think, that an ecological and socialist corrective to the depredations of the 'bourgeois form' of wealth production will depend in part on a highly rational, technically sophisticated intervention in ('mastering' of?) natural forces. To correct soil erosion (whether resulting from human or purely natural causes) we cannot leave nature to itself: we will need positively to do some things (plant trees, build dykes, and so on) and to stop doing others. And one may cite many other examples where a 'hands off nature' approach would have ecologically deleterious consequences.

However, there is a further dimension to Marx's emphasis on the 'negatives' ensuing from the *bourgeois form* of harnessing resources, which is of cardinal pertinence to the green critique of industrialism. This lies in the clarity with which, by exposing this form *as a form* (i.e. as in no sense a necessary mode of production) he also exposes the non-necessity of crystallizing all surplus labour in commodities.

Since profit can only be realized through the sale of commodities (material goods and services almost always involving material resources) any society subject to capital accumulation will be driven into a wholly anti-ecological concretization of surplus labour time (time, we might say, left over after producing the necessities of a decent and modest lifestyle) into surplus product — into proliferating luxury production. But as Marx over and over again makes clear, a socialist economy can enjoy surplus labour time as *free* time: as time not spent on producing, and therefore *a fortiori* not expended in resource-consuming ways. Or to put this less tendentiously, he makes clear that it is not part of the very nature of wealth production that all available social labour time should unceasingly become embodied in new material commodities and services. He makes clear that one could in principle opt for a more reproductive system of 'primary' need satisfaction.

It is true, of course, that what counts as 'primary' or 'necessary' consumption as opposed to 'affluence' and 'luxury' is not fixed by nature but is very much a convention varying for different times and places. All people at all times have a need for water. But the clean water piped into one's home which even the more ecologically ascetic of the greens would seem to regard as part of necessary consumption in the industrialized nations remains a luxury relative to what counts as 'primary' need or necessary consumption in other parts of the globe. In other words, a 'politics of need' is presupposed by any attempt to distinguish for any actual society between the part of social labour time which is 'necessary' because it is essential to the satisfaction of a certain range of goods deemed necessary, and the part which is 'surplus' (and which could be spent either in idleness or in creative/productive activities to satisfy a range of more sophisticated needs). What is needed even in a basic or primary sense is culturally conditioned to a very high degree albeit determined in an abstract and general sense by our common natural physiology as a species.

It is also true that, when Marx analyses necessary and surplus labour time under capitalism and its implications for the release of 'surplus' or 'free' time in a socialist society, he does not actually specify that such surplus time would in fact be spent either literally doing nothing or only in ways that would be sustainable in terms of resource use. His argument in this sense is not explicitly ecological. In other words, there is nothing directly in Marx's argument which associates socialism with a restraint on material and resource-intensive forms of production or with a use of surplus/free time which would be obedient to environmental limitations on the expansion of certain forms of consumption. In this sense, a socialist economy (whether organized in more or less centralized ways) does not in itself guarantee that surplus time will not be devoted to expanding the range of material commodities available to society. And if such a society does opt for this use of its energies, then it will not prove much of a corrective to the 'bourgeois form' from any ecological perspective.

But the important point is that it is only under a socialist economy that a society is placed in a position to *choose* the forms of embodiment of its labour time and therefore in principle able to opt for a more ecologically sustainable pattern of consumption.[28] It may be true that Marx's dialectic of necessary and surplus time under socialism leaves open the question of what is 'needed', but he certainly exposed more clearly than any other theorist the ways in which surplus time *could* be spent not in enhancing 'living standards' in the conventional sense of the term but as 'free' time: as time spent not producing material goods and therefore not expended in resource-consuming ways.

He reveals socialism as the possibility of idleness; and in this idleness, one may argue, lies one of the most important eco-friendly resources available to human societies at the present time. For in the last analysis, it is only if we stop working, in the sense of devoting labour time to the production of resource-hungry material commodities, particularly in the more affluent global regions, that we shall stave off the barbarism of ecological collapse.

This is also, in the last analysis, why a commitment to a Marxian-socialist economic approach, which insists on the necessity of correcting the inequalities and eco-destructiveness of capitalism from the *production* rather than the *distribution* end, should be a *sine qua non* of anyone who is seriously anxious about the future ecological survival of the planet. Redistributing income through heavier taxation on the rich, Basic Income schemes, and similar policies, will correct some of the economic injustices and will help shift investment away from luxury production. But in the first place (as Marx points out in his criticism of Proudhon and the English 'Ricardian Socialists'[29]) full equality in the distribution of wealth is incompatible with the maintenance of the competitive market economy; and, second, any redistribution of wealth which is compatible with the continuation of capitalist relations of production will do rather little to check the expansion of material commodity production. A limited social democratic reallocation from rich to poor cannot in itself halt and reverse the (material) commodifying and (material) consumerist tendencies which are the real enemies of ecological revolution.

I have suggested that in a formal and abstract sense, Marx's argument on the relations between necessary and surplus labour time leaves open the question of the actual forms consumption would take in a socialist society and therefore does not explicitly commit the latter to an ecologically responsible use of labour time. But there is little doubt, all the same, that Marx himself envisaged that freedom from the 'laws' of capitalist accumulation would lead to the emergence of a very different structure of needs: a structure wherein the major source of satisfaction would be the free time released for the cultivation of 'rich individuality' conceived in essentially spiritual and artistic terms. For whatever Marx's more technocratist followers may have advocated as the consumption goals of a 'Marxist' economy, no one who reads Marx's works, I think, can really claim that his is a consumerist perspective. On the contrary, there is even, if one dare say so, something a little old-fashioned and other-worldly about the picture Marx conjures up of the many-sided 'hunter, fisher and critical critic' of the communist future.[30] At any rate, the idea he conveys of 'rich development of individuality' is hardly rampantly materialist, even if the hunting and fishing (presumably in unpolluted waters) will not recommend itself to all green sensibilities.

Finally, it should be recognized that there is an important ambiguity attaching even to Marx's more Promethean and seemingly least green pronouncements. When he refers us, for example, to a communist future 'unmeasurable by all previous yardsticks', and associates this with the escape from 'natural limits' and 'presuppositions', we are inclined to view this as a piece of heady Enlightenment optimism very much at odds with ecological cautions about dwindling resources and the need for a sustainable level of consumption. But there is no reason to interpret the idea of 'breaking with natural limits' primarily, let alone exclusively, in terms of breaking with limits on natural resources; and there is very little, in fact, in Marx's argument which invites us to think of it in that way. On the contrary, the bias of the argument is more towards the idea of transcending a previously self-satisfied, but limited, *human* nature, and the gauges of progress and human wellbeing that have gone together with that 'nature'. If we construe it in this sense, then the argument is by no means so incompatible with ecological demands, and might even be said to be quite consistent with the green call for a 'new philosophy' in our approach to nature. For it would have to be admitted, I think, that if we were indeed to break with 'human nature' as hitherto manifested in our treatment of the rest of nature, we would be breaking with attitudes which had issued in some very wasteful and destructive patterns of use of our environment. Likewise, in respect of previous yardsticks of progress: to move into a future 'unmeasurable' by these standards would be to move into a future which had broken with some profoundly anti-ecological conceptions of the 'good life', 'civilization' and human 'development'.

I would stress here that I am drawing attention to an *ambiguity* in Marx's 'Promethean' discourse, and not trying to claim that the 'eco-friendly' construction I have put upon it is that which Marx himself intended and which we should accept as 'faithful' to Marxism. The point rather is that the ambiguity in Marx's position derives from the same vacuity or lack of content in the projection of a future beyond 'all previous yardsticks' which makes it impossible to claim any one interpretation is definitively Marxist. Where the vision of the future is so under-defined, nothing definite can be said of it. In other words, statements by Marx which have been received as anthropocentric and arrogant in their approach to nature, are often so formally dialectical and devoid of empirical content that they allow of either a more green or a more technocratist interpretation. This is one reason for wanting a synthesis of green and Marxist intellectual forces: it will allow the ecological argument to flood the vacuum. Where Marx failed to blue-print, we can blue-print green.

Notes

1. 'The green movement,' writes Peter Tatchell (see 'Ecological Sustainability' in ed. Felix Dodds, *Into the Twentieth Century*, Basingstoke: Green Print 1988, p.38) is the most important new radical movement since the emergence of socialism nearly two centuries ago'; and cf. Dodds himself; p. xi: 'Just as socialism became the dominant philosophy of this century in reaction to the existing political climate, green politics could well become the philosophy of the twenty-first century'; also Jonathan Porritt, p. 196: 'this multiplicity represents the single most important social and political movement since the birth of socialism'.

2. There are many voices here, among whom one might single out Rousseau, Wordsworth and William Morris. See Keith Thomas, *Man and the Natural World, Changing Attitudes in England 1500–1800*, London: Allen Lane 1983; and also John Passmore, *Man's Responsibility for Nature*, London: Duckworth 1980, Part One.

3. For statistics on pollution in central and eastern Europe see the essays

by Mark Thompson, Kate Soper and Martin Ryle in L. Mackay and M. Thompson, eds, *Something in the Wind: Politics after Chernobyl*, London: Zwan 1988; also essays by Istvan Rev, Kate Soper and Martin Ryle in M. Kaldor, G. Holden, and R. Falk, eds, *The New Detente*, London: Verso 1989.

4. The reorganization of national economies along socialist lines is a precondition of any green revolution because it allows for a *political* control over the use of resources — a control denied to capitalist economies, which in the end are answerable only to the logic of value accumulation. But being in a position to exercise such control does not in itself decide *how* it will be used, and if consumerist economic goals are chosen there will be an ecological price to pay. See the concluding pages of this article.

5. Such as has been given, for example, by Gerry Cohen in his *Karl Marx's Theory of History: A Defence*, Oxford: Blackwell 1978, a work which relies very heavily indeed, in fact, on the argument of the 1859 Preface.

6. R. Bahro, *Socialism and Survival*, London: Heretic 1982, p. 27; cf. Martin Ryle, *Ecology and Socialism*, London: Radius 1988, pp. 68–70.

7. Jonathan Porritt, for example, in his Preface to the Programme of *Die Grünen* (in English translation in *Seeing Green*, Oxford: Blackwell 1984, p.4) hails the end of 'the redundant polemic of class warfare and the mythical immutability of the left/right divide', and also argues at another point (p. 226) that 'genuine redistribution of power can no longer be simplistically interpreted in terms of setting class against class'. In a general sense, as Martin Ryle argues (*Ecology and Socialism*, p. 20), environmental groups and Green Parties 'tend to see themselves as . . . expressing a "general interest" — the interest of nature, of a viable humanity/nature relationship — that is distinct from and even in opposition to the interests of each and every particular group/class within a social formation'.

8. Cited in Martin Ryle, *Ecology and Socialism*, p. 33.

9. In that Hegel defines alienation in terms of the failure of Spirit to realize its own conceptualizing role in what it takes to be 'objective'. For a full discussion of the differing but comparable usage of the term by Hegel, Feuerbach and Marx, see Chris Arthur, *The Dialectics of Labour*, Oxford: Blackwell 1987.

10. These are my own examples, in fact, but the essential idea is central to green thinking from William Morris onwards. For recent examples, see the opening and closing essays of Jeremy Seabrook, *The Race for Riches*, Basingstoke: Green Line 1988; Martin Ryle, *Ecology and Socialism*, pp. 27–31, 43–58, 75–8; William Ophuls, *Ecology and the Politics of Scarcity*, San Francisco: W. H. Freeman 1977, esp. pp. 167–83.

11. Marx, *Collected Works*, London: Lawrence and Wishart 1975, Vol. 3, p. 326.

12. Jeremy Seabrook, *The Race for Riches*, p. 101.

13. Seabrook, pp. 102–3.

14. Marx, *Collected Works*, Vol. 3, p. 277.

15. There is a further question, of course, as to whether we could produce such replicas in a manner allowing the insects concerned actually *to make use* of them.

16. In an interesting article on Marx, humanism and speciesism, *Radical Philosophy* 50, Autumn 1988, pp. 4–18, Ted Benton takes issue with Marx's

human/animal dualism on the grounds that the general qualities attributed exclusively to humanity by Marx are a property of other animal species also. He proposes instead a naturalistic approach deriving from the central insight that 'these things which only humans can do are generally to be understood as rooted in the specifically human *ways* of doing things which other animals do' (p. 14). The capacity to value, which I here associate with Marx's human/animal dualism, is not directly discussed in the article, but Benton suggests that the starting point of any analysis of the distinguishing 'aesthetic, cognitive, normative, "spiritual" — in other words "cultural" dimension to the way in which humans meet their physical needs' is the

> recognition of a need which is common to both humans and non-human animals. The specification of the distinctively human then proceeds not by identifying a further, supervenient class of needs possessed only by humans, but rather by identifying the species-specific *way in which* humans meet the needs they share with other species. (p.15).

But the weak point of this approach, it would seem, is that it cannot explain *why* there is a need for human beings to do things in their more specifically aesthetic ways — *why*, for example, they don't just eat more as animals do. And this weakness emerges, I think, rather clearly in Benton's response to the objection that not all human needs would seem reducible to physical need, since he offers us only the idea of viewing them 'as *in some sense* consequential upon those needs which are common to natural beings' (ibid.), when of course, it is precisely the particular sense which is here in question. For the naturalistic, anti-dualist position to prove compelling, it will need to do more than recognize a human distinctiveness in the ways of doing things other animals do: it will need to offer a cogent naturalistic explanation for the difference itself.

17. I understand, however, that some 'deep ecologists' would regard any destruction of nature's more pestilential aspects as an illegitimate interference in the global eco-balance — and would include even the attempt to develop anti-AIDS drugs and vaccine in this condemnation.

18. My remarks here should not be taken to imply that Marx fully recognized, let alone conceptualized, these implications of his account of the humanity–nature interaction. For some pertinent indications of the conceptual inadequacies of Marx's account as it stands, see Ted Benton's contribution to this volume (chapter 10) — in particular, his criticisms of Marx's emphasis on the 'transformative' and 'intentional' aspects of the labour-process at the expense of more 'eco-regulatory' types of practice in his section on 'Labour: Intentional Structures and Natural Limits?'

19. Felix Guattari, *Les Trois Ecologies*, paper delivered at the Institute of Contemporary Arts, London, November 1988.

20. There is considerable debate, obviously, about the extent to which we are likely to be able to provide substitutes for exhausted or dwindling resources, but there is general agreement (reflected in such authoritative sources as the Brundtland report, *Our Common Future*, 1987) that it is out of the question that alternative forms of energy could be developed sufficient to bring global use generally up to the level of the currently most affluent

nations — even if it were desirable or feasible to do so in other terms. Cf. Martin Ryle, *Ecology*, pp. 3–4. (Any pronouncement on the potential of the recent nuclear fusion experiments would be premature.)

21. Marx, *Collected Works*, Vol. 5, pp. 58–9.

22. Readers will recognize that such arguments rest on attributing an Aristotelian notion of 'essence' to Marx along the lines most systematically defended by Scott Meikle in his *Essentialism in the Thought of Karl Marx*, London: Duckworth 1985. I think, in fact, that there are considerable problems about treating Marx's approach in his later work to human self-realization along such teleological lines (and some of these difficulties are obliquely touched on in my discussion below on the approach of the *Grundrisse* to alienation). But the more Aristotelian approach does indeed seem justified by the earlier argument around the notion of 'species being'.

23. Marx, *Grundrisse*, Harmondsworth: Penguin 1973, pp. 450–56; and see the whole section on Pre-Capitalist Economic Modes of Production, pp. 471–515, where Marx elaborates on this 'theory of personality'. See also my own discussion of this in *On Human Needs*, Brighton: Harvester Press 1981, pp. 125–42.

24. Marx, *Grundrisse*, pp. 409–10.

25. *Grundisse*, pp. 487–8.

26. Ibid.

27. Marx, *Speech at the Anniversary of the 'People's Paper'*, *Selected Works*, Vol. 1, London: Lawrence and Wishart 1972, p. 500.

28. But this level of consumption would not necessarily be without variety or devoid altogether of luxury goods. André Gorz's 'utopia', for example, would include a sphere providing for 'wants' in addition to that satisfying 'basic needs' (see his *Paths to Paradise*, London: Pluto 1985, and his *Farewell to the Working Class*, London: Pluto 1982); and see also Martin Ryle, *Ecology*, pp. 75–8.

29. For Marx's strictures against Proudhon, see *The Poverty of Philosophy*, *Collected Works*, Vol. 6, pp. 120–43; and on the English 'Ricardian Socialists' (Bray, William Thompson, John Gray, Thomas Hodgkin, Thomas Rowe Edmonds, and so on) see pp. 143–50; also *Grundrisse*, p. 319, and *Theories of Surplus Value*, London: Lawrence and Wishart 1972, Part 3, pp. 319–25.

30. As a jibe against Stirner, this is not a phrase to be taken very seriously as a guide to Marx's true views of 'communist man', and I hope readers will appreciate that I use it here myself with a touch of the same irony. But the essential point I think holds good, and Marx was certainly more of a Millian gentleman than a Benthamite sausage-maker in his estimations of the quality of human happiness.

Notes on Contributors

ANTHONY ARBLASTER is Lecturer in Politics at the University of Sheffield. His publications include *The Rise and Decline of Western Liberalism* (1984) and *Democracy* (1987).

TED BENTON is Lecturer in Sociology at the University of Essex. He has published *Philosophical Foundations of the Three Sociologies* (1977) and *The Rise and Fall of Structural Marxism* (1984). He is an editor of *Radical Philosophy*, and is currently working on a book on Marxism and Ecology.

JAY BERNSTEIN is Senior Lecturer in Philosophy at the University of Essex and the editor of the *Bulletin of the Hegel Society of Great Britain*. He is the author of *The Philosophy of the Novel: Lukács, Marxism and the Dialectics of Form* (1984) and *Beauty Bereaved: Aesthetic Alienation from Kant to Derrida and Adorno* (forthcoming).

ROBIN BLACKBURN is Editor of *New Left Review*. He is the author of *The Overthrow of Colonial Slavery, 1776–1884* (1988).

TOM FURNISS is Lecturer in English at the University of Strathclyde. He has published several articles on Edmund Burke and Thomas Paine, and is currently preparing a book on aesthetics, gender and political economy in Burke's writings.

RICHARD NORMAN is Professor of Philosophy at the University of Kent. His publications include *The Moral Philosophers* (1983).

PETER OSBORNE teaches Philosophy and Politics at Middlesex Polytechnic. He is an editor of *Radical Philosophy*, and editor (with Sean Sayers) of *Socialism, Feminism and Philosophy: A Radical Philosophy Reader* (1990) and (with Andrew Benjamin) of *Thinking Art: Beyond Traditional Aesthetics* (1991).

ANNE PHILLIPS is Senior Lecturer in Politics at City of London Polytechnic. She has published *Hidden Hands: Women and Economic Policy* (1983), *Divided Loyalties: Dilemmas of Sex and Class* (1987), and is the editor of *Feminism and Equality* (1987). She is currently working on a book on democracy.

MICHAEL RUSTIN is Professor of Sociology at the Polytechnic of East London. He is the author of *For a Pluralist Socialism* (1985) and *The Good Society and the Inner World* (1991), and an editor of *New Left Review*.

KATE SOPER teaches Philosophy at the Polytechnic of North London. She has published *On Human Needs* (1981), *Humanism and Anti-Humanism* (1986), and *Troubled Pleasures* (1990). She is an editor of *Radical Philosophy* and *New Left Review*.

GAYATRI CHAKRAVORTY SPIVAK is Andrew W. Mellon Professor at the University of Pittsburgh. She is the English translator of Derrida's *Of Grammatology* and a contributor to numerous books and journals. She is the author of *In Other Worlds: Essays in Cultural Politics* (1987).

Index